D1250769

DISCARDED

THE FLOWERS OF EVIL

CHARLES BAUDELAIRE

THE FLOWERS OF EVIL

SELECTED AND EDITED BY

Marthiel and Jackson Mathews

REVISED EDITION

A NEW DIRECTIONS BOOK

REVISED EDITION

Library of Congress Catalog Card Number: 54-9871

Manufactured in the United States of America
New Directions Books are published for James Laughlin
by New Directions Publishing Corporation,
333 Sixth Avenue, New York 10014

Revised edition published in 1963

SECOND PRINTING

ACKNOWLEDGMENTS

For permission to reprint the copyrighted translations in this volume, the editors are indebted to the following translators, their heirs and publishers:

Ernest Benn, Ltd., for the translation "The Death of Lovers" from *Wild Honey from Various Thyme* by Michael Field

Keith B. Bullen for the translation "The Poison" from *Charles Baudelaire, un poète maudit* (Cairo: 1942)

Cassell & Co., Ltd., for translations from Baudelaire's *Les Fleurs du Mal,* translated by Alan Conder

Thomas Cole, editor and publisher of *Imagi,* for the translation "Invitation to the Voyage" by Richard Wilbur

Harper & Brothers for translations by George Dillon and Edna St. Vincent Millay from *Flowers of Evil,* translated from the French of Charles Baudelaire, Copyright 1936 by George Dillon and Edna

St. Vincent Millay; and for "Delphine and Hippolyte" from *The Cicadas and Other Poems,* Copyright 1929, 1931 by Aldous Huxley

The Harvill Press, Ltd., and Pantheon Books, Inc., for translations by Roy Campbell from *Poems of Baudelaire,* Copyright 1952 by Pantheon Books, Inc.

Henry Holt & Co., Inc., for translations by Lewis Piaget Shanks from *Les Fleurs du Mal,* Copyright 1926 by Henry Holt and Co., Inc.

The Limited Editions Club for James Laver's translation for "Sisina," published in 1940 by The Limited Editions Club.

Mr. Michael Maclagan for the translation by Sir Eric Maclagan

Mrs. T. Sturge Moore, and Macmillan and Co., Ltd., London; Macmillan Company of Canada, Ltd.; and St. Martin's Press, Inc., New York, for T. Sturge Moore's translation of "The Blind" from *The Poems of T. Sturge Moore,* Collected Edition, Volume II, Copyright 1932 by Macmillan Co., London

Random House, Inc., for the translation "The Giantess" by Karl Shapiro from *Person, Place and Thing,* Copyright 1942 by Karl Shapiro

The Richards Press, Ltd., for translations by James Elroy Flecker

Charles Scribner's Sons for the translation "A Carrion" by Allen Tate from *Poems, 1922-1947,* Copyright 1932, 1937, 1948 by Charles Scribner's Sons

The University of California Press for translations by C. F. MacIntyre from *One Hundred Poems from Les Fleurs du Mal,* Copyright 1947 by the Regents of the University of California

Miss Ann Wolfe for the translations by Humbert Wolfe

Farrar, Straus & Cudahy for translations by Robert Lowell from *Imitations,* Copyright 1958, 1959, 1960, 1961 by Robert Lowell

Atlantic-Little Brown and Company for the translation by Stanley Kunitz from *Selected Poems 1928-1958,* Copyright 1929, 1930, 1944, 1951, 1953, 1954, 1956, 1957, 1958 by Stanley Kunitz

Doubleday Anchor Books for Frederick Morgan's "Voyage to Cythera" and Robert Fitzgerald's "Music" from *An Anthology of French Poetry from Nerval to Valéry in English Translation,* edited by Angel Flores, Copyright 1958 by Angel Flores

ACKNOWLEDGMENTS

Alan Swallow, publisher, for Yvor Winter's "The Skeleton Laborer," Part II, from *Collected Poems* by Yvor Winters, Copyright 1952 by Yvor Winters

The Hudson Review for Anthony Hecht's "The Swan"

James Laver
Dorothy Martin
David Paul
Graham Reynolds
Lois Saunders
Cyril Scott
and Sir John Squire

Special acknowledgment is made to the following who have allowed the editors to include in this volume their previously unpublished poems:

Doreen Bell
Hilary Corke
Barbara Gibbs
Kenneth Hanson
Desmond Harmsworth
Anthony Hecht
Peter Hellings
Naomi Lewis
Frederick Morgan
David Paul
Ruthven Todd
and Richard Wilbur

PREFACE

The present age of translation began some fifty years ago with Ezra Pound's versions of Cavalcanti, the Troubadours, the Chinese. . . . Then the Greek plays and Homer were recovered from the 19th century by several talented poet-translators writing in a language that was clearly ours. Meanwhile, something was happening in criticism; it developed an intense preoccupation with poetry, and for some years a great deal of poetry was "translated" into critical analysis. That was good in its time, and something important for the art of translation came out of it. I am convinced that the intensive analysis of poetry is what led to the excellent practice of translating foreign poems into plain prose. And this has had one telling effect. It has liberated the poets.

The proper business of prose translations is to come between the poet and the original, to relieve him of being expected to say exactly what the original says, which no translated poem can do and live. As the publication of literal prose versions of the poetry of other languages goes on here and in England, the poets are beginning to enjoy their freedom and poetry is being translated into poetry.

That is my sense of what is happening, and there is evidence of it, I believe, in this collection of Baudelaire's poems. Its aim is to reflect, as it has done from the first, the present state of the art of translation.

Eleven poets are new to this edition: Doreen Bell, Hilary Corke, Robert Fitzgerald, Desmond Harmsworth, Anthony Hecht, Stanley Kunitz, Naomi Lewis, Robert Lowell, Frederick Morgan, Ruthven Todd, and Yvor Winters. We are grateful to them and to others who have sent us their translations.

PREFACE

We have decided to present, side by side, two versions of the first poem, *To the Reader,* by Robert Lowell and Stanley Kunitz. It is not only that the two poems seem equally fine—which they do—but we wish to express in this way our view that there can be many good translations of a single poem.

JACKSON MATHEWS

New York, 1962

A NOTE ON THE FIRST EDITION

The first edition of *Les Fleurs du Mal* was published in 1857. So far as we know and can judge, we offer here the best English translations of Baudelaire's poems done in these hundred years. They have been collected from every published and unpublished source we could find in America and England,* and they range in date from 1869, two years after Baudelaire's death, to 1954. Each translation has been judged on its own merits, without regard to the translator; each has won a competition, some against as many as twenty versions of the same poem.

This edition then is a commentary on the present state of the art of translation. It is our aim to make it a permanent proving ground of the art and a permanent collection of the best Baudelaire in English by including from time to time in later printings any better translations we may find. Our experience does not allow us to believe the changes will be many or rapid. These are the best we know, but surely they are not, all of them, the best that can be done. We invite translators to send us their work.

No one can translate all of the poems of a great poet. A translator's range, even if he is a better poet than the one he is translating, will not coincide with the range of his model; their sensibilities will vibrate together only within limits. Roy Campbell is the first poet of reputation to attempt the whole of *The Flowers of Evil* in English. We believe he succeeds in a large number of poems, but he is most successful in the hard-driving didactic ones. It takes other translators, other sensibilities, to give us a notion of Baudelaire's

* We are obligated to Professor W. T. Bandy of the University of Wisconsin for the use of his bibliographical list.

full range. That is what we believe a composite edition of this kind, containing the best work of thirty different translators, can do better than another. There are translators here with very different styles and notions of their art; but David Paul's creative readings, Richard Wilbur's fine sense of texture and rhythm, and C. F. MacIntyre's stark imagery (despite his sometimes clumsy verse), all represent real and different qualities of Baudelaire. We feel that F. P. Sturm, whose work was done about 1905, is still one of the finest of Baudelaire's translators; his understanding of the poems, his fine workmanship, his poetic sense prevail over any softness or old-fashioned diction in his work. Richard Wilbur, Kenneth Hanson, Jackson Mathews, and David Paul made translations especially for this edition, and Roy Campbell was generous and conscientious in revising his.

This edition is dedicated to the translators. It is bilingual but it is primarily a volume of fine translations, and the format means to show our respect for the poems chosen to represent Baudelaire in English. The French texts are included, for comparison and for themselves, as an appendix. We believe it is a mistake to put verse translations face to face with the original text. This encourages a criss-cross testing of the translation that keeps it from ever being read as a poem, in its own integrity. It is all right for prose to face the original text, and act as a guide to it. But verse is another thing, and it cannot survive such misuse. It is not comparison that is to be avoided, but competition for the reader's attention.

A further bow to the translators: rather than insist on uniformity, we have kept both American and English spellings.

For the arrangement of the poems, we felt that it was better to reflect Baudelaire's original scheme, the "architecture" of *The Flowers of Evil,* rather than attempt to retrace in the order of the poems (as scholarly editions incline to do) the luckless hazards of his publishing career. In short, we have preferred the poet's meaning to the accidents of chronology. We have therefore restored the suppressed poems to their places in the main body of the work. The arrangement of the "further poems" is our own.

The text used for "Three Drafts of a Preface" was taken from the critical edition of *Les Fleurs du Mal* by Jacques Crépet and Georges Blin. This is the first publication in English of these notes for a preface Baudelaire had planned for the second (1861) and again for the third (1868) edition of his poems. He abandoned the project both times, probably at the insistence of his publisher and his mother, who were alarmed at his violence. He was furious at the court's suppression of six poems in the first edition and at certain attacks on him in the press. On October 11, 1860, he wrote to his mother: *"The Flowers of Evil* are at the printer's. But I am *very perplexed*. There is a prose preface which is a violent bit of clowning. I hesitate to print it, and yet I shall never have my fill of insulting France. . . . The matter of that ridiculous *croix d'honneur* has come up again. I hope the preface to the *Flowers* will make the thing forever impossible." About two years later, in a note to Michel Lévy, he wrote again: "In the third edition . . . I shall add a big preface in which I shall explain my tricks and methods, and teach others *the art of doing just as well by themselves*."

Baudelaire's preface is at last, for the first time, put at the head of his poems. A century later and in another country, there is no longer any reason for suppressing his plans.

1955

J.M. & M.M.
University of Washington
Seattle

This book is dedicated to
THE TRANSLATORS

DOREEN BELL
Her Hair
Lethe
The Cat
The Serpent's Tooth

KEITH B. BULLEN
The Poison

ROY CAMPBELL
Elevation
I love the thought . . .
Ill Luck
The Possessed
The Living Torch
To One Who Is Too Gay
Misty Sky
The Cat
(A fine strong gentle cat)
The Splendid Ship
Praises of My Frances
The Owls
Burial
Fantastic Engraving
The Cask of Hate
Obsession
Sympathetic Horror
The Clock
The Red-Haired Beggar Girl
The Seven Old Men
The Little Old Women
Skeletons Digging (Part I)
The Dance of Death
The Martyr
Lesbians
The Two Good Sisters
The Denial of St. Peter
Dream of a Curious Person
Epigraph for a Condemned Book
The Unforeseen
Hymn
On Delacroix's Picture of Tasso in Prison

HILARY CORKE
Moesta et Errabunda
The Ghost

ALAN CONDER
Exotic Perfume
Afternoon Song
Alchemy of Grief
The Murderer's Wine

HENRY CURWEN
The Irremediable

THE TRANSLATORS

GEORGE DILLON
The Vampire
The Voice

MICHAEL FIELD
The Death of Lovers

ROBERT FITZGERALD
Music

JAMES ELROY FLECKER
Don Juan in Hell
Litany to Satan

BARBARA GIBBS
The Wicked Monk
The Dancing Serpent
The Thirst for Extinction

DESMOND HARMSWORTH
De Profundis Clamavi

KENNETH O. HANSON
Spleen *(Old Pluvius, month of rains . . .)*
Abel and Cain
Amina Boschetti

ANTHONY HECHT
Duellum
If by some freak of fortune . . .
To a Madonna
Cats
Spleen *(I have more memories . . .)*
The Swan
Laments of an Icarus

PETER HELLINGS
Semper Eadem
To a Creole Lady

ALDOUS HUXLEY
Lesbians

STANLEY KUNITZ
To the Reader

JAMES LAVER
Sisina

NAOMI LEWIS
Gypsies on the Road
Evening Harmony
Heautontimoroumenos

ROBERT LOWELL
To the Reader
The Ruined Garden
Spleen *(I'm like the king . . .)*
The Servant
My Beatrice
The Voyage
The Injured Moon
Meditation

C. F. MACINTYRE
The Venal Muse
Sed Non Satiata
Song of Autumn
To a Passer-by
The Love of Lies
The Soul of Wine
The Ragpickers' Wine
The Solitary's Wine
Destruction
The Fountain of Blood
To a Malabar Girl

SIR ERIC MACLAGAN
I have not forgotten . . .

DOROTHY MARTIN
Hymn to Beauty

JACKSON MATHEWS
The Gladly Dead
The Metamorphoses of a Vampire
Love and the Skull
The Death of Artists
The End of the Day
The Rebel
The Abyss
Lola de Valence

EDNA ST. VINCENT MILLAY
What shall you say tonight . . .
Mists and Rains
Parisian Dream
The Pagan's Prayer
Ever So Far From Here

T. STURGE MOORE
The Blind

FREDERICK MORGAN
You'd take to bed the whole world . . .
A Voyage to Cythera
Questioning at Midnight
Bertha's Eyes

DAVID PAUL
The Blessing
Beacons
Jewels
The Sun
Comes the Charming Evening
What a Pair of Eyes Can Promise
The Paranymph
About a Bore
A Gay Chophouse
Morning Twilight
The Fountain

GRAHAM REYNOLDS
The Mask
You Whom I Worship

LOIS SAUNDERS
The Confession

CYRIL SCOTT
Lovers' Wine

LEWIS PIAGET SHANKS
A Phantom
Verses for the Portrait of Honoré Daumier

KARL SHAPIRO
Giantess

RICHARD HERNE SHEPHERD
Lesbos

SIR JOHN SQUIRE
The Punishment of Pride
A hideous Jewess lay with me . . .
The Spiritual Dawn
The Irreparable
Conversation
The Pipe
The Cracked Bell

Spleen *(When the low heavy sky . . .)*
The Ransom
To Theodore de Banville

F. P. STURM
The Sick Muse
A Former Life
Beauty
The Ideal
Robed in a silken robe . . .
The Remorse of the Dead
The Balcony
All in One
Reversibility
The Flask
Sonnet of Autumn
The Sadness of the Moon
A Landscape
An Allegory
The Death of the Poor
The Lid
A Madrigal of Sorrow
Romantic Sunset

ALLEN TATE
A Carrion

RUTHVEN TODD
Man and the Sea

RICHARD WILBUR
The Albatross
Correspondences
Invitation to the Voyage

YVOR WINTERS
Skeletons Digging (Part II)

HUMBERT WOLFE
The Gaming Table

CONTENTS

THE FLOWERS OF EVIL

TO THE IMPECCABLE POET
To the perfect magician of French letters
To my very dear and venerated
MASTER AND FRIEND
THÉOPHILE GAUTIER
with a sense
of the deepest humility
I dedicate
THESE STUNTED FLOWERS
C. B.

THREE DRAFTS OF A PREFACE

by Charles Baudelaire

I

NOTES FOR A PREFACE

France is passing through a period of vulgarity. Paris: a center radiating stupidity in every direction. Despite Molière and Béranger, no one would ever have supposed that France would take to the road of *progress* at such a rate. Matters of art: *terrae incognitae*.

Great men are stupid.

My book may have done some good; I do not regret that. It may have done harm; neither do I rejoice at that.

The aim of poetry. This book is not made for my women, my daughters, or my sisters.

Every sin, every crime I have related has been imputed to me.

Hatred and contempt as forms of amusement. Elegists are vulgar scum. *Et verbum caro factum est.* The poet is of no party. Otherwise, he would be a mere mortal.

The Devil. Original sin. Man as good. If you would, you could be the Tyrant's favorite; it is more difficult to love God than to believe in Him. On the other hand, it is harder nowadays for people to believe in the Devil than to love him. Everyone smells him and no one believes in him. Sublime subtlety of the Devil.

A soul to my liking. The scene.—Thus, novelty.—The Epigraph.—D'Aurevilly.—The Renaissance.—Gérard de Nerval.—We are all hanged or should be.

I have included a certain amount of filth to please the gentlemen of the press. They have proved ungrateful.

II

PREFACE TO THE FLOWERS

It is not for my women, my daughters, or my sisters that this book has been written; nor for the wives, daughters, or sisters of my neighbors. I leave that to those who have some reason to confuse good deeds with fine language.

I know the passionate lover of fine style exposes himself to the hatred of the masses; but no respect for humanity, no false modesty, no conspiracy, no universal suffrage will ever force me to speak the unspeakable jargon of the age, or to confuse ink with virtue.

Certain illustrious poets have long since divided among themselves the more flowery provinces of the realm of poetry. I have found it amusing, and the more pleasant because the task was more difficult, to extract *beauty* from *Evil*. This book, which is quintessentially useless and absolutely innocent, was written with no other aim than to divert myself and to practice my passionate taste for the difficult.

Some have told me that these poems might do harm; I have not rejoiced at that. Other good souls, that they might do some good; and that has given me no regret. I was equally surprised at what the former feared and what the latter hoped, which only served to prove once again that this age has lost all sense of the classical notions of literature.

Despite the encouragement given by a few celebrated pedants to man's natural stupidity, I should never have thought our country could take with such speed to the road of *progress*. The world has taken on a thickness of vulgarity that raises a spiritual man's contempt to a violent passion.

But there are those happy hides so thick that even poison could not penetrate them.

I had intended, at first, to answer numerous criticisms and at the same time to explain a few quite simple questions that have been totally obscured by modern enlightenment: What is poetry? What is its aim? On the distinction between the Good and the Beautiful; on the Beauty in Evil; that rhythm and rhyme answer the immortal need in man for monotony, symmetry, and surprise; on adapting style to subject; on the vanity and danger of inspiration, etc., etc.; but this morning I was so rash as to read some of the public newspapers; suddenly an indolence weighing twenty atmospheres fell upon me, and I stopped, faced by the appalling uselessness of explaining anything whatever to anyone whatever. Those who know can divine me, and for those who can not or will not understand, it would be useless to go on explaining.

C.B.

How the artist, by a prescribed series of exercises, can in proportion increase his originality;

How poetry is related to music through prosody, the roots of which go deeper into the human soul than any classical theory indicates;

That French poetry possesses a mysterious and unrecognized prosody, like the Latin and English languages;

Why any poet who does not know exactly how many rhymes each word has is incapable of expressing any idea whatever;

That the poetic phrase can imitate (and in this, poetry is like the art of music and the science of mathematics) a horizontal line, an ascending or descending vertical line; that it can rise straight up to heaven without losing its breath, or fall straight down to hell with the velocity of any weight; that it can follow a spiral, describe a parabola, or can zigzag, making a series of superimposed angles;

That poetry is like the arts of painting, cooking, and cosmetics in its ability to express every sensation of sweetness or bitterness, of beatitude or horror, by coupling a certain noun with a certain adjective, in analogy or contrast;

How, by relying on my principles and using the knowledge which I guarantee to teach him in twenty lessons, any man can learn to compose a tragedy that will be no more hooted at than another, or line up a poem long enough to be as dull as any epic known.

A difficult matter, to rise to that divine callousness! For, despite my most commendable efforts, even I have not been able to resist the desire to please my contemporaries, as witness in several places, laid on like make-up, certain patches of base flattery aimed at democracy, and even a certain amount of filth meant to excuse the dreariness of my subject. But the gentlemen of the press having proved ungrateful for tender attentions of this kind, I have eliminated every trace of both, so far as possible, from this new edition.

I propose, in order to prove again the excellence of my method, to apply it in the near future to celebrating the pleasures of devotion and the raptures of military glory, though I have never known either.

Notes on my plagiarisms. — Thomas Gray. Edgar Poe (2 passages). Longfellow (2 passages). Statius. Virgil (the whole of Andromache). Aeschylus. Victor Hugo.

III

DRAFT OF A PREFACE FOR THE *Flowers of Evil*

(*To be combined perhaps with earlier notes*)

If there is any glory in not being understood, or in being only very slightly so, I may without boasting say that with this little book I have at a single stroke both won and deserved that glory. Submitted several times over to various publishers who rejected it with disgust; put on trial and mutilated in 1857 as a result of a quite bizarre misapprehension; then gradually revived, added to, and strengthened during several years of silence, only to disappear again thanks to my losing interest in it, this discordant product of the *Muse of modern times,* again enlivened with a few violent new touches, dares today for the third time to face the sun of stupidity.

This is not my fault, but that of an insistent publisher who thinks he is strong enough to brave the public distaste. "This book will be a stain on your whole life," one of my friends, a great poet, predicted from the beginning. And indeed all my misadventures have so far justified him. But I have one of those happy natures that enjoy hatred and feel glorified by contempt. My diabolically passionate taste for stupidity makes me take peculiar pleasure in the fabrications of calumny. Being as chaste as paper, as sober as water, as devout as a woman at communion, as harmless as a sacrificial lamb, it would not displease me to be taken for a lecher, a drunkard, an infidel, a murderer. My publisher insists that it might be of some use, to me and to him, to explain why and how I have written this book, what were my means and aim, my plan and method. Such a critical task might well have the luck to interest those minds that love profound rhetoric. For those I shall perhaps write it later on and have it printed in ten copies. But, on second thought, doesn't it seem obvious that this would be a quite superfluous undertaking for everyone concerned since those are the minds that already know or guess and the rest will never understand? I am too much afraid of being ridiculous to wish to inspire the mass of humanity with the understanding of an art object; in doing so, I should fear being like those Utopians who by decree wish to make all Frenchmen rich and virtuous at a single stroke. And moreover, my best, my supreme reason is that it annoys and bores me. Do we invite the crowd, the audience, behind the scenes, into the workshop of costume and scene designers; into the actress's dressing-room? Do we show the public (enthusiastic today, tomorrow indifferent) the mechanisms behind our effects? Do we explain to them all the revisions, or the improvisations adopted in rehearsal, and even to what extent instinct and sincerity are mixed with artifice and charlatanry, all of them indispensable to the mixture that is the work itself? Do we display all the rags, the paint, the pulleys, the chains, the alterations, the scribbled-over proof sheets, in short all the horrors that make up the sanctuary of art?

In any case, such is not my mood today. I have no desire either to demonstrate, to astonish, to amuse, or to persuade. I have my nerves and my vertigo. I aspire to absolute rest and unbroken night. Though I have sung the mad pleasures of wine and opium, I thirst only for a liquor unknown on earth, which the pharmaceutics of heaven itself could not afford me; a liquor that contains neither vitality nor death, neither excitation nor extinction. To know nothing, to teach nothing, to will nothing, to feel nothing, to sleep and still to sleep, this today is my only wish. A base and loathsome wish, but sincere.

Nevertheless, since the best of taste teaches us not to be afraid of contradicting ourselves a bit, I have collected at the end of this abominable book certain testimonials of sympathy from a few of the men I prize most, so that an impartial reader may infer from them that I do not positively deserve excommunication, and that since I have managed to make myself loved by a few, my heart, whatever a certain printed rag may have said of it, is perhaps not "as frightfully hideous as my face."

Finally, the uncommon generosity which those gentlemen, the critics . . .

Since ignorance is on the increase . . .

I take it on myself to point out my imitations . . .

(*Translated by J.M.*)

TO THE READER

Ignorance, error, cupidity, and sin
Possess our souls and exercise our flesh;
Habitually we cultivate remorse
As beggars entertain and nurse their lice.

Our sins are stubborn. Cowards when contrite
We overpay confession with our pains,
And when we're back again in human mire
Vile tears, we think, will wash away our stains.

Thrice-potent Satan in our cursèd bed
Lulls us to sleep, our spirit overkissed,
Until the precious metal of our will
Is vaporized—that cunning alchemist!

Who but the Devil pulls our waking-strings!
Abominations lure us to their side;
Each day we take another step to hell,
Descending through the stench, unhorrified.

Like an exhausted rake who mouths and chews
The martyrized breast of an old withered whore
We steal, in passing, whatever joys we can,
Squeezing the driest orange all the more.

Packed in our brains incestuous as worms
Our demons celebrate in drunken gangs,
And when we breathe, that hollow rasp is Death
Sliding invisibly down into our lungs.

If the dull canvas of our wretched life
Is unembellished with such pretty ware
As knives or poison, pyromania, rape,
It is because our soul's too weak to dare!

But in this den of jackals, monkeys, curs,
Scorpions, buzzards, snakes—this paradise
Of filthy beasts that screech, howl, grovel, grunt—
In this menagerie of mankind's vice

There's one supremely hideous and impure!
Soft-spoken, not the type to cause a scene,
He'd willingly make rubble of the earth
And swallow up creation in a yawn.

I mean *Ennui!* who in his hookah-dreams
Produces hangmen and real tears together.
How well you know this fastidious monster, reader,
—Hypocrite reader, you—my double! my brother!

—Stanley Kunitz

TO THE READER

(For Stanley Kunitz)

Infatuation, sadism, lust, avarice
possess our souls and drain the body's force;
we spoonfeed our adorable remorse,
like whores or beggars nourishing their lice.

Our sins are mulish, our confessions lies;
we play to the grandstand with our promises,
we pray for tears to wash our filthiness,
importantly pissing hogwash through our styes.

The devil, watching by our sickbeds, hissed
old smut and folk-songs to our soul, until
the soft and precious metal of our will
boiled off in vapor for this scientist.

Each day his flattery makes us eat a toad,
and each step forward is a step to hell,
unmoved, though previous corpses and their smell
asphyxiate our progress on this road.

Like the poor lush who cannot satisfy,
we try to force our sex with counterfeits,
die drooling on the deliquescent tits,
mouthing the rotten orange we suck dry.

Gangs of demons are boozing in our brain—
ranked, swarming, like a million warrior-ants,
they drown and choke the cistern of our wants;
each time we breathe, we tear our lungs with pain.

If poison, arson, sex, narcotics, knives
have not yet ruined us and stitched their quick,
loud patterns on the canvas of our lives,
it is because our souls are still too sick.

Among the vermin, jackals, panthers, lice,
gorillas and tarantulas that suck
and snatch and scratch and defecate and fuck
in the disorderly circus of our vice,

there's one more ugly and abortive birth.
It makes no gestures, never beats its breast,
yet it would murder for a moment's rest,
and willingly annihilate the earth.

It's BOREDOM. Tears have glued its eyes together.
You know it well, my Reader. This obscene
beast chain-smokes yawning for the guillotine—
you—hypocrite Reader—my double—my brother!

—Robert Lowell

BILE AND THE IDEAL

I

THE BLESSING

When, by a decree of the sovereign power,
The poet makes his appearance in a bored world,
With fists clenched at the horror, his outraged mother
Calls on a pitying God, at whom these curses are hurled :

" Why was I not made to litter a brood of vipers
Rather than conceive this human mockery ?
My curses on that night whose ephemeral pleasures
Filled my womb with this avenging treachery !

Since I must be chosen among all women that are
To bear the lifetime's grudge of a sullen husband,
And since I cannot get rid of this caricature,
—Fling it away like old letters to be burned,

On what you have devised for my punishment
I will let all your hate of me rebound,
I will torture this stunted growth until its bent
Branches let fall every blighted bud to the ground ! "

And so she prepares for herself in Hell's pit
A place on the pyre made for a mother's crimes,
Blind, in the fury of her foaming hatred,
To the meaning and purpose of the eternal designs.

Meanwhile, under the care of an unseen angel,
The disinherited Child revels in the sun's

Bright force; all that he eats and drinks can fill
Him with memories of the food that was heaven's.

The wind his plaything, any cloud a friend,
The Spirit watching can only weep to see
How in childhood his way of the cross is lightened
With the wild bird-song of his innocent gaiety.

Those he would love look at him with suspicion
Or else, emboldened by his calm, experiment
With various possible methods of exciting derision
By trying out their cruelty on his complaint.

They mix ashes or unspeakable filth with the bread
And the wine of his daily communion, drop
Whatever he may have touched with affected dread,
And studiously avoid wherever he may step.

His mistress, parading her contempt in the street,
Cries : " Since he finds my beauty a thing to worship,
I will be one of the ancient idols he talks about,
And make myself with gold out of the same workshop!

I will never have enough of his kneelings and offerings
Until I am sure that the choice foods, the wines,
The 'nard,' the 'incense,' the 'myrrh' that he brings
He brings as other men would to the Virgin's shrines.

And when I am sick to death of trying not to laugh
At the farce of my black masses, I'll try the force
Of the hand he calls 'frail,' my nails will dig a path
Like harpies', to the heart that beats for me, of course !

Like a nestling trembling and palpitating
I will pull that red heart out of his breast
And throw it down for my favourite dog's eating
—Let him do whatever he likes with the rest!"

A serene piety, lifting the poet's gaze,
Reveals heaven opening on a shining throne,
And the lower vision of the world's ravening rage
Is shut off by the sheet lightnings of his brain.

"Be blessed, oh my God, who givest suffering
As the only divine remedy for our folly,
As the highest and purest essence preparing
The strong in spirit for ecstasies most holy.

I know that among the uplifted legions
Of saints, a place awaits the Poet's arrival,
And that among the Powers, Virtues, Dominations
He too is summoned to Heaven's festival.

I know that sorrow is the one human strength
On which neither earth nor hell can impose,
And that all the universe and all time's length
Must be wound into the mystic crown for my brows.

But all the treasury of buried Palmyra,
The earth's unknown metals, the sea's pearls,
Mounted by Thy hand, would be deemed an inferior
Glitter, to his diadem that shines without jewels.

For Thou knowest it will be made of purest light
Drawn from the holy hearth of every primal ray,

To which all human eyes, if they were one bright
Eye, are only a tarnished mirror's fading day ! "

—David Paul

II

THE ALBATROSS

Often, for pastime, mariners will ensnare
The albatross, that vast sea-bird who sweeps
On high companionable pinion where
Their vessel glides upon the bitter deeps.

Torn from his native space, this captive king
Flounders upon the deck in stricken pride,
And pitiably lets his great white wing
Drag like a heavy paddle at his side.

This rider of winds, how awkward he is, and weak !
How droll he seems, who lately was all grace !
A sailor pokes a pipestem into his beak;
Another, hobbling, mocks his trammeled pace.

The Poet is like this monarch of the clouds,
Familiar of storms, of stars, and of all high things;
Exiled on earth amidst its hooting crowds,
He cannot walk, borne down by his giant wings.

—Richard Wilbur

III

ELEVATION

Above the valleys and the lakes : beyond
The woods, seas, clouds, and mountain-ranges : far
Above the sun, the aethers silver-swanned
With nebulae, and the remotest star,

My spirit ! with agility you move
Like a strong swimmer with the seas to fight,
Through the blue vastness furrowing your groove
With an ineffable and male delight.

Far from these foetid marshes, be made pure
In the pure air of the superior sky,
And drink, like some most exquisite liqueur,
The fire that fills the lucid realms on high.

Beyond where cares and boredom hold dominion,
Which charge our fogged existence with their spleen,
Happy is he who with a stalwart pinion
Can seek those fields so shining and serene :

Whose thoughts, like larks, rise on the freshening breeze,
Who fans the morning with his tameless wings,
Skims over life, and understands with ease
The speech of flowers and other voiceless things.

—Roy Campbell

IV

CORRESPONDENCES

Nature is a temple whose living colonnades
Breathe forth a mystic speech in fitful sighs;
Man wanders among symbols in those glades
Where all things watch him with familiar eyes.

Like dwindling echoes gathered far away
Into a deep and thronging unison
Huge as the night or as the light of day,
All scents and sounds and colors meet as one.

Perfumes there are as sweet as the oboe's sound,
Green as the prairies, fresh as a child's caress,
—And there are others, rich, corrupt, profound

And of an infinite pervasiveness,
Like myrrh, or musk, or amber, that excite
The ecstasies of sense, the soul's delight.

—Richard Wilbur

V

I LOVE THE THOUGHT . . .

I love the thought of those old naked days
When Phoebus gilded torsos with his rays,
When men and women sported, strong and fleet,
Without anxiety or base deceit,
And heaven caressed them, amorously keen
To prove the health of each superb machine.
Cybele then was lavish of her guerdon
And did not find her sons too gross a burden :
But, like a she-wolf, in her love great-hearted,
Her full brown teats to all the world imparted.
Bold, handsome, strong, Man rightly might evince
Pride in the glories that proclaimed him prince—
Fruits pure of outrage, by the blight unsmitten,
With firm, smooth flesh that cried out to be bitten.

Today the Poet, when he would assess
Those native splendours in the nakedness
Of man or woman, feels a sombre chill
Enveloping his spirit and his will.
He meets a gloomy picture, which he loathes,
Wherein deformity cries out for clothes.
Oh comic runts ! Oh horror of burlesque !
Lank, flabby, skewed, pot-bellied, and grotesque !
Whom their smug god, Utility (poor brats!),
Has swaddled in his brazen clouts " ersatz "
As with cheap tinsel. Women tallow-pale,
Both gnawed and nourished by debauch, who trail
The heavy burden of maternal vice,
Or of fecundity the hideous price.

We have (corrupted nations) it is true
Beauties the ancient people never knew—
Sad faces gnawed by cancers of the heart
And charms which morbid lassitudes impart.
But these inventions of our tardy muse
Can't force our ailing peoples to refuse
Just tribute to the holiness of youth
With its straightforward mien, its forehead couth,
The limpid gaze, like running water bright,
Diffusing, careless, through all things, like light
Of azure skies, the birds, the winds, the flowers,
Its songs, and perfumes, and heart-warming powers.

—Roy Campbell

VI

BEACONS

Rubens, garden of idleness watered by oblivion,
Where quick flesh pillows the impotence of dreams,
Where life's affluence writhes in eddying abandon
Like air in the air, or water in streams.

Leonardo da Vinci, deep mirror of darkness,
Where angels appear, their smiles charged with mystery
And tenderness, within the shadowy enclosures
Of pines and glaciers that shut in their country.

Rembrandt, tragic hospital re-echoing round a sigh;
A tall crucifix for only ornament

Traversed obliquely by a single wintry ray
Through which prayers rise, exhaling from excrement.

Michelangelo, no man's land where Hercules and Christ
Are at one; where powerful phantoms in crowds
Erect themselves deliberately in darkening twilights,
With pressed, rigid fingers ripping open their shrouds.

Rage of the wrestler, impudence of the faun;
Puget, the convicts' melancholy emperor,
Caging the lion's pride in a weak, jaundiced man,
Deducing beauty from crime, vice and terror.

Watteau, carnival where many a distinguished soul
Flutters like a moth, lost in the brilliance
Of chandeliers shedding frivolity on the cool,
Clear decors enclosing the changes of the dance.

Goya, nightmare compact of things incredible :
Foetuses being fried for a witch's sabbath feast;
An old woman at a mirror, a little naked girl
Lowering an artful stocking to tempt a devil's lust.

Delacroix, blood lake haunted by evil angels
In the permanent green darkness of a forest of firs,
Where under a stricken sky a muffled sigh fills
The air like a faintly echoed fanfare of Weber's.

Such, O Lord, are the maledictions, the tears,
The ecstasies, the blasphemies, the cries of Te Deum
Re-echoing along labyrinthine corridors :
A dream for mortal hearts distilled from divine opium,

The watchword reiterated by sentinels
A thousand times, the message whispered from post to post,
A beacon burning on a thousand citadels,
A call of all the hunters lost in the great forest.

For is this not indeed, O Lord, the best witness
That our dignity can render to Your pity,
This tide of tears which age after age gathers
To fail and fall on the shore of Your eternity ?

—David Paul

VII

THE SICK MUSE

Poor Muse, alas, what ails thee, then, today ?
Thy hollow eyes with midnight visions burn,
Upon thy brow in alternation play,
Madness and Horror, cold and taciturn.

Have the green lemure and the goblin red,
Poured on thee love and terror from their urn ?
Or with despotic hand the nightmare dread
Deep plunged thee in some fabulous Minturne ?

Would that thy breast, where so deep thoughts arise,
Breathed forth a healthful perfume with thy sighs;
Would that thy Christian blood ran wave by wave

In rhythmic sounds the antique numbers gave,
When Phoebus shared his alternating reign
With mighty Pan, lord of the ripening grain.

—F. P. Sturm

VIII

THE VENAL MUSE

Muse of my heart, lover of grand châteaux,
When January unleashes storm and sleet,
Through the black dreary evenings when it snows,
Will you have coals to warm your violet feet ?

With gleaming starlight that has pierced the blinds
Will you reanimate your shoulders' cold
Marble ? Your palate dry, your purse unlined,
From vaults of azure will you harvest gold ?

To earn your evening bread you'll have to swing
The censer like a choirboy, and sing
Te Deums of which you don't believe a word,

Or, starving clown, show off your charms, your smile
Wet with tears that none see, to beguile
And cheer the sick spleen of the vulgar herd.

—C. F. MacIntyre

IX

THE WICKED MONK

Old cloisters, on their mighty walls, displayed
In tableau, scenes of holy Verity
Which warmed the pious entrails and allayed
The chill of cenobite austerity.

When the seed of Christ flourished long ago,
Many a monk, of small renown today,
Using the churchyard for his studio,
Glorified Death in all simplicity.

My soul's a tomb which, wicked cenobite,
I wander in for all eternity;
Nothing embellishes these odious walls.

O slothful monk ! When shall they learn to make
Of the live pageant of my misery
My hands their labor, my eyes their delight ?

—Barbara Gibbs

X

THE RUINED GARDEN

My childhood was only a menacing shower,
cut now and then by hours of brilliant heat.
All the top soil was killed by rain and sleet,
my garden hardly bore a standing flower.

From now on, my mind's autumn! I must take
the field and dress my beds with spade and rake
and restore order to my flooded grounds.
There the rain raised mountains like burial mounds.

I throw fresh seeds out. Who knows what survives?
What elements will give us life and food?
This soil is irrigated by the tides.

Time and nature sluice away our lives.
A virus eats the heart out of our sides,
digs in and multiplies on our lost blood.

—Robert Lowell

XI

ILL LUCK

So huge a burden to support,
Your courage, Sisyphus, would ask;
Well though my heart attacks its task,
Yet Art is long and Time is short.

Far from the famed memorial arch
Towards a lonely grave I come.
My heart in its funereal march
Goes beating like a muffled drum.

—Yet many a gem lies hidden still
Of whom no pick-axe, spade, or drill
The lonely secrecy invades;

And many a flower, to heal regret,
Pours forth its fragrant secret yet
Amidst the solitary shades.

—Roy Campbell

XII

A FORMER LIFE

Long since, I lived beneath vast porticoes,
By many ocean-sunsets tinged and fired,
Where mighty pillars, in majestic rows,
Seemed like basaltic caves when day expired.

The rolling surge that mirrored all the skies
Mingled its music, turbulent and rich,
Solemn and mystic, with the colours which
The setting sun reflected in my eyes.

And there I lived amid voluptuous calms,
In splendours of blue sky and wandering wave,
Tended by many a naked, perfumed slave,

Who fanned my languid brow with waving palms.
They were my slaves—the only care they had
To know what secret grief had made me sad.

—F. P. Sturm

XIII

GYPSIES ON THE ROAD

The dark-eyed ancient tribe that never rests
Took up the age-old journey yesterday,
The young on the women's backs, and—should they cry—
Treasure awaits them at the hanging breasts.

On foot, the men, whose shouldered weapons gleam,
Trudge by the waggons where their families lie.
Their gaze is heavy as they scan the sky
With nameless shadows of a distant dream.

The cricket, watching from its sandy bower,
Greets their approach with loudest eloquence;
Cybele makes earth greener for their sake;

The rock becomes a spring, the deserts flower
Before these wanderers, as they march to take
The constant empire of the unknown hence.

—Naomi Lewis

XIV

MAN AND THE SEA

Always, unfettered man, you will cherish the sea!
The sea your mirror, you look into your mind
In its eternal billows surging without end,
And as its gulfs are bitter, so must your spirit be.

You plunge with joy into this image of your own:
You hug it with your eyes and arms; your heart
Forgets for a time its noisy beat, becomes a part
Of a greater, more savage and less tameable moan.

In your own ways, you both are brooding and discreet:
Man, no one has mapped your chasm's hidden floor,
Oh sea, no one knows your inmost riches, for
Your jealousy hides secrets none can repeat.

As the uncounted swarm of centuries gathers
You two have fought without pity or remorse, both
From sheer love of the slaughter and of death,
Oh, eternal wrestlers, oh, relentless brothers!

—Ruthven Todd

XV

DON JUAN IN HELL

The night Don Juan came to pay his fees
To Charon, by the caverned water's shore,
A Beggar, proud-eyed as Antisthenes,
Stretched out his knotted fingers on the oar.

Mournful, with drooping breasts and robes unsewn
The shapes of women swayed in ebon skies,
Trailing behind him with a restless moan
Like cattle herded for a sacrifice.

Here, grinning for his wage, stood Sganarelle,
And here Don Luis pointed, bent and dim,

To show the dead who lined the holes of Hell,
This was that impious son who mocked at him.

The hollow-eyed, the chaste Elvira came,
Trembling and veiled, to view her traitor spouse.
Was it one last bright smile she thought to claim,
Such as made sweet the morning of his vows ?

A great stone man rose like a tower on board,
Stood at the helm and cleft the flood profound :
But the calm hero, leaning on his sword,
Gazed back, and would not offer one look round.

—James Elroy Flecker

XVI

THE PUNISHMENT OF PRIDE

In those old times wherein Theology
Flourished with greater sap and energy,
A celebrated doctor — so they say —
Having stirred many careless hearts one day
Down to their dullest depths, and having shown
Strange pathways leading to the heavenly throne —
Tracks he himself had never journeyed on
(Whereby maybe pure spirits alone had gone) —
Frenzied and swollen by a devilish pride,
Like to a man who has climbed too high, outcried :
" Ah, little Jesus, I have lifted thee !
But had I willed to assault thy dignity,

Thy shame had matched thy present fame, and lo !
Thou wouldst be but a wretched embryo ! "

Straightway his reason left him; that keen mind,
Sunbright before, was darkened and made blind;
All chaos whirled within that intellect
Erewhile a shrine with all fair gems bedeckt,
Beneath whose roof such pomp had shone so bright;
He was possessed by silence and thick night
As is a cellar when its key is lost . . .

Thenceforth he was a brute beast; when he crossed
The fields at times, not seeing any thing,
Knowing not if it were winter or green spring,
Useless, repulsive, vile, he made a mock
For infants, a mere children's laughing-stock.

— Sir John Squire

XVII

BEAUTY

I am as lovely as a dream in stone;
My breast on which each finds his death in turn
Inspires the poet with a love as lone
As everlasting clay, and as taciturn.

Swan-white of heart, a sphinx no mortal knows,
My throne is in the heaven's azure deep;
I hate all movement that disturbs my pose;
I smile not ever, neither do I weep.

Before my monumental attitudes,
Taken from the proudest plastic arts,
My poets pray in austere studious moods,

For I, to fold enchantment round their hearts,
Have pools of light where beauty flames and dies,
The placid mirrors of my luminous eyes.

—F. P. Sturm

XVIII

THE IDEAL

Never those beauties in old prints vignetted,
Those shopworn products of a worthless age,
With slippered feet and fingers castanetted,
The thirst of hearts like my heart can assuage.

To Gavarni, the poet of chloroses,
I leave his troupe of beauties sick and wan;
I cannot find among those pale, pale roses,
The red ideal mine eyes would gaze upon.

You, Lady Macbeth, a soul strong in crime,
Aeschylus' dream born in a northern clime—
Ah, you could quench my dark heart's deep desiring;

Or you, Michelangelo's daughter, Night,
In a strange posture dreamily admiring
Your beauty fashioned for a giant's delight!

—F. P. Sturm

XIX

GIANTESS

When Nature once in lustful hot undress
Conceived gargantuan offspring, then would I
Have loved to live near a young giantess,
Like a voluptuous cat at a queen's feet.

To see her body flower with her desire
And freely spread out in its dreadful play,
Guess if her heart concealed some heavy fire
Whose humid smokes would swim upon her eye.

To feel at leisure her stupendous shapes,
Crawl on the cliffs of her enormous knees,
And, when in summer the unhealthy suns

Have stretched her out across the plains, fatigued,
Sleep in the shadows of her breasts at ease
Like a small hamlet at a mountain's base.

—Karl Shapiro

XX

JEWELS

The darling one was naked and, knowing my wish,
Had kept only the regalia of her jewelry
Whose resonant charms can lure and vanquish
Like a Moorish slave-girl's in her moment of glory.

A world of dazzling stones and of precious metals
Flinging, in its quick rhythm, glints of mockery
Ravishes me into ecstasy, I love to madness
The mingling of sounds and lights in one intricacy.

Naked, then, she was to all of my worship,
Smiling in triumph from the heights of her couch
At my desire advancing, as gentle and deep
As the sea sending its waves to the warm beach.

Her eyes fixed as a tiger's in the tamer's trance,
Absent, unthinking, she varied her poses
With an audacity and wild innocence
That gave a strange pang to each metamorphosis.

Her long legs, her hips, shining smooth as oil,
Her arms and her thighs, undulant as a swan,
Lured my serene, clairvoyant gaze to travel
To her belly and breasts, the grapes of my vine.

With a charm as powerful as an evil angel
To trouble the calm where my soul had retreated,
They advanced slowly to dislodge it from its crystal
Rock, where its loneliness meditated.

With the hips of Antiope, the torso of a boy,
So deeply was the one form sprung into the other
It seemed as if desire had fashioned a new toy.
Her farded, fawn-brown skin was perfection to either!

—And the lamp having at last resigned itself to death,
There was nothing now but firelight in the room,

And every time a flame uttered a gasp for breath
It flushed her amber skin with the blood of its bloom.

—David Paul

XXI

THE MASK

(*An allegorical statue in the style of the Renaissance*)

To Ernest Christophe, sculptor.

Observe the Florentine grand style, and trace
How in this body's sinuous soft curves
Twin goddesses are present, Force and Grace;
Truly she is miraculous, deserves
In her delicious strength and suppleness
To be enthroned on some most sumptuous bed
And charm a king's or pontiff's idleness.

Observe again where self-conceit is led
To steal enjoyment from this tempting smile;
This languid, sinister and mocking air;
This coy regard, concealed beneath a veil,
In which victorious lineaments declare
"I am called Pleasure, and am crowned by Love."
What thrilling charm informs her majesty
This moving gentleness goes far to prove.
Let us go near and walk around her beauty.

Oh ! blasphemy of art ! Oh ! fatal shock !
The divine body, which appeared to ask
Us to our pleasure, has two heads that mock !

No ! these exquisite features are a mask,
Mere debased ornament with fine grimace;
Behind, atrociously contorted, is
The veritable head, the sincere face
Turned to the shadow of this face which lies.
Poor perfect beauty, a grand river breaks
As your tears fall into my anxious soul,
I am drunk with your lie, my spirit slakes
Its torture in the stream your eyes unroll.

Why is she weeping ? In her lovely pride
She could have conquered the whole race of man;
What unknown evil harrows her lithe side ?

She weeps, mad girl, because her life began;
Because she lives. One thing she does deplore
So much that she kneels trembling in the dust —
That she must live tomorrow, evermore,
Tomorrow and tomorrow — as we must !

— Graham Reynolds

XXII

HYMN TO BEAUTY

From heaven or hell, O Beauty, come you hence ?
Out from your gaze, infernal and divine,
Pours blended evil and beneficence,
And therefore men have likened you to wine.

Sunset and dawn within your eyes are fair;
Stormlike you scatter perfume into space;
Your kiss, a philtre from an amphora rare,
Charms boys to courage and makes heroes base.

Whence come you, from what spheres, or inky deeps,
With careless hand joy and distress to strew ?
Fate, like a dog at heel, behind you creeps;
You govern all things here, and naught you rue.

You walk upon the dead with scornful glances,
Among your gems Horror is not least fair;
Murder, the dearest of your baubles, dances
Upon your haughty breast with amorous air.

Mothlike around your flame the transient, turning,
Crackles and flames and cries, " Ah, heavenly doom ! "
The quivering lover o'er his mistress yearning
Is but a dying man who woos his tomb.

From heaven or the abyss ? Let questioning be,
O artless monster wreaking endless pain,
So that your smile and glance throw wide to me
An infinite that I have loved in vain.

From Satan or from God ? Holy or vile ?
Let questioning rest. O soft-eyed sprite, my queen,
O rhythm, perfume, light — so you beguile
Time from his slothfulness, the world from spleen.

— Dorothy Martin

XXIII

EXOTIC PERFUME

When, on an autumn evening, with closed eyes,
I breathe the warm dark fragrance of your breast,
Before me blissful shores unfold, caressed
By dazzling fires from blue unchanging skies.

And there, upon that calm and drowsing isle,
Grow luscious fruits amid fantastic trees :
There, men are lithe : the women of those seas
Amaze one with their gaze that knows no guile.

Your perfume wafts me thither like a wind :
I see a harbour thronged with masts and sails
Still weary from the tumult of the gales;

And with the sailors' song that drifts to me
Are mingled odours of the tamarind,
— And all my soul is scent and melody.

— Alan Conder

XXIV

HER HAIR

O fleece, that down the neck waves to the nape!
O curls! O perfume nonchalant and rare!
O ecstacy! To fill this alcove shape
With memories that in these tresses sleep,
I would shake them like pennons in the air!

Languorous Asia, burning Africa,
And a far world, defunct almost, absent,
Within your aromatic forest stay!
As other souls on music drift away,
Mine, o my love! still floats upon your scent.

I shall go there where, full of sap, both tree
And man swoon in the heat of southern climes;
Strong tresses, be the swell that carries me!
I dream upon your sea of ebony
Of dazzling sails, of oarsmen, masts and flames:

A sun-drenched and reverberating port,
Where I imbibe colour and sound and scent;
Where vessels, gliding through the gold and moire,
Open their vast arms as they leave the shore
To clasp the pure and shimmering firmament.

I'll plunge my head, enamoured of its pleasure,
In this black ocean where the other hides;
My subtle spirit then will know a measure
Of fertile idleness and fragrant leisure,
Lulled by the infinite rhythm of its tides!

Pavilion, of blue-shadowed tresses spun,
You give me back the azure from afar;
And where the twisted locks are fringed with down
Lurk mingled odours I grow drunk upon
Of oil of coconut, of musk and tar.

A long time! always! my hand in your hair
Will sow the stars of sapphire, pearl, ruby,
That you be never deaf to my desire,
My oasis and gourd whence I aspire
To drink deep of the wine of memory!

—Doreen Bell

XXV

YOU, WHOM I WORSHIP . . .

You, whom I worship as night's firmament,
Urn of sorrow, beautiful and silent;
I love you more, because you turn from me
Adorning night, but, with large irony
Rather increase the absolute blue space
Which alienates the sky from my embrace.

I leap to your attack, climb in assault
Like corpseworms feeding nimbly in the vault,
And cherish you, relentless, cruel beast
Till that last coldness which delights me best.

— Graham Reynolds

XXVI

YOU'D TAKE TO BED THE WHOLE WORLD . . .

You'd take to bed the whole world as your prize,
you slut of sluts, by boredom brutalized!
To exercise your jaws at this rare sport
each day you must be served a fresh-killed heart.
Lit up like shop-windows in vulgar blaze
or street-lamps glaring on public holidays,
your insolent eyes with borrowed power burn.
Their beauty's proper law they never learn.

Oh blind and deaf machine, rich in torment—
drinker of the world's blood, wholesome instrument,
how can you not feel shame, how can you not
blanch at each mirror from which your charms look out?
This hideous wrong in which you feel secure,
has it not made you shrink one step in fear,—
that nature, strong in her concealed designs,
makes use of you, oh woman, queen of sins,
vile animal! to mould a genius?

Oh foul magnificence—sublime disgrace!

—Frederick Morgan

XXVII

SED NON SATIATA

Bizarre deity, as dark as night,
Scented with musky perfume and Havana,
Work of some obi, the Faust of the savanna,
Witch with ebony flanks, child of black midnight,

Rather than *constance, le nuits,* opium,
The elixir of your mouth where love pavanes;
Your eyes are wells where my desires come
And my ennuis drink in thirsty caravans.

From those black eyes, your soul's smoke-vents, I pray,
Pitiless demon, pour on me less flame;
I am not the Styx to encompass you nine times,

Alas ! I can't, Megaerian libertine,
Break your spirit and bring you to bay,
Transformed in your bed's hell to Proserpine !

—C. F. MacIntyre

XXVIII

ROBED IN A SILKEN ROBE . . .

Robed in a silken robe that shines and shakes,
She seems to dance whenever she treads the sod,
Like the long serpent that a fakir makes
Dance to the waving cadence of a rod.

As the sad sand upon the desert's verge,
Insensible to mortal grief and strife;
As the long weeds that float among the surge,
She folds indifference round her budding life.

Her eyes are carved of minerals pure and cold,
And in her strange symbolic nature where
An angel mingles with the sphinx of old,

Where all is gold and steel and light and air,
For ever, like a vain star, unafraid
Shines the cold hauteur of the sterile maid.

—F. P. Sturm

XXIX

THE DANCING SERPENT

Dear indolent, I love to see,
  In your body bright,
How like shimmering silk the skin
  Reflects the light !

On the deep ocean of your hair
  Where perfume laves,
Odorous and vagabond sea
  Of blue and brown waves,

Like a vessel awakening
  When morning winds rise

My dreaming soul begins to sail
Toward remote skies.

Your two eyes that neither sweetness
Nor bitterness hold
Are two chilly gems mingled of
Iron and gold.

When you walk in rhythm, lovely
With abandonment,
You seem to be swayed by a wand,
A dancing serpent.

Your child's head under the burden
Of your indolence
Sways as delicately as a
Young elephant's,

And your body bends and straightens
Like a slender ship
That, plunging and rolling, lets the
Yards in water dip.

When, like a stream by thawing of
Glaciers made replete,
The water of your mouth rises
Up to your teeth,

I drink a Bohemian wine,
Powerful and tart,
A liquid sky that sows its stars
Within my heart!

—Barbara Gibbs

XXX

A CARRION

Remember now, my Love, what piteous thing
We saw on a summer's gracious day :
By the roadside a hideous carrion, quivering
On a clean bed of pebbly clay,

Her legs flexed in the air like a courtesan,
Burning and sweating venomously,
Calmly exposed its belly, ironic and wan,
Clamorous with foul ecstasy.

The sun bore down upon this rottenness
As if to roast it with gold fire,
And render back to nature her own largess
A hundredfold of her desire.

Heaven observed the vaunting carcass there
Blooming with the richness of a flower;
And that almighty stink which corpses wear
Choked you with sleepy power !

The flies swarmed on the putrid vulva, then
A black tumbling rout would seethe
Of maggots, thick like a torrent in a glen,
Over those rags that lived and seemed to breathe.

They darted down and rose up like a wave
Or buzzed impetuously as before;
One would have thought the corpse was held a slave
To living by the life it bore!

This world had music, its own swift emotion
Like water and the wind running,
Or corn that a winnower in rhythmic motion
Fans with fiery cunning.

All forms receded, as in a dream were still,
Where white visions vaguely start
From the sketch of a painter's long-neglected idyl
Into a perfect art!

Behind the rocks a restless bitch looked on
Regarding us with jealous eyes,
Waiting to tear from the livid skeleton
Her loosed morsel quick with flies.

And even you will come to this foul shame,
This ultimate infection,
Star of my eyes, my being's inner flame,
My angel and my passion!

Yes: such shall you be, O queen of heavenly grace,
Beyond the last sacrament,
When through your bones the flowers and sucking grass
Weave their rank cerement.

Speak, then, my Beauty, to this dire putrescence,
To the worm that shall kiss your proud estate,
That I have kept the divine form and the essence
Of my festered loves inviolate!

—Allen Tate

XXXI

DE PROFUNDIS CLAMAVI

Have pity, You alone whom I adore
From down this black pit where my heart is sped,
A sombre universe ringed round with lead
Where fear and curses the long night explore.

Six months a cold sun hovers overhead;
The other six is night upon this land.
No beast; no stream; no wood; no leaves expand.
The desert Pole is not a waste so dead.

Now in the whole world there's no horror quite
So cold and cruel as this glacial sun,
So like old Chaos as this boundless night;

I envy the least animals that run,
Which can find respite in brute slumber drowned,
So slowly is the skein of time unwound.

—Desmond Harmsworth

XXXII

THE VAMPIRE

Thou who abruptly as a knife
Didst come into my heart; thou who,
A demon horde into my life,
Didst enter, wildly dancing, through

The doorways of my sense unlatched
To make my spirit thy domain —
Harlot to whom I am attached
As convicts to the ball and chain,

As gamblers to the wheel's bright spell,
As drunkards to their raging thirst,
As corpses to their worms — accurst
Be thou ! Oh, be thou damned to hell !

I have entreated the swift sword
To strike, that I at once be freed;
The poisoned phial I have implored
To plot with me a ruthless deed.

Alas ! the phial and the blade
Do cry aloud and laugh at me :
" Thou art not worthy of our aid;
Thou art not worthy to be free.

Though one of us should be the tool
To save thee from thy wretched fate,
Thy kisses would resuscitate
The body of thy vampire, fool ! "

— George Dillon

XXXIII

LETHE

Come to my heart, cruel, insensible one,
Adored tiger, monster with the indolent air;
I would for a long time plunge my trembling fingers
Into the heavy tresses of your hair;

And in your garments that exhale your perfume
I would bury my aching head,
And breathe, like a withered flower,
The sweet, stale reek of my love that is dead.

I want to sleep! sleep rather than live!
And in a slumber, dubious as the tomb's,
I would lavish my kisses without remorse
Upon the burnished copper of your limbs.

To swallow my abated sobs
Nothing equals your bed's abyss;
Forgetfulness dwells in your mouth,
And Lethe flows from your kiss.

My destiny, henceforth my pleasure,
I shall obey, predestined instrument,
Docile martyr, condemned innocent,
Whose fervour but augments his torment.

I shall suck, to drown my rancour,
Nepenthe, hemlock, an opiate,
At the charming tips of this pointed breast
That has never imprisoned a heart.

—Doreen Bell

XXXIV

A HIDEOUS JEWESS LAY WITH ME . . .

A hideous Jewess lay with me for hire
One night : two corpses side by side we seemed
And stretched by that polluted thing I dreamed
Of the sad beauty of my vain desire.

I thought upon her brow clad round with fire
And matchless strength, her native majesty,
Her perfumed helm of hair whose memory
Makes me toward Love's heights to reaspire.

For fervently I would have rained, my Sweet,
Fond kisses over all thy form divine
Even from thy black tresses to thy feet,

If some soft evening, with a single tear,
O cruel queen, thou couldst have dimmed the clear
Cold splendour of those icy eyes of thine.

—Sir John Squire

XXXV

THE REMORSE OF THE DEAD

O shadowy Beauty mine, when thou shalt sleep
In the deep heart of a black marble tomb;
When thou for mansion and for bower shalt keep
Only one rainy cave of hollow gloom;

And when the stone upon thy trembling breast,
And on thy straight sweet body's supple grace,
Crushes thy will and keeps thy heart at rest,
And holds those feet from their adventurous race;

Then the deep grave, who shares my reverie,
(For the deep grave is ever the poet's friend)
During long nights when sleep is far from thee,

Shall whisper : " Ah, thou didst not comprehend
The dead wept thus, thou woman frail and weak " —
And like remorse the worm shall gnaw thy cheek.

—F. P. Sturm

XXXVI

THE CAT

Come, beautiful creature, sheathe your claws;
Rest on my amorous heart,
And let me plunge in your marvellous eyes,
Of mingled metal and agate.

When my fingers caress at leisure
Your supple, elastic back,
And my hand tingles with pleasure
From your body's electric contact,

I seem to see my mistress. Her regard,
Like yours, nice animal,
Deep and cold, cuts and thrusts like a sword,

And from her feet to her head's dark coronal,
A subtile air, a dangerous perfume,
Swim round her brown body's dusky bloom.

—Doreen Bell

XXXVII

DUELLUM

Two warriors engage, their weapons flash,
Spill blood, splash glints of steel into the air,
Such fracas, such encounters are the war
Of puppy-love, the torment of young flesh.

Dearest, our blades are broken, the fine fashion
Of youth is gone, but teeth and fingernails
Take up where the outmoded weapon fails—
Hearts ulcerated by a full-fledged passion.

In a deep gulley, lynx-haunted, forlorn,
Roll our own champions, locked in brute embrace,
Tearing their bloody flesh among the thorns.

That is the pit of Hell, filled with our kind.
Let's roll in it ourselves, with no remorse,
To keep alive our hatred without end.

—Anthony Hecht

XXXVIII

THE BALCONY

Mother of memories, mistress of mistresses,
O thou, my pleasure, thou, all my desire,
Thou shalt recall the beauty of caresses,
The charm of evenings by the gentle fire,
Mother of memories, mistress of mistresses !

The eves illumined by the burning coal,
The balcony where veiled rose-vapour clings —
How soft your breast was then, how sweet your soul !
Ah, and we said imperishable things,
Those eves illumined by the burning coal.

Lovely the suns were in those twilights warm,
And space profound, and strong life's pulsing flood;
In bending o'er you, queen of every charm,
I thought I breathed the perfume of your blood.
The suns were beauteous in those twilights warm.

The film of night flowed round and over us,
And my eyes in the dark did your eyes meet;
I drank your breath, ah ! sweet and poisonous,
And in my hands fraternal slept your feet —
Night, like a film, flowed round and over us.

I can recall those happy days forgot,
And see, with head bowed on your knees, my past.
Your languid beauties now would move me not
Did not your gentle heart and body cast
The old spell of those happy days forgot.

Can vows and perfume, kisses infinite,
Be reborn from the gulf we cannot sound;
As rise to heaven suns once again made bright
After being plunged in deep seas and profound ?
Ah, vows and perfumes, kisses infinite !

—F. P. Sturm

XXXIX

THE POSSESSED

The sun in crêpe has muffled up his fire.
Moon of my life ! Half shade yourself like him.
Slumber or smoke. Be silent and be dim,
And in the gulf of boredom plunge entire;

I love you thus ! However, if you like,
Like some bright star from its eclipse emerging,
To flaunt with Folly where the crowds are surging—
Flash, lovely dagger, from your sheath and strike !

Light up your eyes from chandeliers of glass !
Light up the lustful looks of louts that pass !
Morbid or petulant, I thrill before you.

Be what you will, black night or crimson dawn;
No fibre of my body tautly drawn,
But cries : " Beloved demon, I adore you ! "

—Roy Campbell

XL

A PHANTOM

I. The Shades

Down in the fathomless despair
Where Destiny has locked me in,
Where light nor joy descends, and where
(Sole lodger of Night's dreary inn)

An artist God has set apart
In mockery, I paint the murk;
Where, like a ghoulish cook at work
Boiling and munching on my heart—

At moments gleams and grows apace
A phantom languorous and bright,
A Dream of Oriental grace.

When it attains its utmost height,
I know at last the lovely thing :
It's She ! girl dark yet glimmering.

II. The Perfume

Hast thou inhaled—O reader, say !—
With zest and lazy greed, the old
Incense that chapel arches hold
Or the stale musk of a sachet ?

O magic spell, O ecstasy !
— To make the present yield the past ! —
It's thus on a beloved breast
Love culls the flowers of memory.

The tresses long about her face
— A living censer, left the place
With strange wild odours all astir,

And in her velvet, muslin, lace,
Candid and girlish, over her
Hovered a perfume, faint, of fur.

III. The Frame

A fine frame to a picture brings
(Though from a brush illustrious)
A charm strange and mysterious,
Secluding it from other things.

Thus jewels, metals, gold, became
Adapted to her beauty bright;
Nothing obscured its perfect light,
All things about her seemed a frame.

Often one might have said she found
Her garments loved her, for she drowned
Her naked body in embraces

Of voluptuous silks and laces;
A monkey's childlike grace she gave
To every movement, gay or grave.

IV. The Portrait

Death and Disease make ashes of
The flames that wrapped our youth around.
Of her soft eyes, ablaze with love,
Her mouth, wherein my heart was drowned,

Of her long kisses' magic spell,
Her passion, sharp as Phoebus' dart,
What have I now ? O woeful heart !
Naught but a faded old pastel.

Dying, like me, in solitude,
Paling each day in every part
Beneath Time's tireless pinions rude . . .

Dark murderer of Life and Art,
Never shalt thou in me destroy
Her who was once my fame, my joy !

—Lewis Piaget Shanks

XLI

IF BY SOME FREAK OF FORTUNE . . .

If by some freak of fortune my name should find
The future's murky coast, and find its way
Nosing through human minds of another day
Like a rigged clipper with a good north wind,

These verses which I give you shall preserve
Your memory like vague legends of old time
Suspended from my intricate webs of rhyme
To tease and touch the thoughtful reader's nerve;

Damned in the world's eyes, totally despised,
Rejected by all persons save by me,
Despising all the others equally,

Ignorant fools who thought you a mere shrew,
O jet-eyed creature, shade unrealized,
O great bronze angel of the noble brow!

—Anthony Hecht

XLII

SEMPER EADEM

Whence, did you say, does this strange sadness rise,
Like tides that over naked black rocks flow ?
— When here the heart's once-trampled vintage lies,
Living's a curse. A secret all men know,

A very simple unmysterious pain,
And, like your joy, quite clear for all to know.
Therefore, O curious beauty, search is vain;
And hold your tongue, although your voice is low.

Ignorant, ever charmed one, spare your breath !
O lips of the childlike laugh ! For often Death
Still more than Life, binds us in subtle ways.

Grant that my heart grow drunk on that which *lies,*
Plunge as in fine dreams into your fine eyes
And in those shading lashes ever laze.

—Peter Hellings

XLIII

ALL IN ONE

The Demon, in my chamber high,
This morning came to visit me,
And, thinking he would find some fault,
He whispered : "I would know of thee

Among the many lovely things
That make the magic of her face,
Among the beauties, black and rose,
That make her body's charm and grace,

Which is most fair ?" Thou didst reply
To the Abhorred, O soul of mine :
"No single beauty is the best,
Since she is all one flower divine.

When all things charm me I ignore
Which one alone brings most delight;
She shines before me like the dawn,
And she consoles me like the night.

The harmony is far too great,
That governs all her body fair,

For impotence to analyse
And say which note is sweetest there.

O mystic metamorphosis!
My senses into one sense flow—
Her voice makes perfume when she speaks,
Her breath is music faint and low!"

—F. P. Sturm

XLIV

WHAT SHALL YOU SAY TONIGHT . . .

What shall you say tonight, poor soul so full of care,
What shall you say, my heart, heart hitherto so sad,
To the most kind, to the most dear, to the most fair,
Whose pure serene regard has made you proud and glad?

—We shall set all our pride to sing her holy praise!
What sweetness to be hers! To live beneath her sight!
Half spirit is her flesh, angelic all her ways;
Her glance alone invests us in a robe of light!

Whether in solitude and deep obscurity,
Whether by day among the moving crowd it be,
Her phantom like a torch in air will dance and run;

It speaks: "Beauty is mine; Authority is mine;
Love only, for my sake, the noble and the fine:
I am thine Angel, Muse, Madonna, all in one."

—Edna St. Vincent Millay

XLV

THE LIVING TORCH

Those lit eyes go before me, in full view,
(Some cunning angel magnetised their light) —
Heavenly twins, yet my own brothers too,
Shaking their diamond blaze into my sight.

My steps from every trap or sin to save,
In the strait road of Beauty they conduct me.
They are my servants, and I am their slave,
Obedient in whatever they instruct me.

Delightful eyes, you burn with mystic rays
Like candles in broad day; red suns may blaze,
But cannot quench their still, fantastic light.

Those candles burn for death, but you for waking :
You sing the dawn that in my soul is breaking,
Stars which no sun could ever put to flight !

— Roy Campbell

XLVI

TO ONE WHO IS TOO GAY

Your head, your gestures, and your air
Are lovely as a landscape; smiles
Rimple upon your face at whiles
Like winds in the clear sky up there.

The grumpy passers that you graze
Are dazzled by the radiant health,
And the illimitable wealth
Your arms and shoulders seem to blaze.

The glaring colours that, in showers,
Clash in your clothes with such commotion,
In poets' minds suggest the notion
Of a mad ballet-dance of flowers.

These garish dresses illustrate
Your spirit, striped with every fad.
O madwoman, whom, quite as mad,
I love as madly as I hate.

Sometimes in gardens, seeking rest,
Where I have dragged my soul atonic,
I've felt the sun with gaze ironic
Tearing the heart within my breast.

The spring and verdure, dressed to stagger,
Humiliate me with such power
That I have punished, in a flower,
The insolence of Nature's swagger.

And so, one night, I'd like to sneak,
When darkness tolls the hour of pleasure,
A craven thief, towards the treasure
Which is your person, plump and sleek.

To punish your bombastic flesh,
To bruise your breast immune to pain,

To furrow down your flank a lane
Of gaping crimson, deep and fresh.

And, most vertiginous delight!
Into those lips, so freshly striking
And daily lovelier to my liking—
Infuse the venom of my spite.

—Roy Campbell

XLVII

REVERSIBILITY

Angel of gaiety, have you tasted grief?
Shame and remorse and sobs and weary spite,
And the vague terrors of the fearful night
That crush the heart up like a crumpled leaf?
Angel of gaiety, have you tasted grief?

Angel of kindness, have you tasted hate?
With hands clenched in the dark, and tears of gall,
When Vengeance beats her hellish battle-call,
And makes herself the captain of our fate,
Angel of kindness, have you tasted hate?

Angel of health, did ever you know pain,
Which like an exile trails his tired footfalls
The cold length of the white infirmary walls,
With lips compressed, seeking the sun in vain?
Angel of health, did ever you know pain?

Angel of beauty, do you wrinkles know ?
Know you the fear of age, the torment vile
Of reading secret horror in the smile
Of eyes your eyes have loved since long ago ?
Angel of beauty, do you wrinkles know ?

Angel of happiness, and joy, and light,
Old David would have asked for youth afresh
From the pure touch of your enchanted flesh;
I but implore your prayers to aid my plight,
Angel of happiness, and joy, and light.

—F. P. Sturm

XLVIII

THE CONFESSION

Once, only once, beloved and gentle lady,
 Upon my arm you leaned your arm of snow,
And on my spirit's background, dim and shady,
 That memory flashes now.

The hour was late, and like a medal gleaming
 The full moon showed her face,
And the night's splendour over Paris streaming
 Filled every silent place.

Along the houses, in the doorways hiding,
 Cats passed with stealthy tread
And listening ear, or followed, slowly gliding,
 Like ghosts of dear ones dead.

Sudden, amid our frank and free relation,
Born of that limpid light,
From you, rich instrument, whose sole vibration
Was radiancy and light—

From you, joyous as bugle-call resounding
Across the woods at morn,
With sharp and faltering accent, strangely sounding,
Escaped one note forlorn.

Like some misshapen infant, dark, neglected,
Its kindred blush to own,
And long have hidden, by no eye detected,
In some dim cave unknown.

Your clashing note cried clear, poor, prisoned spirit,
That nothing in the world is sure or fast,
And that man's selfishness, though decked as merit,
Betrays itself at last.

That hard the lot to be a queen of beauty,
And all is fruitless, like the treadmill toil
Of some paid dancer, fainting at her duty,
Still with her vacant smile.

That if one build on hearts, ill shall befall it,
That all things crack, and love and beauty flee,
Until oblivion flings them in his wallet,
Spoil of eternity.

Oft have I called to mind that night enchanted,
The silence and the languor over all,

And that wild confidence, thus harshly chanted,
At the heart's confessional.

—Lois Saunders

XLIX

THE SPIRITUAL DAWN

When upon revellers the stained dawn breaks,
The fierce ideal comes with it; at that hour,
Stirred by some terrible avenging power,
An angel in the sated brute awakes.

Above the stricken, suffering man there glow
Far azure plains of unimagined bliss
Which draw his dreaming spirit like the abyss.
O pure, beloved Goddess, even so

Over smoked wrecks of stupid scenes of shame
Brighter and rosier thy sweet memory
Hovers before my wide eyes hauntingly.

The sun has dimmed and charred the candles' flame,
And thus, my glorious all-conquering one,
Thy shade is peer to the immortal Sun.

—Sir John Squire

L

EVENING HARMONY

Now every flower stem swings a censer chain
And every flower gives incense to the night.
Sounds, perfumes circle in the evening light.
Turning in langourous waltz, again, again;

And every flower gives incense to the night . . .
The violin trembles like a soul in pain.
Round goes the langourous waltz again, again,
The sky is like an altar, vast and bright.

The violin trembles like a soul in pain,
A sorrowing soul, that fears the unknown night.
The sky is like an altar, vast and bright.
In its own darkening blood the sun lies slain.

A sorrowing soul, that fears the unknown night,
Draws from the shining past what dreams remain.
Though in its darkening blood the sun lies slain,
Your memory, like a monstrance, brings me light.

—Naomi Lewis

LI

THE FLASK

There are some powerful odours that can pass
Out of the stoppered flagon; even glass
To them is porous. Oft when some old box
Brought from the East is opened and the locks

And hinges creak and cry, or in a press
In some deserted house where the sharp stress
Of odours old and dusty fills the brain,
An ancient flask is brought to light again

And forth the ghosts of long-dead odours creep—
There, softly trembling in the shadows, sleep
A thousand thoughts, funereal chrysalides,
Phantoms of old the folding darkness hides,

Who make faint flutterings as their wings unfold,
Rose-washed and azure-tinted, shot with gold.
A memory that brings languor flutters here :
The fainting eyelids droop, and giddy Fear

Thrusts with both hands the soul towards the pit
Where, like a Lazarus from his winding-sheet,
Arises from the gulf of sleep a ghost
Of an old passion, long since loved and lost.

So too, when vanished from man's memory
Deep in some dark and sombre chest I lie,
An empty flagon they have cast aside,
Broken and soiled, the dust upon my pride,

I'll be your shroud, beloved pestilence!
The witness of your might and virulence,
Sweet poison mixed by angels; bitter cup
Of life and death my heart has drunken up!

—F. P. Sturm

LII

THE POISON

O wine can clothe in luxury
    The ale-house foul and low,
And build a golden portico
    With its red alchemy . . .
Like cloudy sunset in the evening glow.

And opium dreams can roam and rove
    Past that which has no bourne,
Can plumb eternity, and mourn
    The emptiness of love
And satiate the soul with joys forlorn.

All this is nothing to the bane
    That trickles from your eyes,
True mirrors of my miseries . . .
    Green lakes where dreams in vain
Would quench in bitter gulfs their agonies.

Ah, nothing to the monstrous flow
    That mingles with your breath,
That brings oblivion beneath

Its waves of vertigo,
And bears me fainting to the brink of Death !

—Keith B. Bullen

LIII

MISTY SKY

One would have thought your eyes were veiled in haze,
Strange eyes ! (Grey, green, or azure is their gaze ?)
It seems they would reflect, in each renewal,
The changing skies, dull, dreamy, fond, or cruel.

You know those days both warm and hazy, which
Melt into tears the hearts that they bewitch :
And when the nerves, uneasy to control,
Too wide-awake, upbraid the sleeping soul.

You, too, resemble such a lit horizon
As suns of misty seasons now bedizen . . .
As you shine out, a landscape fresh with rain
With misty sunbeams sparkling on the plain.

Dangerous girl, seductive as the weather !
Shall I adore your snows and frosts together ?
In your relentless winter shall I feel
A kiss more sharp than that of ice and steel ?

—Roy Campbell

LIV

THE CAT

I

A fine strong gentle cat is prowling
As in his bedroom, in my brain;
So soft his voice, so smooth its strain,
That you can scarcely hear him miowling.

But should he venture to complain
Or scold, the voice is rich and deep :
And thus he manages to keep
The charm of his untroubled reign.

This voice, which seems to pearl and filter
Through my soul's inmost shady nook,
Fills me with poems, like a book,
And fortifies me, like a philtre.

His voice can cure the direst pain
And it contains the rarest raptures.
The deepest meanings, which it captures,
It needs no language to explain.

There is no bow that can so sweep
That perfect instrument, my heart :
Or make more sumptuous music start
From its most vibrant cord and deep,

Than can the voice of this strange elf,
This cat, bewitching and seraphic,

Subtly harmonious in his traffic
With all things else, and with himself.

II

So sweet a perfume seems to swim
Out of his fur both brown and bright,
I nearly was embalmed one night
From (only once) caressing him.

Familiar Lar of where I stay,
He rules, presides, inspires and teaches
All things to which his empire reaches.
Perhaps he is a god, or fay.

When to a cherished cat my gaze
Is magnet-drawn and then returns
Back to itself, it there discerns,
With strange excitement and amaze,

Deep down in my own self, the rays
Of living opals, torch-like gleams
And pallid fire of eyes, it seems,
That fixedly return my gaze.

—Roy Campbell

LV

THE SPLENDID SHIP

Oh soft enchantress, I'll record with truth
The diverse beauties that adorn your youth.
Yes, I will paint your charm
Of womanhood with childhood arm in arm.

When you go sweeping your wide skirts, to me
You seem a splendid ship that out to sea
Spreads its full sails, and with them
Goes rolling in a soft, slow, lazy rhythm.

Over your tall, round neck and those plump shoulders,
Your head swans forth its pride to all beholders;
With grace triumphant, mild,
And strange, you go your way, majestic child.

Oh soft enchantress, I'll record with truth
The diverse beauties that adorn your youth.
Yes, I will paint your charm
Of womanhood with childhood arm in arm.

Your bosom juts and stretches every stitch,
Triumphant bosom, like a coffer rich,
With bosses round and rare,
Like shields that draw the lightning from the air.

Provoking shields, with rosy points uplifted!
Coffer of secret charms, superbly gifted,
Whose scents, liqueurs, and wine
Turn heart and brain deliriously thine.

When you go sweeping your wide skirts, to me
You seem a splendid ship that out to sea
Spreads its full sails, and with them
Goes rolling in a soft, slow, lazy rhythm.

Your noble thighs, beneath the silks they swirl,
Torment obscure desires and tease me, girl;
Like sorcerers they are
That stir black philtres in a deep, cool jar.

Your arms precocious Hercules would grace
And vie with pythons in their bright embrace :
The pressure they impart
Would print your lover's image on your heart.

Over your tall, round neck and those plump shoulders,
Your head swans forth its pride to all beholders;
With grace triumphant, mild,
And strange, you go your way, majestic child.

—Roy Campbell

LVI

INVITATION TO THE VOYAGE

My child, my sister, dream
How sweet all things would seem
Were we in that kind land to live together,
And there love slow and long,
There love and die among
Those scenes that image you, that sumptuous weather.

Drowned suns that glimmer there
Through cloud-dishevelled air
Move me with such a mystery as appears
Within those other skies
Of your treacherous eyes
When I behold them shining through their tears.

There, there is nothing else but grace and measure,
Richness, quietness, and pleasure.

Furniture that wears
The lustre of the years
Softly would glow within our glowing chamber,
Flowers of rarest bloom
Proffering their perfume
Mixed with the vague fragrances of amber;
Gold ceilings would there be,
Mirrors deep as the sea,
The walls all in an Eastern splendor hung—
Nothing but should address
The soul's loneliness,
Speaking her sweet and secret native tongue.

There, there is nothing else but grace and measure,
Richness, quietness, and pleasure.

See, sheltered from the swells
There in the still canals
Those drowsy ships that dream of sailing forth;
It is to satisfy
Your least desire, they ply
Hither through all the waters of the earth.

The sun at close of day
Clothes the fields of hay,
Then the canals, at last the town entire
In hyacinth and gold :
Slowly the land is rolled
Sleepward under a sea of gentle fire.

There, there is nothing else but grace and measure,
Richness, quietness, and pleasure.

—Richard Wilbur

LVII

THE IRREPARABLE

I

How shall we kill this old, this long Remorse
Which writhes continually
And feeds on us as worms upon a corse,
Maggots upon a tree ?
How stifle this implacable Remorse ?

What wine, what drug, what philtre known of man
Will drown this ancient foe,
Ruthless and ravenous as a courtesan,
Sure as an ant, and slow ?
What wine ? what drug ? what philtre known of man ?

O tell, fair sorceress, tell if thou dost know
This soul distraught with pain

As a dying soldier crushed and bruised below
    Steel hooves and wounded men !
O tell, fair sorceress, tell if thou dost know;

This poor racked wretch the wolf already flays
    O'er whom the vultures whirr,
This broken warrior ! if in vain he prays
    For cross and sepulchre,
This anguished wretch the wolf already flays.

How should we read dense gulfs which know not dawn
    Nor eve, nor any star ?
How pierce with light skies which abyss-like yawn
    When black as pitch they are ?
How should we read dense gulfs which know not dawn ?

Hope glimmered in the windows of the Inn,
    But Hope is dead for aye !
Moonless and rayless, can poor travellers win
    To shelter from the way ?
The Devil made dark the windows of the Inn !

Dost love the damned, adorable sorceress ?
    Dost know the smitten sore ?
Dost know Remorse that, grim and pitiless,
    Feeds at my heart's red core ?
Dost love the damned, adorable sorceress ?

My soul is prey to the Irreparable,
    It gnaws with tooth accurst,
And, termite-like, the cunning spawn of hell
    Mines the foundations first !
My soul is prey to the Irreparable !

II

Often within a theatre I have seen
'Thwart the orchestral roar,
A dazzling Fairy stand in sudden sheen
Where all was gloom before!
Often within a theatre I have seen

A being made of light and gold and gauze
Fling Demons to their fate!
But on my heart's dark stage an endless pause
Is all, and I await
In vain, in vain the Spirit with wings of gauze!

—Sir John Squire

LVIII

CONVERSATION

You are an autumn sky, suffused with rose . . .
Yet sadness rises in me like the sea,
And on my sombre lip, when it outflows,
Leaves its salt burning slime for memory.

Over my swooning breast your fingers stray;
In vain, alas! My breast is a void pit
Sacked by the tooth and claw of woman. Nay,
Seek not my heart; the beasts have eaten it!

My heart is as a palace plundered
By the wolves, wherein they gorge and rend and kill,
A perfume round thy naked throat is shed . . .

Beauty, strong scourge of souls, O work thy will!
Scorch with thy fiery eyes which shine like feasts
These shreds of flesh rejected by the beasts!

—Sir John Squire

LIX

SONG OF AUTUMN

I

Soon we shall plunge into the chilly fogs;
Farewell, swift light! our summers are too short!
I hear already the mournful fall of logs
Re-echoing from the pavement of the court.

All of winter will gather in my soul:
Hate, anger, horror, chills, the hard forced work;
And, like the sun in his hell by the north pole,
My heart will be only a red and frozen block.

I shudder, hearing every log that falls;
No scaffold could be built with hollower sounds.
My spirit is like a tower whose crumbling walls
The tireless battering-ram brings to the ground.

It seems to me, lulled by monotonous shocks,
As if they were hastily nailing a coffin today.
For whom? — Yesterday was summer. Now autumn knocks.
That mysterious sound is like someone's going away.

II

I love your long eyes with their greenish light,
But, sweetheart, today everything seems bitter to me;
Nothing, neither your love nor your hearth at night,
Is worth as much as the sunshine on the sea.

But love me still, my dear ! Be as a mother
To this ungrateful, even this wicked son;
Be the ephemeral sweetness, sister or lover,
Of a glorious autumn or a setting sun.

The tomb is hungry, and it waits ! Short task !
But with my forehead resting on your knees,
Regretting this torrid summer, let me bask
Awhile in autumn's gentle yellow rays.

— C. F. MacIntyre

LX

TO A MADONNA

Ex-Voto in the Spanish Style

Madonna, mistress, I shall build for you
An altar of my misery, and hew
Out of my heart's remote and midnight pitch,
Far from all worldly lusts and sneers, a niche
Enamelled totally in gold and blue
Where I shall set you up, and worship you.
And of my verse, like hammered silver lace
Studded with amethysts of rhyme, I'll place

A hand-wrought crown upon your head, and I'll
Make you a coat in the barbaric style,
Picked out in seedling tears instead of pearl,
That you shall wear like mail, my mortal girl,
Lined with suspicion, made of jealousy,
Encasing all your charms, that none may see.
As for the intimate part of your attire,
Your dress shall be composed of my desire,
Rising and falling, swirling from your knees
To your round hills and deep declivities.
Of the respect I owe you I shall make
A pair of satin shoes that they may take—
Though most unworthily prepared to do it—
The authentic shape and imprint of your foot.
And if I fail, for all my proffered boon,
To make a silver footstool of the moon,
Victorious queen, I place beneath your heel
The head of this black serpent that I feel
Gnawing at my intestines all the time,
Swollen with hate and venomous with crime.
You shall behold my thoughts like tapers lit
Before your flowered shrine, and brightening it,
Reflected in the semi-dome's clear skies
Like so many fierce stars or fiery eyes.
And I shall be as myrrh and frankincense,
Rising forever in a smokey trance,
And the dark cloud of my tormented hopes
Shall lift in yearning toward your snowy slopes.

And finally, to render you more real,
I shall make seven blades of Spanish steel
Out of the Seven Deadly Sins, and I
Shall mix my love with murderous savagery,

And like a circus knife-thrower, I'll aim
At the pure center of your gentle frame,
And plunge those blades into your beating heart,
Your bleeding, suffering, palpitating heart.

—Anthony Hecht

LXI

AFTERNOON SONG

Though your eyebrows may give rise
To a strange malign impression
(Unangelic's your expression,
Witch with the alluring eyes),

I'm your worshipper at least;
Perilous mad passion mine,
Wild one, yet for me divine,
You're the idol, I the priest!

Desert and thick forest scent
Your rude tresses; in your mien
Mysteries are dimly seen,
Secrets of the Orient;

Perfume floats about your form
As it floats about a censer,
Evening Nymph, adored dispenser
Of enchantments dark and warm.

Ah ! no philtres known to men
With your indolence compare;
Your caresses are so rare
They'd revive the dead again !

By your hips your breasts are wooed,
You fill cushions with delight,
For they're ravished by the sight
Of your languid attitude.

Sometimes, seeking to assuage
Your mysterious sombre rage,
Pouring pain into my bliss,
You will bite me as you kiss;

From your mocking laugh I smart
As you tear me, then I swoon
When your gaze soft as the moon
Falls upon my tortured heart.

'Neath your soft and satin shoe,
'Neath your charming silken foot
All my happiness I put,
And my fate and genius too;

Healer of my soul, you are
Music, colour, living light !
Warm explosion in the night
Of my black Siberia !

—Alan Conder

LXII

SISINA

Think of Diana crashing through the wood,
Wind on her breast and in her tangled hair,
Beating the thicket, finding the tumult good,
The forest's pride, the swiftest steed's despair.

See, see Theroigne, thirsty for tyrant's blood,
Urging to war a troop whose feet are bare,
As, cheeks aflame, she stands where kings have stood,
And mounts, with sword in hand, the royal stair.

Such is Sisina ! with a soul on fire,
But charity is mingled with her ire,
And her gay courage in the battle's heat

Lays down its arms to quiet the suppliant's fears,
And, when she sees the unhappy at her feet,
That flaming heart becomes a fount of tears.

—James Laver

LXIII

PRAISES OF MY FRANCES

(Verses to a learned and devout Milliner)

Upon new chords of you I sing.
And the new-born bud you bring
From solitude, the pure heart's Spring.

Your brows should be with garlands twined,
Woman of delightful mind,
Who our trespasses unbind.

As the wondrous balm of Lethe,
Through thy kisses, I will breathe thee.
All are magnetised who see thee.

When my vices, wild and stormy,
From my wonted courses bore me
It was You appeared before me,

Star of Oceans ! you that alter
Courses, when the pilots falter —
Take my heart upon your altar.

Cistern full of virtuous ruth,
Fountain of eternal youth,
Give to dumbness speech and truth !

What was dirty, you cremated,
What uneven — you equated,
What was weak you re-created.

Inn, on the hungry roads I tramp,
And, in the dark, a guiding lamp
To steer the lost one back to camp.

To my strength add strength, O sweet
Bath, where scents and unguents meet !
Anoint me for some peerless feat !

Holy water most seraphic,
On the lusts in which I traffic
Flash your chastity ecstatic.

Bowl of gems where radiance dances.
Salt that the holy bread enhances,
And sacred wine — your name is Frances!

— Roy Campbell

LXIV

TO A CREOLE LADY

I've known, in scented lands that suns caress,
Under a canopy of reddened trees,
Where palms deluge the eyes with laziness,
A Creole lady's charms that no one sees.

Pale-hued and warm, this brown-skinned sorceress
Bears in her head fine airs and dignities;
A huntress strides in her tall slenderness,
And her smile's quiet and her gaze at ease.

If ever you go where true glories are,
Madame, beside the Seine or the green Loire,
Your beauty our old houses might well prize,

And in some sheltered shady haunt you'd start
A thousand sonnets in each poet's heart,
Subdued more than your slaves by your large eyes.

— Peter Hellings

LXV

MOESTA ET ERRABUNDA

Tell me, Perdita, does not your heart sometimes
From this black ocean of the shameless town
Will to fly far, into another sea
Whose sparkling blue is of a virgin's gown?
Tell me, Perdita, does not your heart sometimes?

O sea, O great sea, after our labouring
Rest us! What spirit gifted you, who high
Howl to the growling organ of the winds,
The holy function of a lullaby,
O sea, O great sea, after our labouring?

Carry me, train! and ferry me, packet-boat,
Far far from here whose mud is of our tears!
Is it not true, your sad heart, Perdita,
Murmurs at times: From evil, guilt and fears,
Carry me, train, and ferry me, packet-boat?

How far you are O heaven of delicate scent
Where love and pleasure gaze without a frown,
And what one loves is worthy to be loved,
And in its pure desire the heart goes down!
How far you are O heaven of delicate scent!

But the grass-greenest heaven of childish loves,
The races, songs, the kisses and the flowers,
The violins that called behind the hills,
The crocks of cider in the evening bowers—
But the grass-greenest heaven of childish loves,

The simple heaven full of stolen joys,
Is it so farther than the China seas
And not to be recalled with bitter cries
Or woken at a treble's silver voice,
The simple heaven full of stolen joys?

—Hilary Corke

LXVI

THE GHOST

Like an angel, feral eyed,
Piercing to your sleeping side,
Gliding down with oily flight
In the inwards of the night,

I shall give you, my dark one,
Kisses frozen as the moon,
Caresses such as snakes give
Slithering round the open grave.

When the livid daylights waken
You will find my place forsaken,
Icy till the evening's here:

As others might with tenderness
Rule your life and your youngness
I shall rule you with a fear.

—Hilary Corke

LXVII

SONNET OF AUTUMN

They say to me, thy clear and crystal eyes :
" Why dost thou love me so, strange lover mine ? "
— Be sweet, be still ! My heart and soul despise
All save that antique brute-like faith of thine;

And will not bare the secret of their shame
To thee whose hand soothes me to slumbers long,
Nor their black legend written out in flame !
Passion I hate, and spirit does me wrong.

Let us love gently. Love, from his retreat,
Ambushed and shadowy, bends his fatal bow,
And I too well his ancient arrows know :

Crime, horror, folly. O pale marguerite,
Thou art as I, an autumn sun brought low,
O my so white, my so cold Marguerite.

— F. P. Sturm

LXVIII

THE SADNESS OF THE MOON

The Moon more indolently dreams tonight
Than a fair woman on her couch at rest,
Caressing, with a hand distraught and light,
Before she sleeps, the contour of her breast.

Upon her silken avalanche of down,
Dying she breathes a long and swooning sigh;
And watches the white visions past her flown,
Which rise like blossoms to the azure sky.

And when, at times, wrapped in her languor deep,
Earthward she lets a furtive tear-drop flow,
Some pious poet, enemy of sleep,

Takes in his hollow hand the tear of snow
Whence gleams of iris and of opal start,
And hides it from the Sun, deep in his heart.

—F. P. Sturm

LXIX

CATS

Feverish lovers, scholars in their lofts,
Both come in their due time to love the cat;
Gentle but powerful, king of the parlor mat,
Lazy, like them, and sensitive to draughts.

Your cat, now, linked to learning and to love,
Exhibits a taste for silences and gloom—
Would make a splendid messenger of doom
If his fierce pride would condescend to serve.

Lost in his day-dream, he assumes the pose
Of sphinxes in the desert, languidly
Fixed in a reverie that has no end.

His loins are lit with the fires of alchemy,
And bits of gold, small as the finest sand,
Fleck, here and there, the mystery of his eyes.

—Anthony Hecht

LXX

THE OWLS

Within the shelter of black yews
The owls in ranks are ranged apart
Like foreign gods, whose eyeballs dart
Red fire. They meditate and muse.

Without a stir they will remain
Till, in its melancholy hour,
Thrusting the level sun from power,
The shade establishes its reign.

Their attitude instructs the sage,
Content with what is near at hand,
To shun all motion, strife, and rage.

Men, crazed with shadows that they chase,
Bear, as a punishment, the brand
Of having wished to change their place.

—Roy Campbell

LXXI

THE PIPE

An author's favourite pipe am I,
My Kaffir woman's countenance
Tells the beholder at a glance
My master smokes incessantly.

If he is mournful or in pain
I smoke as does the ploughman's cot
When the good wife prepares the pot
Before her spouse comes home again.

I bind his soul and rock her well
In the blue twisting skein which slips
And rises from my fiery lips,

And weave a very potent spell
Which soothes his heart in its distress
And heals his spirit's weariness.

—Sir John Squire

LXXII

MUSIC

On music drawn away, a sea-borne mariner,
Star over bowsprit pale,
Beneath a roof of mist or depths of lucid air
I put out under sail;

Breastbone my steady bow and lungs full, running free
    Before a following gale,
I ride the rolling back and mass of every sea
    By Night wrapt in her veil;

All passions and all joys that vessels undergo
    Tremble alike in me;
Fair wind, or waves in havoc when the tempests blow

    On the enormous sea
Rock me, and level calms come silvering sea and air,
    A glass for my despair.

—Robert Fitzgerald

LXXIII

BURIAL

If on a night obscure and deep,
Some decent Christian, out of ruth,
Buries behind some garbage-heap
The vaunted body of your youth :

There, when the chaster stars have set
And the moon to rest has swung,
Will the spider weave his net
And the adder hatch her young.

Your cursèd head beneath the ground
Will hear, through all the seasons then,
The dismal cries of wolves resound,

Old half-starved witches raising spooks,
The antics of obscene old men,
And black conspiracies of crooks.

—Roy Campbell

LXXIV

FANTASTIC ENGRAVING

A monstrous spectre carries on his forehead,
And at a rakish tilt, grotesquely horrid,
A crown such as at carnivals parade.
Without a whip or spur he rides a jade,
A phantom-like apocalyptic moke,
Whose nostrils seem with rabid froth to smoke.
Across unbounded space the couple moves
Spurning infinity with reckless hooves.
The horseman waves a sword that lights the gloom
Of nameless crowds he tramples to their doom,
And, like a prince his mansion, goes inspecting
The graveyard, which, no skyline intersecting,
Contains, beneath a sun that's white and bleak,
Peoples of history, modern and antique.

—Roy Campbell

LXXV

THE GLADLY DEAD

In a soil thick with snails and rich as grease
I've longed to dig myself a good deep grave,
There to stretch my old bones at ease
And sleep in oblivion, like a shark in a wave.

Wills I detest, and tombstones set in rows;
Before I'd beg a tear of anyone,
I'd rather go alive and let the crows
Bleed the last scrap of this old carrion.

O worms ! Black comrades without eye or ear,
Here comes a dead man for you, willing and gay;
Feasting philosophers, sons born of decay,

Come burrow through my ruins, shed not a tear;
But tell me if any torture is left to dread
For this old soulless body, dead as the dead ?

—Jackson Mathews

LXXVI

THE CASK OF HATE

The Cask of the pale Danaïds is Hate.
Vainly Revenge, with red strong arms employed,
Precipitates her buckets, in a spate
Of blood and tears of the dead, to feed the void.

The Fiend bores secret holes in these abysms
By which a thousand years of sweat and strain
Would spill, though Hate revived their organisms
In order just to bleed them once again.

Hate is a drunkard in a tavern staying,
Who feels his thirst born of its very cure,
Like Lerna's hydra, multiplied by slaying.

Gay drinkers of their conqueror are sure,
But Hate is doomed to a sad fate, unable
Ever to fall and snore beneath the table.

—Roy Campbell

LXXVII

THE CRACKED BELL

'Tis bitter-sweet, when nights are long,
To watch, beside the flames which smoke and twist,
The distant memories which slowly throng,
Brought by the chimes soft-singing through the mist.

Happy the sturdy, vigorous-throated bell
Who, spite of age alert and confident,
Cries hourly, like some strong old sentinel
Flinging the ready challenge from his tent.

For me, my soul is cracked; when sick with care
She strives with songs to people the cold air
It happens often that her feeble cries

Are like the harsh rattle of a man who lies
Wounded, forgotten, 'neath a mound of slain
And dies, pinned fast, writhing his limbs in vain.

—Sir John Squire

LXXVIII

SPLEEN

Old Pluvius, month of rains, in peevish mood
Pours from his urn chill winter's sodden gloom
On corpses fading in the near graveyard,
On foggy suburbs pours life's tedium.

My cat seeks out a litter on the stones,
Her mangy body turning without rest.
An ancient poet's soul in monotones
Whines in the rain-spouts like a chilblained ghost.

A great bell mourns, a wet log wrapped in smoke
Sings in falsetto to the wheezing clock,
While from a rankly perfumed deck of cards

(A dropsical old crone's fatal bequest)
The Queen of Spades, the dapper Jack of Hearts
Speak darkly of dead loves, how they were lost.

—Kenneth O. Hanson

LXXIX

SPLEEN

I have more memories than if I had lived a thousand years.

Even a bureau crammed with souvenirs,
Old bills, love letters, photographs, receipts,
Court depositions, locks of hair in plaits,
Hides fewer secrets than my brain could yield.
It's like a tomb, a corpse-filled Potter's Field,
A pyramid where the dead lie down by scores.
I am a graveyard that the moon abhors:
Like guilty qualms, the worms burrow and nest
Thickly in bodies that I loved the best.
I'm a stale boudoir where old-fashioned clothes
Lie scattered among wilted fern and rose,
Where only the Boucher girls in pale pastels
Can breathe the uncorked scents and faded smells.

Nothing can equal those days for endlessness
When in the winter's blizzardy caress
Indifference expanding to Ennui
Takes on the feel of Immortality.
O living matter, henceforth you're no more
Than a cold stone encompassed by vague fear
And by the desert, and the mist and sun;
An ancient Sphinx ignored by everyone,
Left off the map, whose bitter irony
Is to sing as the sun sets in that dry sea.

—Anthony Hecht

LXXX

SPLEEN

I'm like the king of a rain-country, rich
but sterile, young but with an old wolf's itch,
one who escapes his tutor's monologues,
and kills the day in boredom with his dogs;
nothing cheers him, darts, tennis, falconry,
his people dying by the balcony;
the bawdry of the pet hermaphrodite
no longer gets him through a single night;
his bed of fleur-de-lys becomes a tomb;
even the ladies of the court, for whom
all kings are beautiful, cannot put on
shameful enough dresses for this skeleton;
the scholar who makes his gold cannot invent
washes to cleanse the poisoned element;
even in baths of blood, Rome's legacy,
our tyrants' solace in senility,
he cannot warm up his shot corpse, whose food
is syrup-green Lethean ooze, not blood.

—Robert Lowell

LXXXI

SPLEEN

When the low heavy sky weighs like a lid
Upon the spirit aching for the light
And all the wide horizon's line is hid
By a black day sadder than any night;

When the changed earth is but a dungeon dank
Where batlike Hope goes blindly fluttering
And, striking wall and roof and mouldered plank,
Bruises his tender head and timid wing;

When like grim prison bars stretch down the thin,
Straight, rigid pillars of the endless rain,
And the dumb throngs of infamous spiders spin
Their meshes in the caverns of the brain,

Suddenly, bells leap forth into the air,
Hurling a hideous uproar to the sky
As 'twere a band of homeless spirits who fare
Through the strange heavens, wailing stubbornly.

And hearses, without drum or instrument,
File slowly through my soul; crushed, sorrowful,
Weeps Hope, and Grief, fierce and omnipotent,
Plants his black banner on my drooping skull.

—Sir John Squire

LXXXII

OBSESSION

You forests, like cathedrals, are my dread :
You roar like organs. Our curst hearts, like cells
Where death forever rattles on the bed,
Echo your *de Profundis* as it swells.

My spirit hates you, Ocean ! sees, and loathes
Its tumults in your own. Of men defeated
The bitter laugh, that's full of sobs and oaths,
Is in your own tremendously repeated.

How you would please me, Night ! without your stars
Which speak a foreign dialect, that jars
On one who seeks the void, the black, the bare.

Yet even your darkest shade a canvas forms
Whereon my eye must multiply in swarms
Familiar looks of shapes no longer there.

—Roy Campbell

LXXXIII

THE THIRST FOR EXTINCTION

Sad spirit who once loved the battle-ground,
Hope whose bright spur used to arouse your flame
No longer rides you ! Sleep then without shame,
Old horse whose stumbling feet furrow each mound.

Resign yourself my heart, poor beast, sleep sound.

Vanquished spirit with foundered feet, old jade,
You find no joy in love nor in dispute;
Farewell then songs of brass and sighs of flute !
Pleasure, tempt not the heart in sullen shade !

The spring is gone and all its odors fade.

As the immense snows a stiffened body hide,
So Time devours me momentarily;
I contemplate the earth's rotundity,
Seeking no hut's door where I may abide.

Avalanche, take me with you in your slide !

— Barbara Gibbs

LXXXIV

ALCHEMY OF GRIEF

The one lights Nature with his sun,
Another shrouds her in his night :
What whispers " Burial ! " to one
Cries out to others " Life and light ! "

I always stood in awe of thee,
Mysterious Hermes who assists
Me to invert Midas and be
The saddest of all alchemists;

Thou helpest me make iron from gold
And hell from heaven; the very clouds
Are winding-sheets, for in those shrouds

My dear ones' corpses I behold,
And on the shores of heaven I
Rear up immense sarcophagi.

— Alan Conder

LXXXV

SYMPATHETIC HORROR

From livid skies that, without end,
As stormy as your future roll,
What thoughts into your empty soul
(Answer me, libertine !) descend ?

— Insatiable yet for all
That turns on darkness, doom, or dice,
I'll not, like Ovid, mourn my fall,
Chased from the Latin paradise.

Skies, torn like seacoasts by the storm !
In you I see my pride take form,
And the huge clouds that rush in streams

Are the black hearses of my dreams,
And your red rays reflect the hell,
In which my heart is pleased to dwell.

— Roy Campbell

LXXXVI

HEAUTONTIMOROUMENOS

I shall beat you without rage
Or hate, as Moses struck the rock,
As a butcher strikes his block.
I shall make your tears assuage

My drought, my desert in their tide.
You shall weep for my relief,
And on the salt waves of your grief
My longings swollen with hope shall ride,

Like a ship that puts to sea.
My heart, delirious with the sound,
Shall hear your sobs rebound, rebound—
Like a drum that's summoning me.

Am I not a jarring note
In the heavenly symphony
Since devouring Irony
Gnaws me, shakes me by the throat?

Hers is the shrillness in my voice;
Through my blood her poisons race.
I am the unholy mirror
Where the shrew can watch her face.

I am the ulcer and the lance;
I am the bruise; I am the blow;

I am the rack, the limbs also,
Hangman and hanged at once.

I am my own heart's vampire—
One of the vast abandoned host;
Laughter's the doom of those who've lost
The power to smile forever.

—Naomi Lewis

LXXXVII

THE IRREMEDIABLE

I

A Dream, a Form, a Creature, late
Fallen from azure realms, and sped
Into some Styx of mud and lead
No eye from heaven can penetrate;

An angel, rash wanderer, who craves
To look upon deformity,
The vast nightmare's gulf to try
As swimmer struggling with the waves,

And battling (anguish fierce and stark !)
Against gigantic whirlpools
That, singing, go like mad fools
Pirouetting in the dark;

One spellbound in sorcery,
Groping vainly as he makes
To flee a place alive with snakes,
Seeking the candle and the key;

A lost and lampless soul descending,
Within a gulf whose foetid scent
Betrays its damp and deep extent,
A railless staircase never ending,

Where clammy monsters guard the way,
Whose great eyes' phosphoric light
Makes even blacker still the night,
And nothing but themselves betray;

A vessel icebound at the pole,
As in a crystal trap secure,
Seeking the fatal aperture
By which it reached that prison goal :

— Perfect emblems, clear and true,
Of irremediable Fate,
They make us think the Devil's hate
Does well whatever he will do !

II

The dialogue is dark and clear
When a heart becomes its mirror !
Black well of Truth, but none is clearer,
Where that livid star appears,

That ironic and primaeval
Beacon, torch of Satan's grace,
Our sole glory and our solace —
Consciousness in doing Evil !

— Henry Curwen

LXXXVIII

THE CLOCK

The Clock, calm evil god, that makes us shiver,
With threatening finger warns us each apart : —
"*Remember !* Soon the vibrant woes will quiver,
Like arrows in a target, in your heart.

To the horizon Pleasure will take flight
As flits a vaporous sylphide to the wings.
Each instant gnaws a crumb of the delight
That for his season every mortal brings.

Three thousand times and more, each hour, the second
Whispers '*Remember !*' Like an insect shrill
The present chirps, 'With Nevermore I'm reckoned.
I've pumped your lifeblood with my loathsome bill.'

Remember ! Souviens-toi ! Esto Memor !
My brazen windpipe speaks in every tongue.
Each moment, foolish mortal, is like ore
From which the precious metal must be wrung.

Remember. Time the gamester (it's the law)
Wins always, without cheating. Daylight wanes.

Night deepens. The abyss with gulfy maw
Thirsts on unsated, while the hourglass drains.

Sooner or later, now, the time must be
When Hazard, Virtue (your still-virgin mate),
Repentance (your last refuge), or all three —
Will tell you, 'Die, old Coward. It's too late!'"

—Roy Campbell

PARISIAN SCENES

LXXXIX

A LANDSCAPE

I would, when I compose my solemn verse,
Sleep near the heaven as do astrologers,
Near the high bells, and with a dreaming mind
Hear their calm hymns blown upon the wind.
Out of my tower, with chin upon my hands,
I'll watch the singing, babbling human bands;
And see clock-towers like spars against the sky,
And heavens that bring thoughts of eternity;

And softly, through the mist, will watch the birth
Of stars in heaven and lamplight on the earth;
The threads of smoke that rise above the town;
The moon that pours her pale enchantment down.
Seasons will pass till Autumn fades the rose;
And when comes Winter with his weary snows,
I'll shut the doors and window-casements tight,
And build my faery palace in the night.
Then I will dream of blue horizons deep,
Of gardens where the marble fountains weep,
Of kisses, and of ever-singing birds —
A sinless Idyll built of innocent words.
And Trouble, knocking at my window-pane
And at my closet door, shall knock in vain;
I will not heed him with his stealthy tread,
Nor from my reverie uplift my head;
For I will plunge deep in the pleasure still
Of summoning the spring-time with my will,

Drawing the sun out of my heart, and there
With burning thoughts making a summer air.

—F. P. Sturm

XC

THE SUN

Along old terraces where blinds tent the masonry
Each one a separate shelter for private luxury,
When the cruel sun redoubles its sharp stroke
On street and hedgerow, on rooftop and brake,
I walk alone, absorbed in my curious exercise,
Duelling with words that dodge in corners and byways;
Stumbling on rhymes as on crooked setts, colliding
With a sudden clear line which dreams were past finding.

The all-satisfying sun, anaemia's enemy,
Gives life to the worm and the rose impartially;
Evaporating care and sending it skywards
He brings honey to the hive, and to the mute mind words.
It is he who makes the ancient cripples young again
With the gaiety and gentleness of young children;
He orders the harvest to increase and flourish
In that old heart where life is the perpetual wish.

When he comes down into the city like a poet
Transfiguring the values of things the most abject,
He enters like royalty, unaccompanied by officials,
All the palatial hotels and all the hospitals.

—David Paul

XCI

THE RED-HAIRED BEGGAR GIRL

White girl with flame-red hair,
Whose garments, here and there,
Give poverty to view,
And beauty too.

To me, poor puny poet,
Your body, as you show it,
With freckles on your arms,
Has yet its charms.

You wear with prouder mien
Than in Romance a queen
Her velvet buskins could —
Your clogs of wood.

In place of tatters short
Let some rich robe of court
Swirl with its silken wheels
After your heels :

In place of stockings holed,
A dagger made of gold,
To light the lecher's eye,
Flash on your thigh :

Let ribbons slip their bows
And for our sins disclose
A breast whose radiance vies
Even with your eyes.

To show them further charms
Let them implore your arms,
And these, rebuking, humble
    Fingers that fumble

With profferred pearls aglow
And sonnets of Belleau,
Which, fettered by your beauty,
    They yield in duty.

Riffraff of scullion-rhymers
Would dedicate their primers
Under the stairs to view
    Only your shoe.

Each page-boy lucky-starred,
Each marquis, each Ronsard
Would hang about your bower
    To while an hour.

You'd count, among your blisses,
Than lilies far more kisses,
And boast, among your flames,
    Some royal names.

Yet now your beauty begs
For scraps on floors, and dregs
Else destined to the gutter,
    As bread and butter.

You eye, with longing tense,
Cheap gauds for thirty cents,
Which, pardon me, these days
    I cannot raise.

No scent, or pearl, or stone,
But nothing save your own
Thin nudity for dower,
Pass on, my flower!

—Roy Campbell

XCII

THE SWAN

To Victor Hugo

I

Andromache, I think of you. The little stream,
A yellowing mirror that onetime beheld
The huge solemnity of your widow's grief,
(That other Simois your tears have swelled)

Suddenly flooded the memory's dark soil
As I was crossing the new *Place du Carrousel.*
The old Paris is gone (the face of a town
Is more changeable than the heart of mortal man).

I see what seem the ghosts of these royal barracks,
The rough-hewn capitals, the columns waiting to crack,
Weeds, and the big rocks greened with standing water,
And at the window, a jumble of bric-a-brac.

One time a menagerie was on display there,
And there I saw one morning at the hour
Of cold and clarity when Labor rises
And brooms make little cyclones of soot in the air

A swan that had escaped out of his cage,
And there, web-footed on the dry sidewalk,
Dragged his white plumes over the cobblestones,
Lifting his beak at the gutter as if to talk,

And bathing his wings in the sifting city dust,
His heart full of some cool, remembered lake,
Said, "Water, when will you rain? Where is your thunder?"
I can see him now, straining his twitching neck

Skyward again and again, like the man in Ovid,
Toward an ironic heaven as blank as slate,
And trapped in a ruinous myth, he lifts his head
As if God were the object of his hate.

II

Paris changes, but nothing of my melancholy
Gives way. Foundations, scaffoldings, tackle and blocks,
And the old suburbs drift off into allegory,
While my frailest memories take on the weight of rocks.

And so at the Louvre one image weighs me down:
I think of my great swan, the imbecile strain
Of his head, noble and foolish as all the exiled,
Eaten by ceaseless needs—and once again

Of you, Andromache, from a great husband's arms
Fallen to the whip and mounted lust of Pyrrhus,
And slumped in a heap beside an empty tomb,
(Poor widow of Hector, and bride of Helenus)

And think of the consumptive negress, stamping
In mud, emaciate, and trying to see

The vanished coconuts of hidden Africa
Behind the thickening granite of the mist;

Of whoever has lost what cannot be found again,
Ever, ever; of those who lap up the tears
And nurse at the teats of that motherly she-wolf, Sorrow;
Of orphans drying like flowers in empty jars.

So in that forest where my mind is exiled
One memory sounds like brass in the ancient war:
I think of sailors washed up on uncharted islands,
Of prisoners, the conquered, and more, so many more.

—Anthony Hecht

XCIII

THE SEVEN OLD MEN

To Victor Hugo.

Ant-seething city, city full of dreams,
Where ghosts by daylight tug the passer's sleeve.
Mystery, like sap, through all its conduit-streams,
Quickens the dread Colossus that they weave.

One early morning, in the street's sad mud,
Whose houses, by the fog increased in height,
Seemed wharves along a riverside in flood :
When with a scene to match the actor's plight,

Foul yellow mist had filled the whole of space :
Steeling my nerves to play a hero's part,

I coaxed my weary soul with me to pace
The backstreets shaken by each lumbering cart.

A wretch appeared whose tattered, yellow clothing,
Matching the colour of the raining sky,
Could make it shower down alms — but for the loathing
Malevolence that glittered in his eye.

The pupils of his eyes, with bile injected,
Seemed with their glance to make the frost more raw.
Stiff as a sword, his long red beard projected,
Like that of Judas, level with his jaw.

He was not bent, but broken, with the spine
Forming a sharp right-angle to the straight,
So that his stick, to finish the design,
Gave him the stature and the crazy gait

Of a three-footed Jew, or crippled hound.
He plunged his soles into the slush as though
To crush the dead; and to the world around
Seemed less of an indifferent than a foe.

His image followed him (back, stick, and beard
In nothing differed), spawned from the same hole,
A centenarian twin. Both spectres steered
With the same gait to the same unknown goal.

To what foul plot was I exposed ? of what
Humiliating hazard made the jeer ?
For seven times (I counted) was begot
This sinister, self-multiplying fear !

Let him mark well who laughs at my despair
With no fraternal shudder in reply . . .
Those seven loathsome monsters had the air,
Though rotting through, of what can never die.

Disgusting Phoenix, his own son and father !
Could I have watched an eighth instalment spawn
Ironic, fateful, grim — nor perished rather ?
But from that hellish cortege I'd withdrawn.

Perplexed as drunkards when their sight is doubled,
I locked my room, sick, fevered, chilled with fright :
With all my spirit sorely hurt and troubled
By so ridiculous yet strange a sight.

Vainly my reason for the helm was striving :
The tempest of my efforts made a scorn.
My soul like a dismasted wreck went driving
Over a monstrous sea without a bourn.

— Roy Campbell

XCIV

THE LITTLE OLD WOMEN

To Victor Hugo.

I

In sinuous folds of cities old and grim,
Where all things, even horror, turn to grace,
I follow, in obedience to my whim,
Strange, feeble, charming creatures round the place.

These crooked freaks were women in their pride,
Fair Eponine or Laïs ! Humped and bent,
Love them ! Because they still have souls inside.
Under their draughty skirts in tatters rent,

They crawl : a vicious wind their carrion rides;
From the deep roar of traffic see them cower,
Pressing like precious relics to their sides
Some satchel stitched with mottoes or a flower.

They trot like marionettes along the level,
Or drag themselves like wounded deer, poor crones !
Or dance, against their will, as if the devil
Were swinging in the belfry of their bones.

Cracked though they are, their eyes are sharp as drills
And shine, like pools of water in the night, —
The eyes of little girls whom wonder thrills
To laugh at all that sparkles and is bright.

The coffins of old women very often
Are near as small as those of children are.
Wise Death, who makes a symbol of a coffin
Displays a taste both charming and bizarre.

And when I track some feeble phantom fleeing
Through Paris's immense ant-swarming Babel,
I always think that such a fragile being
Is moving softly to another cradle.

Unless, sometimes, in geometric mood,
To see the strange deformities they offer,
I muse how often he who saws the wood
Must change the shape and outline of the coffer.

Those eyes are wells a million teardrops feed,
Crucibles spangled by a cooling ore,
Invincible in charm to all that breed
Whom stern Misfortune suckled with her lore.

II

Vestal whom old Frascati could enamour :
Thalia's nun, whose name was only known
To her dead prompter : madcap full of glamour
Whom Tivoli once sheltered as its own —

They all elate me. But of these a few,
Of sorrow having made a honeyed leaven,
Say to Devotion, " Lend me wings anew,
O powerful Hippogriff, and fly to heaven."

One for her fatherland a martyr : one
By her own husband wronged beyond belief :
And one a pierced Madonna through her son —
They all could make a river with their grief.

III

Yes, I have followed them, time and again !
One, I recall, when sunset, like a heart,
Bled through the sky from wounds of ruddy stain,
Pensively sat upon a seat apart,

To listen to the music, rich in metal,
That's played by bands of soldiers in the parks

On golden, soul-reviving eves, to fettle,
From meek civilian hearts, heroic sparks.

This one was straight and stiff, in carriage regal,
She breathed the warrior-music through her teeth,
Opened her eye like that of an old eagle,
And bared a forehead moulded for a wreath.

IV

Thus then, you journey, uncomplaining, stoic
Across the strife of modern cities flung,
Sad mothers, courtesans, or saints heroic,
Whose names of old were heard on every tongue,

You once were grace, and you were glory once.
None know you now. Derisory advances
Some drunkard makes you, mixed with worse affronts.
And on your heels a child-tormentor prances.

Ashamed of living, shrivelled shades, who creep
Timidly sidling by the walls, bent double;
Nobody greets you, ripe for endless sleep,
Strange destinies, and shards of human rubble !

But I who watch you tenderly : and measure
With anxious eye, your weak unsteady gait
As would a father — get a secret pleasure
On your account, as on your steps I wait.

I see your passionate and virgin crazes;
Sombre or bright, I see your vanished prime;

My soul, resplendent with your virtue, blazes,
And revels in your vices and your crimes.

Poor wrecks ! My family ! Kindred in mind, you
Receive from me each day my last addresses.
Eighty-year Eves, will yet tomorrow find you
On whom the claw of God so fiercely presses ?

—Roy Campbell

XCV

THE BLIND

Consider them, my soul, how horrible !
Like draper's dummies vaguely ludicrous;
Singular as somnambulists; still thus
Rolling vain eyeballs, wherefore ? who can tell ?

Do pupils whence the spark divine has fled
Yet long to scan afar and, ill at ease,
Probe upward ? Never o'er the pavement these
In pensive reverie droop the full-charged head.

They ford across an endless black abyss
That brother is to silence. Hear they this
City around them laugh and howl, and grind

At pleasure as at some atrocious task ?
I too drag on, more stultified I ask :
What can we seek in Heaven, all we blind ?

—T. Sturge Moore

XCVI

TO A PASSER-BY

Amid the deafening traffic of the town,
Tall, slender, in deep mourning, with majesty,
A woman passed, raising, with dignity
In her poised hand, the flounces of her gown;

Graceful, noble, with a statue's form.
And I drank, trembling as a madman thrills,
From her eyes, ashen sky where brooded storm,
The softness that fascinates, the pleasure that kills.

A flash . . . then night ! — O lovely fugitive,
I am suddenly reborn from your swift glance;
Shall I never see you till eternity ?

Somewhere, far off ! too late ! *never,* perchance !
Neither knows where the other goes or lives;
We might have loved, and you knew this might be !

— C. F. MacIntyre

XCVII

SKELETONS DIGGING

I

Quaint anatomic plates are sold
Along the quays in third-hand stalls
Where tomes cadaverous and old
Slumber like mummies in their palls.

In them the craftsman's skill combines
With expert knowledge in a way
That beautifies these chill designs
Although the subject's far from gay.

One notes that, consummating these
Mysterious horrors, God knows how,
Skeletons and anatomies
Peel off their skins to delve and plough.

—Roy Campbell

II

Out of the earth at which you spade,
Funereal laborers, tired and done,
Out of your straining naked bone,
Out of your muscles bare and frayed,

Tell me, what harvest do you win?
Slaves snatched from the charnel ground,
Who is the farmer drives this round
To fill his barn? And what your sin?

You, the terrible sign we're shown
Of our destiny's greater dearth,
Wish you to say that in the earth
The promised sleep is never known?

That the end has betrayed us here,
That even death himself has lied?
That though eternity betide,
Alas! we have again to fear

That in some unknown land we'll meet
A knotted earth that needs be flayed—
To drive again the heavy spade
Beneath our bleeding naked feet?

—Yvor Winters

XCVIII

COMES THE CHARMING EVENING

Comes the charming evening, the criminal's friend,
Comes conspirator-like on soft wolf tread.
Like a large alcove the sky slowly closes,
And man approaches his bestial metamorphosis.

To arms that have laboured, evening is kind enough,
Easing the strain of sinews that have borne their rough
Share of the burden; it is evening that relents
To those whom an angry obsession daily haunts.
The solitary student now raises a burdened head
And the back that bent daylong sinks into its bed.
Meanwhile darkness dawns, filled with demon familiars
Who rouse, reluctant as business-men, to their affairs,
Their ponderous flight rattling the shutters and blinds.
Against the lamplight, whose shivering is the wind's,
Prostitution spreads its light and life in the streets :
Like an anthill opening its issues it penetrates
Mysteriously everywhere by its own occult route;
Like an enemy mining the foundations of a fort,
Or a worm in an apple, eating what all should eat,
It circulates securely in the city's clogged heart.

The heat and hiss of kitchens can be felt here and there,
The panting of heavy bands, the theatres' clamour.
Cheap hotels, the haunts of dubious solaces,
Are filling with tarts, and crooks, their sleek accomplices,
And thieves, who have never heard of restraint or remorse,
Return now to their work as a matter of course,
Forcing safes behind carefully re-locked doors,
To get a few days' living and put clothes on their whores.

Collect yourself, my soul, this is a serious moment,
Pay no further attention to the noise and movement.
This is the hour when the pains of the sick sharpen,
Night touches them like a torturer, pushes them to the open
Trapdoor over the gulf that is all too common.
Their groans overflow the hospital. More than one
Will not come back to taste the soup's familiar flavour
In the evening, with some friendly soul, by his own fire.

Indeed, many a one has never even known
The hearth's warm charm. Pity such a one.

—David Paul

XCIX

THE GAMING TABLE

On tarnished chairs the pale old harlots quiver,
Sly fatal eyes under the eyebrows painted
Dreadfully mincing : as their lean ears shiver
With hateful jewelled peal the air is tainted.

Round the green tables a frieze of lipless faces,
Of blue-cold lips, if lips, of toothless gums,
And fingers, fevered with Hell's last disgraces,
Fumbling in pockets — or in deliriums.

Dull chandeliers in the soot-mottled ceiling
And swollen lamps pick out with violet
Shadow the brows of famous poets, reeling
To waste the guerdon of art's blood-stained sweat.

My eye, turned inward, darkly can discern
This Hellish picture self-distorted thus,
The while I see in yonder taciturn
Corner myself, cold, mute — and envious.

Envying these creatures their tenacious lust,
These rattling skeletons their deadly mirth,
Envying all of those who gaily thrust
Honour or beauty to rot beneath the earth.

Envious, my heart ! O dark and dreadful word !
When these with passion their bright destruction bless,
Who, drunk with the pulse of their own blood, preferred
Deep pain to death and Hell to nothingness.

— Humbert Wolfe

C

THE DANCE OF DEATH

To Ernest Christophe.

Proud, as a living person, of her height,
Her scarf and gloves and huge bouquet of roses,
She shows such nonchalance and ease as might
A thin coquette excessive in her poses.

Who, at a ball, has seen a form so slim ?
Her sumptuous skirts extravagantly shower
To a dry foot that, exquisitely trim,
Her footwear pinches, dainty as a flower.

The frills that rub her collarbone, and feel,
Like a lascivious rill against a rock,
The charms she is so anxious to conceal,
Defend them, too, from ridicule and mock.

Her eyes are formed of emptiness and shade.
Her skull, with flowers so deftly decked about,
Upon her dainty vertebrae is swayed.
Oh what a charm when nullity tricks out !

" Caricature, " some might opine, but wrongly,
Whose hearts, too drunk with flesh that runs to waste,
Ignore the grace of what upholds so strongly.
Tall skeleton, you match my dearest taste !

Come you to trouble with your strong grimace
The feast of life ? Or has some old desire
Rowelled your living carcase from its place
And sent you, credulous, to feed its fire ?

With tunes of fiddles and the flames of candles,
Hope you to chase the nightmare far apart,
Or with a flood of orgies, feasts, and scandals
To quench the hell that's lighted in your heart ?

Exhaustless well of follies and of faults,
Of the old woe the alembic and the urn,
Around your trellised ribs, in new assaults,
I see the insatiable serpent turn.

I fear your coquetry's not worth the strain,
The prize not worth the effort you prolong.
Could mortal hearts your railleries explain ?
The joys of horror only charm the strong.

The pits of your dark eyes dread fancies breathe,
And vertigo. Among the dancers prudent,
Hope not your sixteen pairs of smiling teeth
Will ever find a contemplative student.

Yet who's not squeezed a skeleton with passion ?
Nor ravened with his kisses on the meat
Of charnels. What of costume, scent, or fashion ?
The man who feigns disgust, betrays conceit.

O noseless geisha, unresisted gouge !
Tell these fastidious feigners, from your husk —

"Proud fondling fools, in spite of talc and rouge,
You smell of death. Anatomies of musk,

Withered Antinoüses, beaux of dunder,
Corpses in varnish, Lovelaces of bone,
The dance of death, with universal thunder,
Is whirling you to places yet unknown!

From Seine to Ganges frolicking about,
You see not, through a black hole in the ceiling,
Like a great blunderbuss, with funnelled snout,
The Angel's trumpet, on the point of pealing.

In every clime, Death studies your devices
And vain contortions, laughable Humanity,
And oft, like you, perfumes herself with spices
Mixing her irony with your insanity!"

—Roy Campbell

CI

THE LOVE OF LIES

Dear indolent creature, when I watch you go,
To the sound of music broken against the ceiling,
With lingering charm, harmonious and slow,
Your ennui in your somber gaze revealing;

When I see how the gas adorns your wan
Forehead with a delicate new lure,
Where evening torches kindle a false dawn,
And like a portrait's eyes your eyes allure,

I think : How beautiful, bizarre, and fresh !
Massive memory, royal and heavy tower,
Crowns her, and her heart, like bruised peach-flesh,
Is ripe now, as her body, for love's lore.

Are you the autumn fruit with sovereign taste ?
Are you a funeral urn awaiting tears,
A perfumed dream-oasis in the waste,
A caressing pillow, or a basket of flowers ?

I know there are most melancholy eyes
Hiding no precious secrets; splendid caskets
Without gems, unconsecrated lockets,
More deep and empty than yourselves, O Skies !

But is it not enough your looks prevail
To gladden a heart that flees from verity ?
What matter indifference or stupidity ?
I adore your beauty. Mask or semblance, hail !

—C. F. MacIntyre

CII

I HAVE NOT FORGOTTEN . . .

I have not forgotten the house I shared with you
In the suburbs, small and white, but quiet too.
A Venus and Pomona hid their bare
Worn stucco limbs in the scant shrubbery there;
And the sun at evening splendidly ablaze

Behind the panes that caught the glittering rays
As if he watched with open, curious eye
Our long and silent dinners, from the sky,
Like candle-gleams his lavish glories shed
On the hanging serge, the frugal cloth we spread.

—Sir Eric Maclagan

CIII

THE SERVANT

My old nurse and servant, whose great heart
made you jealous, is dead and sleeps apart
from us. Shouldn't we bring her a few flowers?
The dead, the poor dead, they have their bad hours,
and when October stripper of old trees,
poisons the turf and makes their marble freeze,
surely they find us worse than wolves or curs
for sleeping under mountainous warm furs . . .
These, eaten by the earth's black dream, lie dead,
without a wife or friend to warm their bed,
old skeletons sunk like shrubs in burlap bags—
and feel the ages trickle through their rags.
They have no heirs or relatives to chase
with children round their crosses and replace
the potted refuse, where they lie beneath
their final flower, the interment wreath.

The oak log sings and sputters in my chamber,
and in the cold blue half-light of December,
I see her tiptoe through my room, and halt

humbly, as if she'd hurried from her vault
with blankets for the child her sleepless eye
had coaxed and mothered to maturity.
What can I say to her to calm her fears?
My nurse's hollow sockets fill with tears.

—Robert Lowell

CIV

MISTS AND RAINS

O ends of autumn, winters, springtimes deep in mud,
Seasons of drowsiness, — my love and gratitude
I give you, that have wrapped with mist my heart and brain
As with a shroud, and shut them in a tomb of rain.

In this wide land when coldly blows the bleak south-west
And weather-vanes at night grow hoarse on the house-crest,
Better than in the time when green things bud and grow
My mounting soul spreads wide its black wings of a crow.

The heart filled up with gloom, and to the falling sleet
Long since accustomed, finds no other thing more sweet —
O dismal seasons, queens of our sad climate crowned —

Than to remain always in your pale shadows drowned;
(Unless it be, some dark night, kissing an unseen head,
To rock one's pain to sleep upon a hazardous bed.)

— Edna St. Vincent Millay

CV

PARISIAN DREAM

I

That marvellous landscape of my dream—
Which no eye knows, nor ever will—
At moments, wide awake, I seem
To grasp, and it excites me still.

Sleep, how miraculous you are—
A strange caprice had urged my hand
To banish, as irregular,
All vegetation from that land;

And, proud of what my art had done,
I viewed my painting, knew the great
Intoxicating monotone
Of marble, water, steel and slate.

Staircases and arcades there were
In a long labyrinth, which led
To a vast palace; fountains there
Were gushing gold, and gushing lead.

And many a heavy cataract
Hung like a curtain,—did not fall,
As water does, but hung, compact,
Crystal, on many a metal wall.

Tall nymphs with Titan breasts and knees
Gazed at their images unblurred,
Where groves of colonnades, not trees,
Fringed a deep pool where nothing stirred.

Blue sheets of water, left and right,
Spread between quays of rose and green,
To the world's end and out of sight,
And still expanded, though unseen.

Enchanted rivers, those — with jade
And jasper were their banks bedecked;
Enormous mirrors, dazzled, made
Dizzy by all they did reflect.

And many a Ganges, taciturn
And heedless, in the vaulted air,
Poured out the treasure of its urn
Into a gulf of diamond there.

As architect, it tempted me
To tame the ocean at its source;
And this I did, — I made the sea
Under a jeweled culvert course.

And every colour, even black,
Became prismatic, polished, bright;
The liquid gave its glory back
Mounted in iridescent light.

There was no moon, there was no sun, —
For why should sun and moon conspire
To light such prodigies ? — each one
Blazed with its own essential fire !

A silence like eternity
Prevailed, there was no sound to hear;
These marvels all were for the eye,
And there was nothing for the ear.

II

I woke; my mind was bright with flame;
I saw the cheap and sordid hole
I live in, and my cares all came
Burrowing back into my soul.

Brutally the twelve strokes of noon
Against my naked ear were hurled;
And a grey sky was drizzling down
Upon this sad, lethargic world.

—Edna St. Vincent Millay

CVI

MORNING TWILIGHT

Reveille rang thinly from across a barrack square,
And a breath of morning troubled the street-lamps' stare.

It was that hour of the night when guilty dreams
Rise from brown, restless adolescents in swarms,
When, quaking and cringing like a blood-shot eye,
The lamp stains the coming day with its dye;
When under the body's reluctant, stubborn weight

The soul, like the lamp, renews its unequal fight;
When the air shivers as if to escape, to efface
Itself in furtive breezes drying a tear-stung face;
When woman is sick of love, as the writer of his work.

Here and there a house sent up a thin smoke.
Women of the streets, sunk in stupid sleep,
Seemed all raw eyelid, and gasping lip.
—And the poor's womenfolk, hugging the chilly droop
Of lank breasts, blew on their fingers, and their soup.
The extra pinch of cold, amid that of penury,
Added, for women in labour, its insult to injury.
Slitting the fogged air, the cry of a distant cock
Broke like a jet of blood through the spasm of a cough.
Buildings still swam in vague tides of mist;
And in silenced hospitals, with a last
Convulsive rattle, the dying gave up breath,
—While night revellers staggered home, tired to death.

Morning, shivering in her robe of rose and green,
Made her hesitant way along the deserted Seine,
While Paris, rubbing tired eyes in its dark,
Woke like an ancient drudge to another day's work.

—David Paul

WINE

CVII

THE SOUL OF WINE

One night the soul of wine sang in the flask :
" I bring you, man, dear disinherited,
From my vermilion wax and prison of glass,
A song all full of light and brotherhood !

I know the flaming hill where painfully
And sweating under the boiling sun you bent
To give me life and grow a soul in me;
I am not ungrateful or malevolent,

For I feel a mighty pleasure when I lave
The gullet of a man worn by his labor,
And his hot body is a cheerful grave
Which I like better than a cold wine-cellar.

You hear resounding strains from Sabbath eves
And hopes that murmur in my trembling breast ?
Elbows on the table, with rolled sleeves,
Glorify me and be content to rest;

I'll light the eyes of your enraptured wife;
Give your son strength and make his pale cheeks ruddy
And for this delicate athlete of life
Will be the oil that toughens the wrestler's body.

I'll pour my living nectar, precious seed
To quicken in you, from the eternal Sower,

So that the poetry our loves may breed
Shall spring toward God like a great, strange flower."

—C. F. MacIntyre

CVIII

THE RAGPICKERS' WINE

In the muddy maze of some old neighborhood,
Often, where the street lamp gleams like blood,
As the wind whips the flame, rattles the glass,
Where human beings ferment in a stormy mass,

One sees a ragpicker knocking against the walls,
Paying no heed to the spies of the cops, his thralls,
But stumbling like a poet lost in dreams;
He pours his heart out in stupendous schemes.

He takes great oaths and dictates sublime laws,
Casts down the wicked, aids the victims' cause;
Beneath the sky, like a vast canopy,
He is drunken of his splendid qualities.

Yes, these people, plagued by household cares,
Bruised by hard work, tormented by their years,
Each bent double by the junk he carries,
The jumbled vomit of enormous Paris,—

They come back, perfumed with the smell of stale
Wine-barrels, followed by old comrades, pale

From war, mustaches like limp flags, to march
With banners, flowers, through the triumphal arch

Erected for them, by some magic touch!
And in the dazzling, deafening debauch
Of bugles, sunlight, of huzzas and drum,
Bring glory to the love-drunk folks at home!

Even so, wine pours its gold to frivolous
Humanity, a shining Pactolus;
Then through man's throat of high exploits it sings
And by its gifts reigns like authentic kings.

To lull these wretches' sloth and drown the hate
Of all who mutely die, compassionate,
God has created sleep's oblivion;
Man added Wine, divine child of the Sun.

—C. F. MacIntyre

CIX

THE MURDERER'S WINE

My wife is dead; I am free!
I can drink to my heart's content.
When I came home without a cent
Her crying was torture to me.

With air pure and a sky that is clear,
I'm as gay as a king could be . . .

This summer recalls the year
That we fell in love — I and she !

The grave of that wife of mine
Would hardly hold enough wine
To quench the thirst that I've got;
— And that is saying a lot.

I threw her corpse down a well
With the stones that rimmed it yonder.
She lies asleep where she fell.
— Shall I ever forget her, I wonder ?

By our sweetest vows of yore
(And nothing annuls such an oath)
And to patch things up so that both
Could be drunk with love as before,

I begged for a rendezvous
At night, in a lonely lane.
She came, mad thing ! — no ado !
— We're all more or less insane !

She still was pretty, although
Worn out with working — while I,
I loved her past bearing; and so
I said : " You've got to die ! "

Who understands me ? Has one
'Mong those fellow sots of mine
Ever dreamt in his nights, as I've done,
Of weaving a shroud out of wine ?

How could hopeless debauchees
As soulless as things of steel
Ever know the love I feel,
True love with its mysteries,

Its black enchantments and fears,
Its hellish procession of pains,
Its poison phials and tears,
Its rattle of bones and of chains!

At last I'm alone and free!
Tonight dead drunk I shall be;
Without fear or remorse, like a dog
On the ground I shall lie; like a log

I shall sleep — as dead men do.
And maybe some skidding truck
Or great cart piled with muck
And stones will cut me in two,

Or crush in my guilty head.
— But why worry about the Hereafter?
The thought of it moves me to laughter!
— To hell with the Devil and God!

— Alan Conder

CX

THE SOLITARY'S WINE

The look from a courtesan, the peculiar glance
That glides upon us like the shining ray
The tossing moon sends to the trembling lake,
When she would bathe her beauty's nonchalance;

The final bag of gold in the gambler's fingers;
A bawdy kiss from the thin Adeline;
The sounds of music with caressing languor
Resembling some distant human whine,—

These are worth nothing, O deep flask, beside
The mighty nostrum your rich belly guards
For the holy poet's thirsty heart.

You pour him hope and youth and life—and pride,
That treasure giving all us beggars odds
To make us conquerors, peers of the Gods!

—C. F. MacIntyre

CXI

LOVERS' WINE

Today the distance is superb,
Without bridle, spur or curb,
Let us mount on the back of wine
For regions fairy and divine!

Let us, two angels tortured by
Some dark, delirious phantasy,
Pursue the distant mirage drawn
Over the blue crystal of dawn !

And gently balanced on the wing
Of some obliging whirlwind, we
— In equal rapture revelling —

My sister, side by side will flee,
Without repose, or truce, where gleams
The golden paradise of my dreams !

— Cyril Scott

FLOWERS OF EVIL

CXII

DESTRUCTION

At my side the Demon writhes forever,
Swimming around me like impalpable air;
As I breathe, he burns my lungs like fever
And fills me with an eternal guilty desire.

Knowing my love of Art, he snares my senses,
Appearing in woman's most seductive forms,
And, under the sneak's plausible pretenses,
Lips grow accustomed to his lewd love-charms.

He leads me thus, far from the sight of God,
Panting and broken with fatigue into
The wilderness of Ennui, deserted and broad,

And into my bewildered eyes he throws
Visions of festering wounds and filthy clothes,
And all Destruction's bloody retinue.

—C. F. MacIntyre

CXIII

THE MARTYR

(*Drawing by an unknown Master*)

Amongst gilt fabrics, flasks of scent and wine,
Rich furniture, white marble, precious moulds,
Fine paintings, and rich, perfumed robes that shine
Swirled into sumptuous folds,

In a warm room, that like a hothouse stifles
With dangerous and fatal breath, where lie
Pale flowers in crystal tombs, exquisite trifles,
Exhaling their last sigh—

A headless corpse, cascading in a flood
Hot, living blood, that soaks, with crimson stain
A pillow slaked and sated as the mud
Of a wet field with rain.

Like those pale visions which the gloom aborts
Which fix us in a still, hypnotic stare,
The head, tricked out with gems of various sorts,
In its huge mass of hair,

Like a ranunculus beside the bed,
Rests on the table, empty of all thought.
From eyes revulsed, like twilight, seems to spread
A gaze that looks at naught.

Upon the bed the carcase, unabashed,
Shows, in complete abandon, without shift,

The secret splendour that, in life, it flashed
Superbly, Nature's gift.

A rosy stocking, freaked with clocks of gold,
Clings to one leg : a souvenir, it seems :
The garter, from twin diamonds, with the cold
Stare of a viper gleams.

The singular effect of solitude
And of a languorous portrait, with its eyes
Provocative as is its attitude,
Dark loves would advertise —

And guilty joys, with feasts of strange delight,
Full of infernal kisses, omens certain
To please the gloating angels of the Night
Who swim behind each curtain.

And yet to see her nimble strength, the risky
Swerve of the rounded shoulder, and its rake,
The tented haunch, the figure lithe and frisky,
Flexed like an angry snake,

You'd know that she was young. Her soul affronted,
Her senses stung with boredom — were they bayed
By packs of wandering, lost desires, and hunted,
And finally betrayed ?

The vengeful man, whose lust you could not sate,
(In spite of much love) nor quench his fire —
Did he on your dead flesh then consummate
His monstrous, last desire ? —

Answer me, corpse impure ! With fevered fist,
Grim visage, did he raise you up on high,
And, as your silver frosty teeth he kissed,
Bid you his last goodbye ?

Far from inquiring magistrates that sneer,
Far from this world of raillery and riot,
Sleep peacefully, strange creature, on your bier,
Of mystery and quiet.

Your lover roams the world. Your deathless shape
Watches his sleep and hears each indrawn breath.
No more than you can ever he escape
From constancy till death !

—Roy Campbell

CXIV

LESBOS

Mother of Latin sports and Greek delights,
Where kisses languishing or pleasureful,
Warm as the suns, as the watermelons cool,
Adorn the glorious days and sleepless nights,
Mother of Latin sports and Greek delights,

Lesbos, where kisses are as waterfalls
That fearless into gulfs unfathomed leap,
Now run with sobs, now slip with gentle brawls,
Stormy and secret, manifold and deep;
Lesbos, where kisses are as waterfalls !

Lesbos, where Phryne Phryne to her draws,
Where never a sigh did echoless expire,
As Paphos' equal, thee the stars admire,
Nor Venus envies Sappho without cause !
Lesbos, where Phryne Phryne to her draws,

Lesbos, the land of warm and languorous nights,
Where by their mirrors seeking sterile good,
The girls with hollow eyes, in soft delights,
Caress the ripe fruits of their womanhood,
Lesbos, the land of warm and languorous nights,

Leave, leave old Plato's austere eye to frown;
Pardon is thine for kisses' sweet excess,
Queen of the land of amiable renown,
And for exhaustless subtleties of bliss,
Leave, leave old Plato's austere eye to frown.

Pardon is thine for the eternal pain
That on the ambitious hearts for ever lies,
Whom far from us the radiant smile could gain,
Seen dimly on the verge of other skies;
Pardon is thine for the eternal pain !

Which of the gods will dare thy judge to be,
And to condemn thy brow with labour pale,
Not having balanced in his golden scale
The flood of tears thy brooks poured in the sea ?
Which of the gods will dare thy judge to be ?

What boot the laws of just and of unjust ?
Great-hearted virgins, honour of the isles,
Lo, your religion also is august,

And love at hell and heaven together smiles !
What boot the laws of just and of unjust ?

For Lesbos chose me out from all my peers,
To sing the secret of her maids in flower,
Opening the mystery dark from childhood's hour
Of frantic laughter, mixed with sombre tears;
For Lesbos chose me out from all my peers.

And since I from Leucate's top survey,
Like a sentinel with piercing eye and true,
Watching for brig and frigate night and day,
Whose distant outlines quiver in the blue,
And since I from Leucate's top survey,

To learn if kind and merciful the sea,
And midst the sobs that make the rock resound,
Brings back some eve to pardoning Lesbos, free
The worshipp'd corpse of Sappho, who made her bound
To learn if kind and merciful the sea !

Of her the manlike lover-poetess,
In her sad pallor more than Venus fair !
The azure eye yields to that black eye, where
The cloudy circle tells of the distress
Of her the manlike lover-poetess !

Fairer than Venus risen on the world,
Pouring the treasures of her aspect mild,
The radiance of her fair white youth unfurled
On Ocean old, enchanted with his child;
Fairer than Venus risen on the world !

Of Sappho who, blaspheming, died that day
When trampling on the rite and sacred creed,
She made her body fair the supreme prey
Of one whose pride punished the impious deed
Of Sappho who, blaspheming, died that day.

And since that time it is that Lesbos moans,
And, spite the homage which the whole world pays,
Is drunk each night with cries of pain and groans,
Her desert shores unto the heavens do raise,
And since that time it is that Lesbos moans!

—Richard Herne Shepherd

CXV

LESBIANS

(*Delphine and Hippolyta*)

The lamps had languisht and their light was pale;
On cushions deep Hippolyta reclined.
Those potent kisses that had torn the veil
From her young candour filled her dreaming mind.

With tempest-troubled eyes she sought the blue
Heaven of her innocence, how far away!
Like some sad traveller, who turns to view
The dim horizons passed at dawn of day.

Tears and the muffled light of weary eyes,
The stupor and the dull voluptuous trance,

Limp arms, like weapons dropped by one who flies—
All served her fragile beauty to enhance.

Calm at her feet and joyful, Delphine lay
And gazed at her with ardent eyes and bright,
Like some strong beast that, having mauled its prey,
Draws back to mark the imprint of its bite.

Strong and yet bowed, superbly on her knees,
She snuffed her triumph, on that frailer grace
Poring voluptuously, as though to seize
The signs of thanks upon the other's face.

Gazing, she sought in her pale victim's eye
The speechless canticle that pleasure sings,
The infinite gratitude that, like a sigh,
Mounts slowly from the spirit's deepest springs.

"Now, now you understand (for love like ours
Is proof enough) that 'twere a sin to throw
The sacred holocaust of your first flowers
To those whose breath might parch them as they blow.

Light falls my kiss, as the ephemeral wing
That scarcely stirs the shining of a lake.
What ruinous pain your lover's kiss would bring!
A plough that leaves a furrow in its wake.

Over you, like a herd of ponderous kine,
Man's love will pass and his caresses fall
Like trampling hooves. Then turn your face to mine;
Turn, oh my heart, my half of me, my all!

Turn, turn, that I may see their starry lights,
Your eyes of azure; turn. For one dear glance
I will reveal love's most obscure delights,
And you shall drowse in pleasure's endless trance."

"Not thankless, nor repentant in the least
Is your Hippolyta." She raised her head.
"But one who from some grim nocturnal feast
Returns at dawn feels less disquieted.

I bear a weight of terrors, and dark hosts
Of phantoms haunt my steps and seem to lead.
I walk, compelled, behind these beckoning ghosts
Down sliding roads and under skies that bleed.

Is ours so strange an act, so full of shame?
Explain the terrors that disturb my bliss.
When you say, Love, I tremble at the name;
And yet my mouth is thirsty for your kiss.

Ah, look not so, dear sister, look not so!
You whom I love, even though that love should be
A snare for my undoing, even though
Loving I am lost for all eternity."

Delphine looked up, and fate was in her eye.
From the god's tripod and beneath his spell,
Shaking her tragic locks, she made reply:
"Who in love's presence dares to speak of hell?

Thinker of useless thoughts, let him be cursed,
Who in his folly, venturing to vex

A question answerless and barren, first
With wrong and right involved the things of sex!

He who in mystical accord conjoins
Shadow with heat, dusk with the noon's high fire,
Shall never warm the palsy of his loins
At that red sun which mortals call desire.

Go, seek some lubber groom's deflowering lust;
Take him your heart and leave me here despised!
Go — and bring back, all horror and disgust,
The livid breasts man's love has stigmatized.

One may not serve two masters here below."
But the child answered: "I am torn apart,
I feel my inmost being rent, as though
A gulf had yawned — the gulf that is my heart.

Naught may this monster's desperate thirst assuage, —
As fire 'tis hot, as space itself profound —
Naught stay the Fury from her quenchless rage,
Who with her torch explores its bleeding wound.

Curtain the world away and let us try
If lassitude will bring the boon of rest.
In your deep bosom I would sink and die,
Would find the grave's fresh coolness on your breast."

Hence, lamentable victims, get you hence!
Hells yawn beneath, your road is straight and steep.
Where all the crimes receive their recompense
Wind-whipped and seething in the lowest deep

With a huge roaring as of storms and fires,
Go down, mad phantoms, doomed to seek in vain
The ne'er-won goal of unassuaged desires,
And in your pleasures find eternal pain!

Sunless your caverns are; the fever damps
That filter in through every crannied vent
Break out with marsh-fire into sudden lamps
And steep your bodies with their frightful scent.

The barrenness of pleasures harsh and stale
Makes mad your thirst and parches up your skin;
And like an old flag volleying in the gale,
Your whole flesh shudders in the blasts of sin.

Far from your kind, outlawed and reprobate,
Go, prowl like wolves through desert worlds apart!
Disordered souls, fashion your own dark fate,
And flee the god you carry in your heart.

—Aldous Huxley

CXVI

LESBIANS

Like pensive cattle lying on the sand
They scan the far horizon of the ocean,
Foot seeking foot, hand magnetising hand,
With sweet or bitter tremors of emotion.

Some with their hearts absorbed in confidences,
Deep in the woods, where streamlets chatter free,
Spell the loved names of childish, timid fancies,
And carve the green wood of the fresh, young tree.

Others like sisters wander, slow and grave,
Through craggy haunts of ghostly emanations,
Where once Saint Anthony was wont to brave
The purple-breasted pride of his temptations.

Some by the light of resin-scented torches
In the dumb hush of caverns seek their shrine,
Invoking Bacchus, killer of remorses,
To liven their delirium with wine.

Others who deal with scapulars and hoods
Hiding the whiplash under their long train,
Mingle, on lonely nights in sombre woods,
The foam of pleasure with the tears of pain.

O demons, monsters, virgins, martyrs, you
Who trample base reality in scorn,
Whether as nuns or satyrs you pursue
The infinite, with cries or tears forlorn,

You, whom my soul has tracked to lairs infernal,
Poor sisterhood, I pity and adore,
For your despairing griefs, your thirst eternal,
And love that floods your hearts for evermore!

—Roy Campbell

CXVII

THE TWO GOOD SISTERS

Debauchery and Death are pleasant twins,
And lavish with their charms, a buxom pair !
Under the rags that clothe their virgin skins,
Their wombs, though still in labour, never bear.

For the curst poet, foe to married rest,
The friend of hell, and courtier on half-pay—
Brothels and tombs reserve for such a guest
A bed on which repentance never lay.

Both tomb and bed, in blasphemy so fecund,
Each other's hospitality to second,
Prepare grim treats, and hatch atrocious things.

Debauch, when will you bury me ? When, Death,
Mingle your Cypress in the selfsame wreath
With the infected Myrtles that she brings ?

—Roy Campbell

CXVIII

THE FOUNTAIN OF BLOOD

It sometimes seems to me as if my blood
Flowed like a rhythmic fountain's sobbing flood.
I hear it run with a long murmuring sound,
But vainly do I try to find the wound.

Across the town, as through the lists, it flows,
Transforming the pavement to archipelagoes,
Slaking the thirst of every living creature,
And staining red the various forms of nature.

I have asked often the insidious
Wine to put to sleep my wasting fear;
Wine makes the ear more sharp, the eye more clear !

I have sought in love for an oblivious
Slumber — it's only a bed of needles whence pours
My blood to be drunken by the cruel whores !

— C. F. MacIntyre

CXIX

AN ALLEGORY

Here is a woman, richly clad and fair,
Who in her wine dips her long, heavy hair;
Love's claws, and that sharp poison which is sin,
Are dulled against the granite of her skin.
Death she defies, Debauch she smiles upon,
For their sharp scythe-like talons every one
Pass by her in their all-destructive play;
Leaving her beauty till a later day.
Goddess she walks; sultana in her leisure;
She has Mohammed's faith that heaven is pleasure,
And bids all men forget the world's alarms
Upon her breast, between her open arms.
She knows, and she believes, this sterile maid

Without whom the world's onward dream would fade,
That bodily beauty is the supreme gift
Which may from every sin the terror lift.
Hell she ignores, and Purgatory defies;
And when black Night shall roll before her eyes,
She will look straight in Death's grim face forlorn,
Without remorse or hate — as one newborn.

—F. P. Sturm

CXX

MY BEATRICE

While I was walking in a pitted place,
crying aloud against the human race,
letting thoughts ramble here and there apart—
knives singing on the whetstone of my heart—
I saw a cloud descending on my head
in the full noon, a cloud inhabited
by black devils, sharp, humped, inquisitive
as dwarfs. They knew where I was sensitive,
now idling there, and looked me up and down,
as cool delinquents watch a madman clown.
I heard them laugh and snicker blasphemies,
while swapping signs and blinking with their eyes.

"Let's stop and watch this creature at our leisure—
all sighs and sweaty hair. We'll take his measure.
It's a great pity that this mountebank
and ghost of Hamlet strutting on his plank
should think he's such an artist at his role
he has to rip the lining from his soul

and paralyze the butterflies and bees
with a peepshow of his indecencies—
and even we, who gave him his education,
must listen to his schoolboy declamation."

Wishing to play a part (my pride was high
above the mountains and the devil's cry)
like Hamlet now, I would have turned my back,
had I not seen among the filthy pack
(Oh crime that should have made the sun drop dead!)
my heart's queen and the mistress of my bed
there purring with the rest at my distress,
and sometimes tossing them a stale caress.

—Robert Lowell

CXXI

THE METAMORPHOSES OF A VAMPIRE

Meanwhile the woman, from her strawberry lips,
(Like a snake on redhot coals, writhing her hips
And working her breasts against the stays of her busk)
Let flow these words, with a heavy scent of musk:
"My mouth is wet; and I know deep in my bed
How to bury old conscience till he's dead.
On these proud breasts I wipe all tears away
And old men laugh like children at their play.
For the man who sees me naked, I replace
The moon, the sun, and all the stars of space!
And I am so expert in voluptuous charms
That when I hush a man in my terrible arms

Yielding my bosom to his biting lust,
(Shy but provocative, frail and yet robust)
The mattress swoons in commotion under me,
And the helpless angels would be damned for me!

When she had sucked the marrow from every bone,
I turned to her as languid as a stone
To give her one last kiss . . . and saw her thus:
A slimy rotten wineskin, full of pus!
I shut my eyes, transfixed in a chill of fright,
And when I opened them to the living light . . .
Beside me there, that powerful robot
That fed its fill out of my blood . . . was not!
Instead, the cold ruins of a skeleton
Shivered, creaking like a weather vane
Or like a sign hung out on an iron arm
Swinging through long winter nights in the storm.

—Jackson Mathews

CXXII

A VOYAGE TO CYTHERA

My heart, like a bird, ahover joyously,
circled the rigging, soaring light and free;
beneath a cloudless sky the ship rolled on
like an angel drunk with blazing rays of sun.

What is that black, sad island?—We are told
it is Cythera, famed in songs of old,
trite El Dorado of worn-out roués.
Look, after all, it's but a paltry place.

—Isle of sweet mysteries and festal loves,
above your waters antique Venus moves;
like an aroma, her imperious shade
burdens the soul with love and lassitude.

Green-myrtled island, fair with flowers in bloom,
revered by every nation for all time,
where sighing hearts send up their fervent praises
afloat like incense over beds of roses

or like a ringdove's endless cooing call!
—Cythera now was but a meager soil,
a flinty desert moiled with bitter cries.
And yet, half-glimpsed, a strange shape met my eyes.

It was no temple couched in shady groves
where the young priestess, lover of flowers, moves,
her body fevered by obscure desires,
her robe half opened to the fleeting airs;

but as we passed, skirting the coast so near
that our white canvas set the birds astir,
we saw it was a three-branched gibbet, high
and black-etched, like a cypress, on the sky.

Perched on their prey, ferocious birds were mangling
with frenzied thrusts a hanged man, ripe and dangling,
each driving like a tool his filthy beak
all through that rot, in every bleeding crack;

the eyes were holes, and from the ruined gut
across the thighs the heavy bowels poured out,

and crammed with hideous pleasures, peck by peck,
his butchers had quite stripped him of his sex.

Beneath his feet, a pack of four-legged brutes
circled and prowled, with upraised avid snouts;
a larger beast was ramping in the midst
like a hangman flanked by his apprentices.

Child of Cythera, born of so fair a sky,
you suffered these defilements silently:
atonement for your impure rituals
and sins that have forbid you burial.

Ridiculous corpse, I know your pains full well.
At sight of your loose-hanging limbs I felt
the bitter-flowing bile of ancient grief
rise up, like a long puke, against my teeth;

poor wretch, so dear-remembered, in your presence
I felt each beak-thrust of those stabbing ravens,
and the black panthers' jaws—each rip and gash—
that once took such delight to grind my flesh.

The sky was suave, and level was the sea,
yet all was blood and blackness then to me,
alas! and my heart in this parable,
as in a heavy shroud, found burial.

On your isle, Venus, I saw but one thing standing,
gallows-emblem from which my shape was hanging . . .
God! give me strength and will to contemplate
heart, body—without loathing, without hate.

—Frederick Morgan

CXXIII

LOVE AND THE SKULL

(*An old cul-de-lampe*)

Love is seated on the skull
    Of humanity,
And on that throne the obscene fool
    In effrontery

Laughs and blows bubbles in gay swirls
    That rise and fly
Up in the air to look for worlds
    Deep in the sky.

Each luminous and fragile whole
    Lifts like a thought,
Then spits its little spray of soul
    Out and is not.

I hear the skull, at every spurt,
    Beg his friend:
"When is this brutal, ridiculous sport
    Going to end?

"That stuff that from your mouth you scatter
    In the air like rain,
You blind murderer, is the matter
    Of my blood and my brain!"

—Jackson Mathews

REVOLT

CXXIV

THE DENIAL OF SAINT PETER

What does God do with that huge storm of curses
That rises daily to the seraphim ?
Like some gorged tyrant, while his guts he nurses,
Our blasphemies are lullabies to him.

Martyrs and tortured victims with their cries
Compose delicious symphonies, no doubt,
Because, despite the blood they cost, the skies
Can always do with more when they give out.

Jesus, remember, in the olive trees —
In all simplicity you prayed afresh
To One whom your own butchers seemed to please
In hammering the nails into your flesh.

To see your godhead spat on by the like
Of scullions, and of troopers, and such scum,
And feel the thorns into your temples strike
Which held, of all Humanity, the sum :

To feel your body's horrifying weight
Lengthen your arms, to feel the blood and sweat
Itching your noble forehead pale with fate,
And as a target to the world be set,

Then did you dream of brilliant days of song,
When, the eternal promise to fulfill,

You mounted on an ass and rode along,
Trampling the flowers and palms beneath your feet,

When whirling your whips, and full of valiant force,
The moneylenders quailed at your advance :
When you, in short, were master ? Did remorse
Not pierce your body further than the lance ?

I am quite satisfied to leave so bored
A world, where dream and action disunite.
I'd use the sword, to perish by the sword.
Peter denied his Master ? . . . He did right !

—Roy Campbell

CXXV

ABEL AND CAIN

I

Race of Abel, eat, sleep and drink;
God smiles on you approvingly.

Race of Cain, in filth and stink
Grovel and die, miserably.

Race of Abel, your offering
Flatters the angelic nose !

Race of Cain, what time will bring
The end of your torment and woes ?

Race of Abel, your seeds take root,
And see how all your cattle prosper;

Race of Cain, within your gut
Howls hunger like an ancient cur.

Race of Abel, your innards take
Warmth from the patriarchal hearth;

Race of Cain, poor jackal, shake
With cold, crouched in the hollowed earth!

Race of Abel, make love and spawn!
Your gold spawns also in its right.

Race of Cain, you hearts that burn,
Beware of such great appetite.

Race of Abel, you browse and breed
As wanton as an orchard pest.

Race of Cain, along the roadside
Drag your family, hard pressed.

II

Ah! race of Abel, your fat carcass
Will enrich the reeking soil!

Race of Cain, your hard work is
Not finished yet in spite of all;

Race of Abel, here your shame lies :
The sword lost to the hunter's rod !

Race of Cain, mount to the skies
And down upon the earth cast God !

—Kenneth O. Hanson

CXXVI

LITANY TO SATAN

O grandest of the Angels, and most wise,
O fallen God, fate-driven from the skies,
Satan, at last take pity on our pain.

O first of exiles who endurest wrong,
Yet growest, in thy hatred, still more strong,
Satan, at last take pity on our pain !

O subterranean King, omniscient,
Healer of man's immortal discontent,
Satan, at last take pity on our pain.

To lepers and to outcasts thou dost show
That Passion is the Paradise below.
Satan, at last take pity on our pain.

Thou, by thy mistress Death, hast given to man
Hope, the imperishable courtesan.
Satan, at last take pity on our pain.

Thou givest to the Guilty their calm mien
Which damns the crowd around the guillotine.
Satan, at last take pity on our pain.

Thou knowest the corners of the jealous Earth
Where God has hidden jewels of great worth.
Satan, at last take pity on our pain.

Thou stretchest forth a saving hand to keep
Such men as roam upon the roofs in sleep.
Satan, at last take pity on our pain.

Thy power can make the halting Drunkard's feet
Avoid the peril of the surging street.
Satan, at last take pity on our pain.

Thou, to console our helplessness, didst plot
The cunning use of powder and of shot.
Satan, at last take pity on our pain.

Thy awful name is written as with pitch
On the unrelenting foreheads of the rich.
Satan, at last take pity on our pain.

In strange and hidden places thou dost move
Where women cry for torture in their love.
Satan, at last take pity on our pain.

Father of those whom God's tempestuous ire
Has flung from Paradise with sword and fire,
Satan, at last take pity on our pain.

PRAYER

Satan, to thee be praise upon the Height
Where thou wast king of old, and in the night
Of Hell, where thou dost dream on silently.
Grant that one day beneath the Knowledge-tree,
When it shoots forth to grace thy royal brow,
My soul may sit, that cries upon thee now.

—James Elroy Flecker

DEATH

CXXVII

THE DEATH OF LOVERS

There will be beds, full of light odours blent,
Divans, great couches, deep, profound as tombs,
And, grown for us in light magnificent,
Over the flower stand there will droop strange blooms.

Careful of our last flame declining
As two vast torches our two hearts shall flare,
And our two spirits in their double shining
Reflect the double lights enchanted there.

One night, a night of mystic blue and rose,
A look will pass, supreme, from me to you,
Like a long sob, laden with long adieux.

And later on an angel will unclose
The door and entering joyously relight
The tarnished mirrors and the flames blown to the night.

—Michael Field

CXXVIII

THE DEATH OF THE POOR

Death is consoler and Death brings to life;
The end of all, the solitary hope;
We, drunk with Death's elixir, face the strife,
Take heart, and mount till eve the weary slope.

Across the storm, the hoarfrost, and the snow,
Death on our dark horizon pulses clear;
Death is the famous hostel we all know,
Where we may rest and sleep and have good cheer.

Death is an angel whose magnetic palms
Bring dreams of ecstasy and slumberous calms
To smooth the beds of naked men and poor.

Death is the mystic granary of God;
The poor man's purse; his fatherland of yore;
The Gate that opens into heavens untrod!

—F. P. Sturm

CXXIX

THE DEATH OF ARTISTS

How often must I shake my bells and kiss
Your low forehead, O dismal Caricature?
How many arrows must I shoot amiss
Before I strike the target's mystic lure?

We must wear out our souls in subtle schemes,
We must dismantle many a scaffolding,
Before we know the Creature of our dreams
That fills our hearts with sobs and sorrowing.

Some never know the Idol of their soul;
Like sculptors damned and branded for disgrace
Who hammer upon their own breast and face,

They have *one* hope—their somber Capitol!
That Death may rise, a sun of another kind,
And bring to blossom the flowers of their mind.

—Jackson Mathews

CXXX

THE END OF THE DAY

In the waning deathpale daylight,
Convulsive Life runs, dances without reason,
Blatant and brawling, shrill with spite.
—As soon as over the horizon

Night, voluptuous and vast,
Arises, making hunger tame,
Hiding all things, even shame,
The Poet to himself: "At last!

My spirit and my jaded spine
Plead hungrily for rest. I'll go,
With dreams darkening my mind,

And lie full length upon my back,
O cooling curtains of deep shadow,
And roll and wrap me in your black."

—Jackson Mathews

CXXXI

DREAM OF A CURIOUS PERSON

To F. N.

Have you known such savoury grief as I ?
Do people say " Strange fellow ! " whom you meet ?
— My amorous soul, when I was due to die,
Felt longing mixed with horror; pain seemed sweet.

Anguish and ardent hope (no factious whim)
Were mixed : and as the sands of life ran low
My torture grew delicious yet more grim;
And of this world my heart was letting go.

I seemed a child, so keen to see the Show
He feels a deadly hatred of the Curtain . . .
And then I saw the hard, cold truth for certain :

I felt that dreadful dawn around me grow
With no surprise or vestige of a thrill.
The curtain rose — and I stayed waiting still.

— Roy Campbell

CXXXII

THE VOYAGE

(For T. S. Eliot)

I

For the boy playing with his globe and stamps,
the world is equal to his appetite—
how grand the world in the blaze of the lamps,
how petty in tomorrow's small dry light!

One morning we lift anchor, full of brave
prejudices, prospects, ingenuity—
we swing with the velvet swell of the wave,
our infinite is rocked by the fixed sea.

Some wish to fly a cheapness they detest,
others, their cradles' terror—others stand
with their binoculars on a woman's breast,
reptilian Circe with her junk and wand.

Not to be turned to reptiles, such men daze
themselves with spaces, light, the burning sky;
cold toughens them, they bronze in the sun's blaze
and dry the sores of their debauchery.

But the true voyagers are those who move
simply to move—like lost balloons! Their heart
is some old motor thudding in one groove.
It says its single phrase, "Let us depart!"

They are like conscripts lusting for the guns;
our sciences have never learned to tag
their projects and designs—enormous, vague
hopes grease the wheels of these automatons!

II

We imitate, oh horror! tops and bowls
in their eternal waltzing marathon;
even in sleep, our fever whips and rolls—
like a black angel flogging the brute sun.

Strange sport! where destination has no place
or name, and may be anywhere we choose—
where man, committed to his endless race,
runs like a madman diving for repose!

Our soul is a three-master seeking port:
a voice from starboard shouts, "We're at the dock!"
Another, more elated, cries from port,
"Here's dancing, gin and girls!" Balls! it's a rock!

The islands sighted by the lookout seem
the El Dorados promised us last night;
imagination wakes from its drugged dream,
sees only ledges in the morning light.

Poor lovers of exotic Indias,
shall we throw you in chains or in the sea?
Sailors discovering new Americas,
who drown in a mirage of agony!

The worn-out sponge, who scuffles through our slums
sees whiskey, paradise and liberty
wherever oil-lamps shine in furnished rooms—
we see Blue Grottoes, Caesar and Capri.

III

Stunningly simple Tourists, your pursuit
is written in the tear-drops in your eyes!
Spread out the packing cases of your loot,
your azure sapphires made of seas and skies!

We want to break the boredom of our jails
and cross the oceans without oars or steam—
give us visions to stretch our minds like sails,
the blue, exotic shoreline of your dream!

Tell us, what have you seen?

IV

"We've seen the stars,
a wave or two—we've also seen some sand;
although we peer through telescopes and spars,
we're often deadly bored as you on land.

The shine of sunlight on the violet sea,
the roar of cities when the sun goes down:
these stir our hearts with restless energy;
we worship the Indian Ocean where we drown!

No old chateau or shrine besieged by crowds
of crippled pilgrims sets our souls on fire,
as these chance countries gathered from the clouds.
Our hearts are always anxious with desire.

(Desire, that great elm fertilized by lust,
gives its old body, when the heaven warms
its bark that winters and old age encrust;
green branches draw the sun into its arms.

Why are you always growing taller, Tree—
Oh longer-lived than cypress!) Yet we took
one or two sketches for your picture-book,
Brothers who sell your souls for novelty!

We have salaamed to pagan gods with horns,
entered shrines peopled by a galaxy
of Buddhas, Slavic saints, and unicorns,
so rich Rothschild must dream of bankruptcy!

Priests' robes that scattered solid golden flakes,
dancers with tattooed bellies and behinds,
charmers supported by braziers of snakes . . ."

V

Yes, and what else?

VI

Oh trivial, childish minds!
You've missed the more important things that we
were forced to learn against our will. We've been
from top to bottom of the ladder, and see
only the pageant of immortal sin:

there women, servile, peacock-tailed, and coarse,
marry for money, and love without disgust
horny, pot-bellied tyrants stuffed on lust,
slaves' slaves—the sewer in which their gutter pours!

old maids who weep, playboys who live each hour,
state banquets loaded with hot sauces, blood and trash,
ministers sterilized by dreams of power,
workers who love their brutalizing lash;

and everywhere religions like our own
all storming heaven, propped by saints who reign
like sybarites on beds of nails and frown—
all searching for some orgiastic pain!

Many, self-drunk, are lying in the mud—
mad now, as they have always been, they roll
in torment screaming to the throne of God:
"My image and my lord, I hate your soul!"

And others, dedicated without hope,
flee the dull herd—each locked in his own world
hides in his ivory-tower of art and dope—
this is the daily news from the whole world!

VII

How sour the knowledge travellers bring away!
The world's monotonous and small; we see
ourselves today, tomorrow, yesterday,
an oasis of horror in sands of ennui!

Shall we move or rest? Rest, if you can rest;
move if you must. One runs, but others drop
and trick their vigilant antagonist.
Time is a runner who can never stop,

the Wandering Jew or Christ's Apostles. Yet
nothing's enough; no knife goes through the ribs
of this retarius throwing out his net;
others can kill and never leave their cribs.

And even when Time's heel is on our throat
we still can hope, still cry, "On, on, let's go!"
Just as we once took passage on the boat
for China, shivering as we felt the blow,

so we now set our sails for the Dead Sea,
light-hearted as the youngest voyager.
If you look seaward, Traveller, you will see
a spectre rise and hear it sing, "Stop, here,

and eat my lotus-flowers, here's where they're sold.
Here are the fabulous fruits; look, my boughs bend;
eat yourself sick on knowledge. Here we hold
time in our hands, it never has to end."

We know the accents of this ghost by heart;
our comrade spreads his arms across the seas;
"On, on, Orestes. Sail and feast your heart—
here's Clytemnestra." Once we kissed her knees.

VIII

It's time. Old Captain, lift anchor, sink!
The land rots; we shall sail into the night;
if now the sky and sea are black as ink
our hearts, as you must know, are filled with light.

Only when we drink poison are we well—
we want, this fire so burns our brain tissue,
to drown in the abyss—heaven or hell,
who cares? Through the unknown, we'll find the *new.*

—Robert Lowell

FURTHER POEMS

I

EPIGRAPH FOR A CONDEMNED BOOK

Dear reader, peaceful and bucolic,
Ingenuous, sober, hierophantic,
Lay by this book so corybantic,
So Saturnine, and melancholic.

If elsewhere than in Satan's school
You learned your syntax and your grammar,
Lay by ! You'll think I rave and stammer
And am a stark, hysteric fool.

But if, not yielding to their charm,
Your eye can plumb the gulfs of harm —
Then learn to love me, read my verses.

Inquiring sufferer, who seek
Your paradise, to you I speak :
Pity me ! . . . else, receive my curses !

— Roy Campbell

II

THE VOICE

I grew up in the shadow of a big bookcase : a tall
Babel, where verses, novels, histories, row upon row —
The immemorial ashes of Greek and Latin — all

Mingled and murmured. When I was as high as a folio,
I heard two voices speaking. The first one said : " Be wise;
The world is but a large, delicious cake, my friend !
It calls for an appetite of corresponding size —
And whoso heeds my counsel, his joys shall have no end."
The other voice spoke softly : " Come, travel with me in
[dreams,
Far, far beyond the range of the possible and the known ! "
And in that voice was the senseless music of winds and
[streams
Blown suddenly out of nowhere and into nowhere blown —
A phantom cry, a sound to frighten and captivate.
And I replied : " I will, O lovely voice ! " And from
That hour was sealed for ever the disastrous fate
Which still attends me : Always, behind the tedium
Of finite semblances, beyond the accustomed zone
Of time and space, I see distinctly another world —
And I must wear with loathing these mortal toils, as one
Dragging a weight of serpents about his ankles curled.
And from that hour, like the old prophets of Palestine,
I love extravagantly the wilderness and the sea;
I find an ineffable joy in the taste of harsh, sour wine;
I smile at the saddest moments; I weep amid gaiety;
I take facts for illusions — and often as not, with my eyes
Fixed confidently upon the heavens, I fall into holes.
But the Voice comforts me : " Fool, guard thy dreams ! The
[wise
Have none so beautiful as thou hast." And the Voice consoles.

— George Dillon

III

QUESTIONING AT MIDNIGHT

The clock, striking the midnight hour,
ironically summons us
to call to mind how we made use
of this *today* that's here no more:
—we have, today, prophetic day,
Friday the thirteenth!—in despite
of all we know that's good and right—
of heresy made great display;

yes, we've blasphemed the name of Jesus,
unquestionable God and Lord,
and, like a sycophant at the board
of some repulsive bloated Croesus,
to give the brute his filthy sport
we, Satan's loyal subject, have
affronted everything we love
and flattered what disgusts our heart;

and, cringing torturer, we've hurt
the weak, whom we scorned wrongfully,
but bowed low to Stupidity,
great bull-browed beast, throned and inert;
for it's brute Matter, dull as clay,
that these our pious lips have kissed,
and the pale radiance we've blessed
is but the corpse-light of decay;

and last, to drown our vertigo
in the full madness of despair,

we, haughty high-priest of the Lyre,
whose fitting glory is to show
the raptures of the works of death,
thirstless have drunk, and hungerless eaten!
Quick, quick! Blow out the lamp! Stay hidden
here in this gloom till our last breath.

—Frederick Morgan

IV

THE SERPENT'S TOOTH

Each man worthy of the part
Has a Serpent in his heart,
Installed as on a throne, and who,
If he says: "I will!" says: "No!"

Plunge into the eyes—so bright!—
Of Satyress or Water-sprite,
The Tooth says: "Think of what is right!"

Beget a child or plant a tree,
Sculp marble, polish poetry,
The Tooth says: "Will you outlive tonight?"

No matter what he hope or plan,
There is no moment left when man
Is not subject to the constant
Warnings of this odious Serpent.

—Doreen Bell

V

THE REBEL

A furious Angel plunged from the sky like a hawk,
Gripped the sinner with rough hands by the hair,
And shaking him, shouted, "You shall obey, do you hear?
I am your Guardian Angel. No back talk!

Learn to love (you must, and no grimaces!)
The poor, the spiteful, the deformed, the dumb;
For you must spread for Jesus when he comes
A rich carpet of Charity where he passes.

That is true Love! Before your heart expires,
Let the glory of God set it afire;
That is the true Delight that cannot rot!"

Then the Angel, cruel as he was kind,
With giant hands twisted him till he whined;
But the damned soul still answered, "I will not!"

—Jackson Mathews

VI

THE ABYSS

Pascal's abyss went with him, yawned in the air—
Everything's an abyss! Desire, acts, dreams,
Words! I have felt the wind of terror stream
Many a time across my standing hair.

On all sides around me shores are descending . . .
Silence . . . terrible, terrifying Space . . .
At night I watch God's knowing finger trace
Unending nightmares on the dark unending.

Sleep itself is an enormous lair
Full of vague horrors, leading who knows where?
All windows open on Infinity;

My spirit, haunted now by vertigo,
Yearns for extinction, insensibility.
—Ah! never to be free of Being, Ego!

—Jackson Mathews

VII

LAMENTS OF AN ICARUS

Men who lie with a whore
Have satisfied their needs,
But my poor arms are sore
From clutching at mere clouds.

Thanks to the priceless stars
That flicker one by one
My burnt-out eyes can see
Dim memories of the sun.

Hopelessly I have sought
To touch the end of all;

Beneath some melting heat
I feel my pinions fail.

And, burnt by beauty's fire,
I shall not fall to fame
Or drop into death's pit
Bearing an honored name.

—Anthony Hecht

VIII

THE LID

Wherever he be, on water or on land,
Under pale suns or climes that flames enfold;
One of Christ's own, or of Cythera's band,
Shadowy beggar or Croesus rich with gold;

Citizen, peasant, student, tramp, whatever
His little brain may be, alive or dead;
Man knows the fear of mystery everywhere,
And peeps, with trembling glances, overhead.

The heaven above ? A strangling cavern wall;
The lighted ceiling of a music-hall
Where every actor treads a bloody soil;

The hermit's hope; the terror of the sot;
The sky : the black lid of the mighty pot
Where the vast human generations boil !

—F. P. Sturm

IX

THE PAGAN'S PRAYER

Ah, damp not yet the living coals!
Heat once again my heart in thee!
Voluptuousness, thou scourge of souls,
Goddess, incline thine ear to me!

Spirit abroad in the bright air,
Flame in our dark and secret ways,
Freezing I bring thee — grant my prayer! —
A song of brass to bruit thy praise!

Siren, be still my sovereign; keep
Thy kingdom; wear thy mask, whose mesh
Is half of velvet, half of flesh!

Or pour me out thy heavy sleep,
In mystic and amorphous wine:
Phantom elastic and divine.

— Edna St. Vincent Millay

X

THE INJURED MOON

Oh Moon, discreetly worshipped by our sires,
still riding through your high blue countries, still
trailed by the shining harem of your stars,
old Cynthia, the lamp of our retreats . . .

the lovers sleep open-mouthed! When they breathe,
they show the white enamel of their teeth.
The writer breaks his teeth on his work-sheets,
the vipers couple under the hot hill.

Dressed in your yellow hood, do you pursue
your boy from night to dawn, till the sun climbs
skyward, where dim Endymion disappears?

"I see your mother, Child of these poor times,
crushed to her mirror by the heavy years.
She cunningly powders the breast that nourished you."

—Robert Lowell

XI

THE RANSOM

To pay his ransom man must toil
With Reason's implement alone
To plough and rake and free from stone
Two plots of hard volcanic soil.

And if he would from out them wrench
A few thorns or a meagre flower,
Continually a heavy shower
Of his salt sweat their roots must drench.

The one is Art, the other Love;
And on that last and terrible day

The wrath of the stern judge to stay,
To escape the vengeance from above,

He must show barns whose uttermost
Recesses swell with ripened grain,
And blooms whose shapes and hues will gain
The suffrage of the Heavenly Host.

—Sir John Squire

XII

THE UNFORESEEN

Harpagon watched his father slowly dying
And musing on his white lips as they shrunk,
Said, " There is lumber in the outhouse lying
It seems : old boards and junk. "

Celimene cooed, and said, " How good I am
And, naturally, God made my looks excel. "
(Her callous heart, thrice-smoked like salted ham,
And cooked in the fires of Hell !)

A smoky scribbler, to himself a beacon,
Says to the wretch whom he has plunged in shade—
" Where's the Creator you so loved to speak on,
The Saviour you portrayed ? "

But best of all I know a certain rogue
Who yawns and weeps, lamenting night and day

(Impotent fathead) in the same old brogue,
" I will be good — one day ! "

The clock says in a whisper, " He is ready
The damned one, whom I warned of his disaster.
He's blind, and deaf, and like a wall unsteady,
Where termites mine the plaster."

Then one appeared whom all of them denied
And said with mocking laughter, " To my manger
You've *all* come; to the Black Mass I provide
Not one of you's a stranger.

You've built me temples in your hearts of sin.
You've kissed my buttocks in your secret mirth.
Know me for Satan by this conquering grin,
As monstrous as the Earth.

D'you think, poor hypocrites surprised red-handed,
That you can trick your lord without a hitch;
And that by guile two prizes can be landed —
Heaven, and being rich ?

The wages of the huntsman is his quarry,
Which pays him for the chill he gets while stalking.
Companions of my revels grim and sorry
I am going to take you walking,

Down through the denseness of the soil and rock,
Down through the dust and ash you leave behind,
Into a palace, built in one solid block,
Of stone that is not kind :

For it is built of Universal Sin
And holds of me all that is proud and glorious."
—Meanwhile an angel, far above the din,
Sends forth a peal victorious

For all whose hearts can say, "I bless thy rod;
And blessèd be the griefs that on us fall.
My soul is not a toy, Eternal God,
Thy wisdom's all in all!"

And so deliciously that trumpet blows
On evenings of celestial harvestings,
It makes a rapture in the hearts of those
Whose love and praise it sings.

—Roy Campbell

XIII

EVER SO FAR FROM HERE

This is the house, the sacred box,
Where, always draped in languorous frocks,
And always at home if someone knocks,

One elbow into the pillow pressed,
She lies, and lazily fans her breast,
While fountains weep their soulfullest:

This is the chamber of Dorothy.
—Fountain and breeze for her alone
Sob in that soothing undertone.
Was ever so spoiled a harlot known?

With odorous oils and rosemary,
Benzoin and every unguent grown,
Her skin is rubbed most delicately.
— The flowers are faint with ecstasy.

— Edna St. Vincent Millay

XIV

MEDITATION

Calm down, my Sorrow, we must move with care.
You called for evening; it descends, it's here.
The town is coffined in its atmosphere,
bringing relief to some, to others care.

Now while the common multitude strips bare,
feels pleasure's cat o' nine tails on its back,
and fights off anguish at the great bazaar,
give me your hand, my Sorrow. Let's stand back;

back from these people! Look, the dead years dressed
in old clothes crowd the balconies of the sky.
Regret emerges smiling from the sea,

the sick sun slumbers underneath an arch,
and like a shroud strung out from east to west,
listen, my Dearest, hear the sweet night march!

—Robert Lowell

XV

A MADRIGAL OF SORROW

I

What do I care though you be wise?
Be sad, be beautiful; your tears
But add one more charm to your eyes,
As streams to valleys where they rise;
And fairer every flower appears

After the storm. I love you most
When joy has fled your brow downcast;
When your heart is in horror lost,
And over your present like a ghost
Floats the dark shadow of the past.

I love you when the teardrop flows,
Hot as blood, from your large eye;
When I would hush you to repose
Your heavy pain breaks forth and grows
Into a loud and tortured cry.

And then, voluptuousness divine!
Delicious ritual and profound!
I drink in every sob like wine,
And dream that in your deep heart shine
The pearls wherein your eyes were drowned.

II

I know your heart, which overflows
With outworn loves long cast aside,
Still like a furnace flames and glows,
And you within your breast enclose
A damned soul's unbending pride;

But till your dreams without release
Reflect the leaping flames of hell;
Till in a nightmare without cease
You dream of poison to bring peace,
And love cold steel and powder well;

And tremble at each opened door,
And feel for every man distrust,
And shudder at the striking hour —
Till then you have not felt the power
Of Irresistible Disgust.

My queen, my slave, whose love is fear,
When you awaken shuddering,
Until that awful hour be here,
You cannot say at midnight drear :
"I am your equal, O my King!"

— F. P. Sturm

XVI

THE FOUNTAIN

Stay one moment as you are
In the tired pose where pleasure
Touched you, closing your sad stare,
Leaving you innocent, gay and pure.
In the courtyard the perpetual fountain
Ruminates nightly and daily;
Its whisper prolongs the ecstasy
Which you and the evening have given.

The fountain's lifted sheaf
    Of wavering flowers
Where moonlight darts as if
    To disclose all its colours
Falls in a wide scarf
    Of shining tears.

So your secret soul, summoned
By the electric touch of pleasure,
Springs, confident of its end,
To the huge sky's mysterious lure;
Then pauses, hesitates, expands
In a wide reluctant shower
Which invisibly descends
To where my heart hides for its hour.

The fountain's lifted sheaf
    Of wavering flowers
Where moonlight darts as if
    To disclose all its colours

Falls in a wide scarf
    Of shining tears.

Oh you whom the dark brightens, my heart
Swaying between your breasts, listens
To that other heart whose beat
Is heard incessantly in the fountain's.
Musical water, moon, trees
Whose shiver surrounds the dark shine
Of night opening into mysteries,
Your sad clarity mirrors mine.

The fountain's lifted sheaf
    Of wavering flowers
Where moonlight darts as if
    To disclose all its colours
Falls in a wide scarf
    Of shining tears.

—David Paul

XVII

TO A MALABAR GIRL

Your feet are delicate as your hands, your heavy
Haunch would fill the loveliest white with envy;
To the thoughtful artist your body is sweet and fresh;
Your velvet eyes are browner than your flesh.
Born beneath hot blue skies, your only tasks
Are to keep cool water and perfume in the flasks,
To light your master's pipe and chase away

Mosquitoes from his bed; when the new day
Makes the plane-trees sing, already you are
Buying pineapples and bananas in the bazaar.
All day, here and there, on naked feet
You wander as you wish and hum those sweet
Outlandish songs. On scarlet-mantled eves
You stretch your body on soft mats of leaves,
In drifting dreams where hummingbirds dart through
A landscape gracious, flowery as you.

Happy child, why wish to see our France,
Its too many people mowed down by mischance,
And bidding goodbye to your dear tamarinds,
Trust your life to lusty sailors and rough winds ?
There, half-dressed in muslins, you would go
Shivering beneath the brunt of hail and snow.
How you'd regret your happy carefree pranks
When brutal corsets prison your soft flanks !
When you must glean your supper from our mud
By selling the fragrance of your exotic blood.
Through our dirty fog you would follow with sad eyes
A mirage of cocoa palms from absent skies.

—C. F. MacIntyre

XVIII

BERTHA'S EYES

All other famous eyes you may despise,
fair eyes of my love where, gentle as night,
a shadowy sweetness filters and takes flight.
Pour over me your pleasing gloom, fair eyes!

Great eyes of my child, shrines of mystery,
you seem like those enchanted caverns where
behind a heap of drowsy shadows, rare
forgotten treasures glimmer hazily.

My child's eyes are profound, mysterious, vast,
and bright with stars, oh boundless Night, like you.
For thoughts of Love, mingled with Faith, shine through
their depths and shimmer—sensual or chaste.

—Frederick Morgan

XIX

HYMN

To the most lovely, the most dear,
The Angel, and the deathless grail
Who fill my heart with radiance clear—
In immortality all hail!

Into my life she flows translated
As saline breezes fill the sky,
And pours into my soul unsated
The taste of what can never die.

Sachet, forever fresh, perfuming
Some quiet nook of hid delight;
A lone forgotten censer fuming
In secrecy across the night.

How, flawless love, with truth impart
Your purity and keep it whole,
O unseen grain of musk who art
The core of my eternal soul ?

To the most lovely, the most dear,
The angel, and the deathless grail,
Who fill my life with radiance clear —
In immortality all hail !

— Roy Campbell

XX

ROMANTIC SUNSET

Fair is the sun when first he flames above,
Flinging his joy down in a happy beam;
And happy he who can salute with love
The sunset far more glorious than a dream.

Flower, stream, and furrow ! — I have seen them all
In the sun's eye swoon like one trembling heart —
Though it be late let us with speed depart
To catch at least one last ray ere it fall !

But I pursue the fading god in vain,
For conquering Night makes firm her dark domain,
Mist and gloom fall, and terrors glide between,

And graveyard odours in the shadow swim,
And my faint footsteps on the marsh's rim,
Bruise the cold snail and crawling toad unseen.

—F. P. Sturm

XXI

TO THEODORE DE BANVILLE

(1842)

So proud your port, your arm so powerful,
With such a grip you grip the goddess' hair,
That one might take you, from your casual air,
For a young ruffian flinging down his trull.

Your clear eye flashing with precocity,
You have displayed yourself proud architect
Of fabrics so audaciously correct
That we may guess what your ripe prime will be.

Poet, our blood ebbs out through every pore;
Is it, perchance, the robe the Centaur bore,
Which made a sullen streamlet of each vein,

Was three times dipped within the venom fell
Of those old reptiles fierce and terrible
Whom, in his cradle, Hercules had slain?

—Sir John Squire

XXII

VERSES FOR THE PORTRAIT OF HONORE DAUMIER

The artist of this pictured page,
Whose pencil, rich in subtlety,
Teaches us self-mockery,
— This artist, reader, is a sage.

A mocker, yes, a satirist;
And yet his sketches, which pursue
Evil and all her retinue,
Prove him a genial humourist.

Not thus did Melmoth sneer, nor thus
Snickered grim Mephistopheles,
The torch of the Eumenides
Burning their faces, chilling us.

Their glee, alas ! their merriment
Is but a doleful travesty :
His mirth is sunny, vast and free,
A kindly spirit's testament !

— Lewis Piaget Shanks

XXIII

LOLA DE VALENCE

(*An inscription for her portrait by Edouard Manet.*)

Desire, my friends, must find it hard to choose
Among so many beauties everywhere;
But Lola de Valence shines with that most rare
Beauty of a jewel black and rose.

—Jackson Mathews

XXIV

ON DELACROIX'S PICTURE OF TASSO IN PRISON

The poet, sick, and with his chest half bare
Tramples a manuscript in his dark stall,
Gazing with terror at the yawning stair
Down which his spirit finally must fall.

Intoxicating laughs which fill his prison
Invite him to the Strange and the Absurd.
With ugly shapes around him have arisen
Both Doubt and Terror, multiform and blurred.

This genius cooped in an unhealthy hovel,
These cries, grimaces, ghosts that squirm and grovel
Whirling around him, mocking as they call,

This dreamer whom these horrors rouse with screams,
They are your emblem, Soul of misty dreams,
Round whom the Real erects its stifling wall.

—Roy Campbell

XXV

WHAT A PAIR OF EYES CAN PROMISE

I love, pale one, your lifted eyebrows bridging
Twin darknesses of flowing depth.
But however deep they are, they carry me
Another way than that of death.

Your eyes, doubly echoing your hair's darkness
—That leaping, running mane—
Your eyes, though languidly, instruct me : "Poet
And connoisseur of love made plain,

If you desire fulfilment of the promise,
The ecstasy that is your trade,
You can confirm the truth, from thigh to navel,
Of all that we have said.

You will find my white breasts heavy
With the weight of their rough, bronze coins,
And, under a soft as velvet, rounded belly,
Poised between ambered loins,

A fleece, not golden, but for richness sister
To that hair with darkness bright,

Supple and springing — and as boundless
As a deep, starless night ! "

— David Paul

XXVI

THE PARANYMPH

I

No, my dear, you're certainly not
What some might call a dainty dish.
You simmer like an ancient pot
With leavings of lust, and worldly relish.
Fresh and sweet you're certainly not,

My raddled old infanta ! Yet
The cavortings of your crazy career
Have given you the greasy sweat
Of things worn out with common wear,
Which hold their tattered value yet.

The green sap of your forty years
Has a tang to wake the jaded palate.
The ripe old fruit that autumn bears
Makes all spring's virgin bloom look pallid !
— There's plenty of sap in your forty years !

Your carcase has its peculiar charms,
Little graces all its own.
Your pepper-pots give me the qualms

— But the flesh is sweetest near the bone !
Yes, your carcase has its charms !

Cock a snook at the connoisseurs
Of the pumpkin and the watermelon !
I'd rather those collarbones of yours
Than all the Songs of Solomon,
— And I'm sorry for those connoisseurs !

You wear your hair like a blue helmet,
Hanging over your blushless brow,
Swathing your empty head with its pelmet
— And then at the back it lifts its prow
Like the plumes of a blue helmet !

Your eyes are black as a street puddle
Catching the glitter of a lamp.
Against the rouge on your cheekbone's middle
They shine with the threat of Hell's fire-damp,
And yet they're black as a street puddle.

The curl of your lip lures and shocks
With its lech, and its look of " You keep out ! "
Like the Tree of Knowledge it provokes
The longing to know what we'd better not !
Yes, the lust in you both lures and shocks.

Your legs are sinewy enough
To scale the heights of a volcano,
And, rain or snow, in cold or cough,
To dance a can-can as only they know
Whose legs are hard and dry enough.

Your skin is hot, and quite as sweet
As that of a seasoned brigadier,
And it's as innocent of sweat
As your eyes are of a tear
—And yet, and yet I've found it sweet!

II

Deviless, you're heading for the devil!
I'd gladly keep you company,
If only the pace at which you travel
Didn't leave me somewhat dizzy.
So get on, alone, with you to the Devil!

My sciatica, asthma, rheumatism
Won't let me render as I ought
His Lordship's homage, without a spasm.
"Now isn't that a shame!" cry out
My asthma and my rheumatism.

Oh you can't guess how much I suffer
To miss your sabbatical conference.
To watch you, when he lets go his sulphur
Kissing his royal circumstance!
Yes, truly and indeed I suffer!

It's damnably sad to bid farewell
To you, my dear, at such a juncture.
No more, my old flambeau of Hell,
To be your holder! Judge what torture
It is, my dear, to say farewell,

For you've been my passion many a year,
A passion sufficiently logical!
I wanted to skim the cream, my dear,
Of all that could be perfectly evil.
—My monster, I've loved you many a year.

—David Paul

XXVII

AMINA BOSCHETTI

Amina bounds . . . is startled . . . whirls and smiles.
The Belgian says, "That's fraud, a pure deceit.
As for your woodland nymphs, I know the wiles
Only of those on Brussels' Market Street."

From shapely foot and lively, laughing eye
Amina spills light elegance and wit.
The Belgian says, "Be gone, ye joys that fly!
My wife's attractions have more solid merit."

Oh, you forget, nymph of the winsome stance,
That though you'd teach an elephant to dance,
Teach owls new melodies, make dull birds shine,

All glimmering grace brings but a Belgian sneer:
Bacchus himself could pour bright southern wine,
This Boor would say, "Give me thick Brussels beer."

—Kenneth O. Hanson

XXVIII

ABOUT A BORE WHO CLAIMED HIS ACQUAINTANCE

To M. Eugene Fromentin.

He told me just how rich he was,
But nervous of the cholera;
—That he took good care where the money goes,
But he liked a seat at the Opera.

—That he was simply wild about nature,
Monsieur Corot being quite an old chum;
—That a carriage was still a missing feature
Among his goods—but it would come;

—That marble and brick divided his fancy,
Along with ebony and gilded wood;
—That there were in his factory
Three foremen who had been decorated;

—That, not to mention all the rest,
He had twenty thousand shares in the *Nord;*
—That he'd found some picture-frames for next
To nothing, and all by Oppenord;

—That he'd go as far even as Luzarches
To steep himself in bric-a-brac;
—That the Marché des Patriarches
Had more than once proved his collector's knack;

—That he didn't care much for his wife
Nor for his mother, but—theirs apart—
He believed in the soul's immortal life.
Niboyet's works he *had* by heart!

—That he quite approved of physical passion,
And once, on a tedious stay in Rome,
A consumptive lady, much in fashion,
Had died away for love of him.

—For three solid hours and a half,
This chatterer, born in Tournai,
Dished up to me the whole of his life,
Until my brain almost fainted away.

If I had to tell you all I suffered
I would never be able to give up.
I sat in helpless hate, and muttered
"If only I could lie down and sleep!"

Like someone whose seat can give no rest
But who cannot get up and make his escape,
I squirmed and brooded on all the best
Methods of torturing the ape.

Bastogne this monstrosity's called;
He was running away from the infection.
I would drown myself, or take the road
To Gascony, or in any direction

If, when everybody gets back
To the Paris he's so much afraid of,

I should happen to cross the track
Of this pest that Tournai bore—and got rid of!
Brussels, 1865

—David Paul

XXIX

A GAY CHOPHOUSE

(*On the road from Brussels to Uccle*)

You who adore the skeleton
And all such horrible devices
As so many relishes and spices
To tickle the delicate palate on,

You old Pharaoh, Monselet,
Here's a sign I saw that will surely whet
Your appetite for an omelette;
It read : *Cemetery View. Estaminet.*

—David Paul

INDEX

TO ENGLISH TITLES

INDEX TO ENGLISH TITLES

The French texts are those established by Yves Gérard Le Dantec for the edition of Baudelaire's *Oeuvres* in the "Bibliothèque de la Pléiade" Series, Librarie Gallimard, 1951.

LES FLEURS DU MAL

AU POËTE IMPECCABLE

AU PARFAIT MAGICIEN ÈS LETTRES FRANÇAISES

A MON TRÈS-CHER ET TRÈS-VÉNÉRÉ

MAITRE ET AMI

THÉOPHILE GAUTIER

AVEC LES SENTIMENTS

DE LA PLUS PROFONDE HUMILITÉ

JE DÉDIE

CES FLEURS MALADIVES

C. B.

AU LECTEUR

La sottise, l'erreur, le péché, la lésine,
Occupent nos esprits et travaillent nos corps,
Et nous alimentons nos aimables remords,
Comme les mendiants nourrissent leur vermine.

Nos péchés sont têtus, nos repentirs sont lâches;
Nous nous faisons payer grassement nos aveux,
Et nous rentrons gaiement dans le chemin bourbeux,
Croyant par de vils pleurs laver toutes nos taches.

Sur l'oreiller du mal c'est Satan Trismégiste
Qui berce longuement notre esprit enchanté,
Et le riche métal de notre volonté
Est tout vaporisé par ce savant chimiste.

C'est le Diable qui tient les fils qui nous remuent !
Aux objets répugnants nous trouvons des appas;
Chaque jour vers l'Enfer nous descendons d'un pas,
Sans horreur, à travers des ténèbres qui puent.

Ainsi qu'un débauché pauvre qui baise et mange
Le sein martyrisé d'une antique catin,
Nous volons au passage un plaisir clandestin
Que nous pressons bien fort comme une vieille orange.

Serré, fourmillant, comme un million d'helminthes,
Dans nos cerveaux ribote un peuple de Démons,
Et, quand nous respirons, la Mort dans nos poumons
Descend, fleuve invisible, avec de sourdes plaintes.

Si le viol, le poison, le poignard, l'incendie,
N'ont pas encor brodé de leurs plaisants dessins
Le canevas banal de nos piteux destins,
C'est que notre âme, hélas ! n'est pas assez hardie.

Mais parmi les chacals, les panthères, les lices,
Les singes, les scorpions, les vautours, les serpents,
Les monstres glapissants, hurlants, grognants, rampants,
Dans la ménagerie infâme de nos vices,

Il en est un plus laid, plus méchant, plus immonde !
Quoiqu'il ne pousse ni grands gestes ni grands cris,
Il ferait volontiers de la terre un débris
Et dans un bâillement avalerait le monde;

C'est l'Ennui ! — l'œil chargé d'un pleur involontaire,
Il rêve d'échafauds en fumant son houka.
Tu le connais, lecteur, ce monstre délicat,
— Hypocrite lecteur, — mon semblable, — mon frère !

SPLEEN ET IDÉAL

I

BÉNÉDICTION

Lorsque, par un décret des puissances suprêmes,
Le Poëte apparaît en ce monde ennuyé,
Sa mère épouvantée et pleine de blasphèmes
Crispe ses poings vers Dieu, qui la prend en pitié :

— " Ah ! que n'ai-je mis bas tout un nœud de vipères,
Plutôt que de nourrir cette dérision !
Maudite soit la nuit aux plaisirs éphémères
Où mon ventre a conçu mon expiation !

Puisque tu m'as choisie entre toutes les femmes
Pour être le dégoût de mon triste mari,
Et que je ne puis pas rejeter dans les flammes,
Comme un billet d'amour, ce monstre rabougri,

Je ferai rejaillir ta haine qui m'accable
Sur l'instrument maudit de tes méchancetés,
Et je tordrai si bien cet arbre misérable,
Qu'il ne pourra pousser ses boutons empestés ! "

Elle ravale ainsi l'écume de sa haine,
Et, ne comprenant pas les desseins éternels,
Elle-même prépare au fond de la Géhenne
Les bûchers consacrés aux crimes maternels.

Pourtant, sous la tutelle invisible d'un Ange,
L'Enfant déshérité s'enivre de soleil,
Et dans tout ce qu'il boit et dans tout ce qu'il mange
Retrouve l'ambroisie et le nectar vermeil.

Il joue avec le vent, cause avec le nuage,
Et s'enivre en chantant du chemin de la croix;
Et l'Esprit qui le suit dans son pèlerinage
Pleure de le voir gai comme un oiseau des bois.

Tous ceux qu'il veut aimer l'observent avec crainte,
Ou bien, s'enhardissant de sa tranquillité,
Cherchent à qui saura lui tirer une plainte,
Et font sur lui l'essai de leur férocité.

Dans le pain et le vin destinés à sa bouche
Ils mêlent de la cendre avec d'impurs crachats;
Avec hypocrisie ils jettent ce qu'il touche,
Et s'accusent d'avoir mis leurs pieds dans ses pas.

Sa femme va criant sur les places publiques :
“ Puisqu'il me trouve assez belle pour m'adorer,
Je ferai le métier des idoles antiques,
Et comme elles je veux me faire redorer;

Et je me soûlerai de nard, d'encens, de myrrhe,
De génuflexions, de viandes et de vins,
Pour savoir si je puis dans un cœur qui m'admire
Usurper en riant les hommages divins !

Et, quand je m'ennuierai de ces farces impies,
Je poserai sur lui ma frêle et forte main;
Et mes ongles, pareils aux ongles des harpies,
Sauront jusqu'à son cœur se frayer un chemin.

Comme un tout jeune oiseau qui tremble et qui pal-
J'arracherai ce cœur tout rouge de son sein, [pite,
Et, pour rassasier ma bête favorite,
Je le lui jetterai par terre avec dédain ! ”

Vers le Ciel, où son œil voit un trône splendide,
Le Poëte serein lève ses bras pieux,
Et les vastes éclairs de son esprit lucide
Lui dérobent l'aspect des peuples furieux :

— " Soyez béni, mon Dieu, qui donnez la souffrance
Comme un divin remède à nos impuretés
Et comme la meilleure et la plus pure essence
Qui prépare les forts aux saintes voluptés !

Je sais que vous gardez une place au Poëte
Dans les rangs bienheureux des saintes Légions,
Et que vous l'invitez à l'éternelle fête
Des Trônes, des Vertus, des Dominations.

Je sais que la douleur est la noblesse unique
Où ne mordront jamais la terre et les enfers,
Et qu'il faut pour tresser ma couronne mystique
Imposer tous les temps et tous les univers.

Mais les bijoux perdus de l'antique Palmyre,
Les métaux inconnus, les perles de la mer,
Par votre main montés, ne pourraient pas suffire
A ce beau diadème éblouissant et clair;

Car il ne sera fait que de pure lumière,
Puisée au foyer saint des rayons primitifs,
Et dont les yeux mortels, dans leur splendeur entière,
Ne sont que des miroirs obscurcis et plaintifs ! "

II

L'ALBATROS

Souvent, pour s'amuser, les hommes d'équipage
Prennent des albatros, vastes oiseaux des mers,
Qui suivent, indolents compagnons de voyage,
Le navire glissant sur les gouffres amers.

A peine les ont-ils déposés sur les planches,
Que ces rois de l'azur, maladroits et honteux,
Laissent piteusement leurs grandes ailes blanches
Comme des avirons traîner à côté d'eux.

Ce voyageur ailé, comme il est gauche et veule !
Lui, naguère si beau, qu'il est comique et laid !
L'un agace son bec avec un brûle-gueule,
L'autre mime, en boitant, l'infirme qui volait !

Le Poëte est semblable au prince des nuées
Qui hante la tempête et se rit de l'archer;
Exilé sur le sol au milieu des huées,
Ses ailes de géant l'empêchent de marcher.

III

ÉLÉVATION

Au-dessus des étangs, au-dessus des vallées,
Des montagnes, des bois, des nuages, des mers,
Par delà le soleil, par delà les éthers,
Par delà les confins des sphères étoilées,

Mon esprit, tu te meus avec agilité,
Et, comme un bon nageur qui se pâme dans l'onde,
Tu sillonnes gaiement l'immensité profonde
Avec une indicible et mâle volupté.

Envole-toi bien loin de ces miasmes morbides;
Va te purifier dans l'air supérieur,
Et bois, comme une pure et divine liqueur,
Le feu clair qui remplit les espaces limpides.

Derrière les ennuis et les vastes chagrins
Qui chargent de leur poids l'existence brumeuse,
Heureux celui qui peut d'une aile vigoureuse
S'élancer vers les champs lumineux et sereins !

Celui dont les pensers, comme des alouettes,
Vers les cieux le matin prennent un libre essor,
— Qui plane sur la vie, et comprend sans effort
Le langage des fleurs et des choses muettes !

IV

CORRESPONDANCES

La Nature est un temple où de vivants piliers
Laissent parfois sortir de confuses paroles;
L'homme y passe à travers des forêts de symboles
Qui l'observent avec des regards familiers.

Comme de longs échos qui de loin se confondent
Dans une ténébreuse et profonde unité,
Vaste comme la nuit et comme la clarté,
Les parfums, les couleurs et les sons se répondent.

Il est des parfums frais comme des chairs d'enfants,
Doux comme les hautbois, verts comme les prairies,
— Et d'autres, corrompus, riches et triomphants,

Ayant l'expansion des choses infinies,
Comme l'ambre, le musc, le benjoin et l'encens,
Qui chantent les transports de l'esprit et des sens.

V

J'aime le souvenir de ces époques nues,
Dont Phœbus se plaisait à dorer les statues.
Alors l'homme et la femme en leur agilité
Jouissaient sans mensonge et sans anxiété,
Et, le ciel amoureux leur caressant l'échine,
Exerçaient la santé de leur noble machine.
Cybèle alors, fertile en produits généreux,
Ne trouvait point ses fils un poids trop onéreux,
Mais, louve au cœur gonflé de tendresses communes,
Abreuvait l'univers à ses tétines brunes.
L'homme, élégant, robuste et fort, avait le droit
D'être fier des beautés qui le nommaient leur roi;
Fruits purs de tout outrage et vierges de gerçures,
Dont la chair lisse et ferme appelait les morsures !

Le Poëte aujourd'hui, quand il veut concevoir
Ces natives grandeurs, aux lieux où se font voir
La nudité de l'homme et celle de la femme,
Sent un froid ténébreux envelopper son âme
Devant ce noir tableau plein d'épouvantement.
O monstruosités pleurant leur vêtement !
O ridicules troncs ! torses dignes des masques !

O pauvres corps tordus, maigres, ventrus ou flasques,
Que le dieu de l'Utile, implacable et serein,
Enfants, emmaillota dans ses langes d'airain !
Et vous, femmes, hélas ! pâles comme des cierges,
Que ronge et que nourrit la débauche, et vous, vierges,
Du vice maternel traînant l'hérédité
Et toutes les hideurs de la fécondité !

Nous avons, il est vrai, nations corrompues,
Aux peuples anciens des beautés inconnues :
Des visages rongés par les chancres du cœur,
Et comme qui dirait des beautés de langueur;
Mais ces inventions de nos muses tardives
N'empêcheront jamais les races maladives
De rendre à la jeunesse un hommage profond,
— A la sainte jeunesse, à l'air simple, au doux front,
A l'œil limpide et clair ainsi qu'une eau courante,
Et qui va répandant sur tout, insouciante
Comme l'azur du ciel, les oiseaux et les fleurs,
Ses parfums, ses chansons et ses douces chaleurs !

VI

LES PHARES

Rubens, fleuve d'oubli, jardin de la paresse,
Oreiller de chair fraîche où l'on ne peut aimer,
Mais où la vie afflue et s'agite sans cesse,
Comme l'air dans le ciel et la mer dans la mer;

Léonard de Vinci, miroir profond et sombre,
Où des anges charmants, avec un doux souris
Tout chargé de mystère, apparaissent à l'ombre
Des glaciers et des pins qui ferment leur pays;

Rembrandt, triste hôpital tout rempli de murmures,
Et d'un grand crucifix décoré seulement,
Où la prière en pleurs s'exhale des ordures,
Et d'un rayon d'hiver traversé brusquement;

Michel-Ange, lieu vague où l'on voit des Hercules
Se mêler à des Christs, et se lever tout droits
Des fantômes puissants qui dans les crépuscules
Déchirent leur suaire en étirant leurs doigts;

Colères de boxeur, impudences de faune,
Toi qui sus ramasser la beauté des goujats,
Grand cœur gonflé d'orgueil, homme débile et jaune,
Puget, mélancolique empereur des forçats;

Watteau, ce carnaval où bien des cœurs illustres,
Comme des papillons, errent en flamboyant,
Décors frais et légers éclairés par des lustres
Qui versent la folie à ce bal tournoyant;

Goya, cauchemar plein de choses inconnues,
De fœtus qu'on fait cuire au milieu des sabbats,
De vieilles au miroir et d'enfants toutes nues,
Pour tenter les démons ajustant bien leurs bas;

Delacroix, lac de sang hanté des mauvais anges,
Ombragé par un bois de sapins toujours vert,
Où, sous un ciel chagrin, des fanfares étranges
Passent, comme un soupir étouffé de Weber;

Ces malédictions, ces blasphèmes, ces plaintes,
Ces extases, ces cris, ces pleurs, ces *Te Deum*,
Sont un écho redit par mille labyrinthes;
C'est pour les cœurs mortels un divin opium !

C'est un cri répété par mille sentinelles,
Un ordre renvoyé par mille porte-voix;
C'est un phare allumé sur mille citadelles,
Un appel de chasseurs perdus dans les grands bois !

Car c'est vraiment, Seigneur, le meilleur témoignage
Que nous puissions donner de notre dignité
Que cet ardent sanglot qui roule d'âge en âge
Et vient mourir au bord de votre éternité !

VII

LA MUSE MALADE

Ma pauvre muse, hélas ! qu'as-tu donc ce matin ?
Tes yeux creux sont peuplés de visions nocturnes,
Et je vois tour à tour réfléchis sur ton teint
La folie et l'horreur, froides et taciturnes.

Le succube verdâtre et le rose lutin
T'ont-ils versé la peur et l'amour de leurs urnes ?
Le cauchemar, d'un poing despotique et mutin,
T'a-t-il noyée au fond d'un fabuleux Minturnes ?

Je voudrais qu'exhalant l'odeur de la santé
Ton sein de pensers forts fût toujours fréquenté,
Et que ton sang chrétien coulât à flots rhythmiques

Comme les sons nombreux des syllabes antiques,
Où règnent tour à tour le père des chansons,
Phœbus, et le grand Pan, le seigneur des moissons.

VIII

LA MUSE VÉNALE

O muse de mon cœur, amante des palais,
Auras-tu, quand Janvier lâchera ses Borées,
Durant les noirs ennuis des neigeuses soirées,
Un tison pour chauffer tes deux pieds violets ?

Ranimeras-tu donc tes épaules marbrées
Aux nocturnes rayons qui percent les volets ?
Sentant ta bourse à sec autant que ton palais,
Récolteras-tu l'or des voûtes azurées ?

Il te faut, pour gagner ton pain de chaque soir,
Comme un enfant de chœur, jouer de l'encensoir,
Chanter des *Te Deum* auxquels tu ne crois guère,

Ou, saltimbanque à jeun, étaler tes appas
Et ton rire trempé de pleurs qu'on ne voit pas,
Pour faire épanouir la rate du vulgaire.

IX

LE MAUVAIS MOINE

Les cloîtres anciens sur leurs grandes murailles
Étalaient en tableaux la sainte Vérité,
Dont l'effet, réchauffant les pieuses entrailles,
Tempérait la froideur de leur austérité.

En ces temps où du Christ florissaient les semailles,
Plus d'un illustre moine, aujourd'hui peu cité,
Prenant pour atelier le champ des funérailles,
Glorifiait la Mort avec simplicité.

— Mon âme est un tombeau que, mauvais cénobite,
Depuis l'éternité je parcours et j'habite;
Rien n'embellit les murs de ce cloître odieux.

O moine fainéant ! quand saurai-je donc faire
Du spectacle vivant de ma triste misère
Le travail de mes mains et l'amour de mes yeux ?

X

L'ENNEMI

Ma jeunesse ne fut qu'un ténébreux orage,
Traversé çà et là par de brillants soleils;
Le tonnerre et la pluie ont fait un tel ravage,
Qu'il reste en mon jardin bien peu de fruits vermeils.

Voilà que j'ai touché l'automne des idées,
Et qu'il faut employer la pelle et les râteaux
Pour rassembler à neuf les terres inondées,
Où l'on creuse des trous grands comme des tombeaux.

Et qui sait si les fleurs nouvelles que je rêve
Trouveront dans ce sol lavé comme une grève
Le mystique aliment qui ferait leur vigueur ?

— O douleur ! ô douleur ! Le Temps mange la vie,
Et l'obscur Ennemi qui nous ronge le cœur
Du sang que nous perdons croît et se fortifie !

XI

LE GUIGNON

Pour soulever un poids si lourd,
Sisyphe, il faudrait ton courage !
Bien qu'on ait du cœur à l'ouvrage,
L'Art est long et le Temps est court.

Loin des sépultures célèbres,
Vers un cimetière isolé,
Mon cœur, comme un tambour voilé,
Va battant des marches funèbres.

— Maint joyau dort enseveli
Dans les ténèbres et l'oubli,
Bien loin des pioches et des sondes;

Mainte fleur épanche à regret
Son parfum doux comme un secret
Dans les solitudes profondes.

XII

LA VIE ANTÉRIEURE

J'ai longtemps habité sous de vastes portiques
Que les soleils marins teignaient de mille feux,
Et que leurs grands piliers, droits et majestueux,
Rendaient pareils, le soir, aux grottes basaltiques.

Les houles, en roulant les images des cieux,
Mêlaient d'une façon solennelle et mystique
Les tout-puissants accords de leur riche musique
Aux couleurs du couchant reflété par mes yeux.

C'est là que j'ai vécu dans les voluptés calmes,
Au milieu de l'azur, des vagues, des splendeurs
Et des esclaves nus, tout imprégnés d'odeurs,

Qui me rafraîchissaient le front avec des palmes,
Et dont l'unique soin était d'approfondir
Le secret douloureux qui me faisait languir.

XIII

BOHÉMIENS EN VOYAGE

La tribu prophétique aux prunelles ardentes
Hier s'est mise en route, emportant ses petits
Sur son dos, ou livrant à leurs fiers appétits
Le trésor toujours prêt des mamelles pendantes.

Les hommes vont à pied sous leurs armes luisantes
Le long des chariots où les leurs sont blottis,
Promenant sur le ciel des yeux appesantis
Par le morne regret des chimères absentes.

Du fond de son réduit sablonneux, le grillon,
Les regardant passer, redouble sa chanson;
Cybèle, qui les aime, augmente ses verdures,

Fait couler le rocher et fleurir le désert
Devant ces voyageurs, pour lesquels est ouvert
L'empire familier des ténèbres futures.

XIV

L'HOMME ET LA MER

Homme libre, toujours tu chériras la mer !
La mer est ton miroir; tu contemples ton âme
Dans le déroulement infini de sa lame,
Et ton esprit n'est pas un gouffre moins amer.

Tu te plais à plonger au sein de ton image;
Tu l'embrasses des yeux et des bras, et ton cœur
Se distrait quelquefois de sa propre rumeur
Au bruit de cette plainte indomptable et sauvage.

Vous êtes tous les deux ténébreux et discrets :
Homme, nul n'a sondé le fond de tes abîmes,
O mer, nul ne connaît tes richesses intimes,
Tant vous êtes jaloux de garder vos secrets !

Et cependant voilà des siècles innombrables
Que vous vous combattez sans pitié ni remord,
Tellement vous aimez le carnage et la mort,
O lutteurs éternels, ô frères implacables !

XV

DON JUAN AUX ENFERS

Quand don Juan descendit vers l'onde souterraine
Et lorsqu'il eut donné son obole à Charon,
Un sombre mendiant, l'œil fier comme Antisthène,
D'un bras vengeur et fort saisit chaque aviron.

Montrant leurs seins pendants et leurs robes ouvertes,
Des femmes se tordaient sous le noir firmament,
Et, comme un grand troupeau de victimes offertes,
Derrière lui traînaient un long mugissement.

Sganarelle en riant lui réclamait ses gages,
Tandis que Don Luis avec un doigt tremblant
Montrait à tous les morts errant sur les rivages
Le fils audacieux qui railla son front blanc.

Frissonnant sous son deuil, la chaste et maigre Elvire,
Près de l'époux perfide et qui fut son amant,
Semblait lui réclamer un suprême sourire
Où brillât la douceur de son premier serment.

Tout droit dans son armure, un grand homme de pierre
Se tenait à la barre et coupait le flot noir;
Mais le calme héros, courbé sur sa rapière,
Regardait le sillage et ne daignait rien voir.

XVI

CHATIMENT DE L'ORGUEIL

En ces temps merveilleux où la Théologie
Fleurit avec le plus de sève et d'énergie,
On raconte qu'un jour un docteur des plus grands,
— Après avoir forcé les cœurs indifférents;
Les avoir remués dans leurs profondeurs noires;
Après avoir franchi vers les célestes gloires
Des chemins singuliers à lui-même inconnus,
Où les purs Esprits seuls peut-être étaient venus, —
Comme un homme monté trop haut, pris de panique,
S'écria, transporté d'un orgueil satanique :

" Jésus, petit Jésus ! Je t'ai poussé bien haut !
Mais, si j'avais voulu t'attaquer au défaut
De l'armure, ta honte égalerait ta gloire,
Et tu ne serais plus qu'un fœtus dérisoire ! "

Immédiatement sa raison s'en alla.
L'éclat de ce soleil d'un crêpe se voila;
Tout le chaos roula dans cette intelligence,
Temple autrefois vivant, plein d'ordre et d'opulence,
Sous les plafonds duquel tant de pompe avait lui.
Le silence et la nuit s'installèrent en lui,
Comme dans un caveau dont la clef est perdue.
Dès lors il fut semblable aux bêtes de la rue,
Et, quand il s'en allait sans rien voir, à travers
Les champs, sans distinguer les étés des hivers,
Sale, inutile et laid comme une chose usée,
Il faisait des enfants la joie et la risée.

XVII

LA BEAUTÉ

Je suis belle, ô mortels ! comme un rêve de pierre,
Et mon sein, où chacun s'est meurtri tour à tour,
Est fait pour inspirer au poëte un amour
Éternel et muet ainsi que la matière.

Je trône dans l'azur comme un sphinx incompris;
J'unis un cœur de neige à la blancheur des cygnes;
Je hais le mouvement qui déplace les lignes,
Et jamais je ne pleure et jamais je ne ris.

Les poëtes, devant mes grandes attitudes,
Que j'ai l'air d'emprunter aux plus fiers monuments,
Consumeront leurs jours en d'austères études;

Car j'ai, pour fasciner ces dociles amants,
De purs miroirs qui font toutes choses plus belles :
Mes yeux, mes larges yeux aux clartés éternelles !

XVIII

L'IDÉAL

Ce ne seront jamais ces beautés de vignettes,
Produits avariés, nés d'un siècle vaurien,
Ces pieds à brodequins, ces doigts à castagnettes,
Qui sauront satisfaire un cœur comme le mien.

Je laisse à Gavarni, poëte des chloroses,
Son troupeau gazouillant de beautés d'hôpital,
Car je ne puis trouver parmi ces pâles roses
Une fleur qui ressemble à mon rouge idéal.

Ce qu'il faut à ce cœur profond comme un abîme,
C'est vous, Lady Macbeth, âme puissante au crime,
Rêve d'Eschyle éclos au climat des autans;

Ou bien toi, grande Nuit, fille de Michel-Ange,
Qui tors paisiblement dans une pose étrange
Tes appas façonnés aux bouches des Titans !

XIX

LA GÉANTE

Du temps que la Nature en sa verve puissante
Concevait chaque jour des enfants monstrueux,
J'eusse aimé vivre auprès d'une jeune géante,
Comme aux pieds d'une reine un chat voluptueux.

J'eusse aimé voir son corps fleurir avec son âme
Et grandir librement dans ses terribles jeux;
Deviner si son cœur couve une sombre flamme
Aux humides brouillards qui nagent dans ses yeux;

Parcourir à loisir ses magnifiques formes;
Ramper sur le versant de ses genoux énormes,
Et parfois en été, quand les soleils malsains,

Lasse, la font s'étendre à travers la campagne,
Dormir nonchalamment à l'ombre de ses seins,
Comme un hameau paisible au pied d'une montagne.

XX

LES BIJOUX

La très-chère était nue, et, connaissant mon cœur,
Elle n'avait gardé que ses bijoux sonores,
Dont le riche attirail lui donnait l'air vainqueur
Qu'ont dans leurs jours heureux les esclaves des Mores.

Quand il jette en dansant son bruit vif et moqueur,
Ce monde rayonnant de métal et de pierre
Me ravit en extase, et j'aime à la fureur
Les choses où le son se mêle à la lumière.

Elle était donc couchée et se laissait aimer,
Et du haut du divan elle souriait d'aise
A mon amour profond et doux comme la mer,
Qui vers elle montait comme vers sa falaise.

Les yeux fixés sur moi, comme un tigre dompté,
D'un air vague et rêveur elle essayait des poses,
Et la candeur unie à la lubricité
Donnait un charme neuf à ses métamorphoses;

Et son bras et sa jambe, et sa cuisse et ses reins,
Polis comme de l'huile, onduleux comme un cygne,
Passaient devant mes yeux clairvoyants et sereins;
Et son ventre et ses seins, ces grappes de ma vigne,

S'avançaient, plus câlins que les Anges du mal,
Pour troubler le repos où mon âme était mise,
Et pour la déranger du rocher de cristal
Où, calme et solitaire, elle s'était assise.

Je croyais voir unis par un nouveau dessin
Les hanches de l'Antiope au buste d'un imberbe,
Tant sa taille faisait ressortir son bassin.
Sur ce teint fauve et brun le fard était superbe !

— Et la lampe s'étant résignée à mourir,
Comme le foyer seul illuminait la chambre,
Chaque fois qu'il poussait un flamboyant soupir,
Il inondait de sang cette peau couleur d'ambre !

XXI

LE MASQUE

STATUE ALLÉGORIQUE DANS LE GOUT DE LA RENAISSANCE

A Ernest Christophe, statuaire.

Contemplons ce trésor de grâces florentines;
Dans l'ondulation de ce corps musculeux
L'Élégance et la Force abondent, sœurs divines.
Cette femme, morceau vraiment miraculeux,
Divinement robuste, adorablement mince,
Est faite pour trôner sur des lits somptueux,
Et charmer les loisirs d'un pontife ou d'un prince.

— Aussi, vois ce souris fin et voluptueux
Où la Fatuité promène son extase;
Ce long regard sournois, langoureux et moqueur;
Ce visage mignard, tout encadré de gaze,
Dont chaque trait nous dit avec un air vainqueur:
"La Volupté m'appelle et l'Amour me couronne!"
A cet être doué de tant de majesté
Vois quel charme excitant la gentillesse donne!
Approchons, et tournons autour de sa beauté.

O blasphème de l'art! ô surprise fatale!
La femme au corps divin, promettant le bonheur,
Par le haut se termine en monstre bicéphale!

—Mais non! ce n'est qu'un masque, un décor subor-
Ce visage éclairé d'une exquise grimace, [neur,
Et, regarde, voici, crispée atrocement,
La véritable tête, et la sincère face
Renversée à l'abri de la face qui ment.
Pauvre grande beauté ! le magnifique fleuve
De tes pleurs aboutit dans mon cœur soucieux;
Ton mensonge m'enivre, et mon âme s'abreuve
Aux flots que la Douleur fait jaillir de tes yeux!

—Mais pourquoi pleure-t-elle? Elle, beauté parfaite
Qui mettrait à ses pieds le genre humain vaincu,
Quel mal mystérieux ronge son flanc d'athlète?

—Elle pleure, insensé, parce qu'elle a vécu!
Et parce qu'elle vit! Mais ce qu'elle déplore
Surtout, ce qui la fait frémir jusqu'aux genoux,
C'est que demain, hélas! il faudra vivre encore!
Demain, après-demain et toujours! — comme nous!

XXII

HYMNE A LA BEAUTÉ

Viens-tu du ciel profond ou sors-tu de l'abîme,
O Beauté ? ton regard, infernal et divin,
Verse confusément le bienfait et le crime,
Et l'on peut pour cela te comparer au vin.

Tu contiens dans ton œil le couchant et l'aurore;
Tu répands des parfums comme un soir orageux;
Tes baisers sont un philtre et ta bouche une amphore
Qui font le héros lâche et l'enfant courageux.

Sors-tu du gouffre noir ou descends-tu des astres ?
Le Destin charmé suit tes jupons comme un chien;
Tu sèmes au hasard la joie et les désastres
Et tu gouvernes tout et ne réponds de rien.

Tu marches sur des morts, Beauté, dont tu te moques;
De tes bijoux l'Horreur n'est pas le moins charmant,
Et le Meurtre, parmi tes plus chères breloques,
Sur ton ventre orgueilleux danse amoureusement.

L'éphémère ébloui vole vers toi, chandelle,
Crépite, flambe et dit : Bénissons ce flambeau !
L'amoureux pantelant incliné sur sa belle
A l'air d'un moribond caressant son tombeau.

Que tu viennes du ciel ou de l'enfer, qu'importe,
O Beauté ! monstre énorme, effrayant, ingénu !
Si ton œil, ton souris, ton pied, m'ouvrent la porte
D'un Infini que j'aime et n'ai jamais connu ?

De Satan ou de Dieu, qu'importe ? Ange ou Sirène,
Qu'importe, si tu rends, — fée aux yeux de velours,
Rhythme, parfum, lueur, ô mon unique reine ! —
L'univers moins hideux et les instants moins lourds ?

XXIII

PARFUM EXOTIQUE

Quand, les deux yeux fermés, en un soir chaud d'au-
Je respire l'odeur de ton sein chaleureux, [tomne,
Je vois se dérouler des rivages heureux
Qu'éblouissent les feux d'un soleil monotone;

Une île paresseuse où la nature donne
Des arbres singuliers et des fruits savoureux;
Des hommes dont le corps est mince et vigoureux,
Et des femmes dont l'œil par sa franchise étonne.

Guidé par ton odeur vers de charmants climats,
Je vois un port rempli de voiles et de mâts
Encor tout fatigués par la vague marine,

Pendant que le parfum des verts tamariniers,
Qui circule dans l'air et m'enfle la narine,
Se mêle dans mon âme au chant des mariniers.

XXIV

LA CHEVELURE

O toison, moutonnant jusque sur l'encolure !
O boucles ! O parfum chargé de nonchaloir !
Extase ! Pour peupler ce soir l'alcôve obscure
Des souvenirs dormant dans cette chevelure,
Je la veux agiter dans l'air comme un mouchoir !

La langoureuse Asie et la brûlante Afrique,
Tout un monde lointain, absent, presque défunt,
Vit dans tes profondeurs, forêt aromatique !
Comme d'autres esprits voguent sur la musique,
Le mien, ô mon amour ! nage sur ton parfum.

J'irai là-bas où l'arbre et l'homme, pleins de sève,
Se pâment longuement sous l'ardeur des climats;
Fortes tresses, soyez la houle qui m'enlève !
Tu contiens, mer d'ébène, un éblouissant rêve
De voiles, de rameurs, de flammes et de mâts :

Un port retentissant où mon âme peut boire
A grands flots le parfum, le son et la couleur;
Où les vaisseaux, glissant dans l'or et dans la moire,
Ouvrent leurs vastes bras pour embrasser la gloire
D'un ciel pur où frémit l'éternelle chaleur.

Je plongerai ma tête amoureuse d'ivresse
Dans ce noir océan où l'autre est enfermé;
Et mon esprit subtil que le roulis caresse
Saura vous retrouver, ô féconde paresse !
Infinis bercements du loisir embaumé !

Cheveux bleus, pavillon de ténèbres tendues,
Vous me rendez l'azur du ciel immense et rond;
Sur les bords duvetés de vos mèches tordues
Je m'enivre ardemment des senteurs confondues
De l'huile de coco, du musc et du goudron.

Longtemps ! toujours ! ma main dans ta crinière
Sèmera le rubis, la perle et le saphir, [lourde
Afin qu'à mon désir tu ne sois jamais sourde !
N'es-tu pas l'oasis où je rêve, et la gourde
Où je hume à longs traits le vin du souvenir ?

XXV

Je t'adore à l'égal de la voûte nocturne,
O vase de tristesse, ô grande taciturne,
Et t'aime d'autant plus, belle, que tu me fuis,
Et que tu me parais, ornement de mes nuits,
Plus ironiquement accumuler les lieues
Qui séparent mes bras des immensités bleues.

Je m'avance à l'attaque, et je grimpe aux assauts,
Comme après un cadavre un chœur de vermisseaux,
Et je chéris, ô bête implacable et cruelle !
Jusqu'à cette froideur par où tu m'es plus belle !

XXVI

Tu mettrais l'univers entier dans ta ruelle,
Femme impure ! L'ennui rend ton âme cruelle.
Pour exercer tes dents à ce jeu singulier,
Il te faut chaque jour un cœur au râtelier.
Tes yeux, illuminés ainsi que des boutiques
Et des ifs flamboyants dans les fêtes publiques,
Usent insolemment d'un pouvoir emprunté,
Sans connaître jamais la loi de leur beauté.

Machine aveugle et sourde, en cruautés féconde !
Salutaire instrument, buveur du sang du monde,
Comment n'as-tu pas honte et comment n'as-tu pas
Devant tous les miroirs vu pâlir tes appas ?
La grandeur de ce mal où tu te crois savante
Ne t'a donc jamais fait reculer d'épouvante,
Quand la nature, grande en ses desseins cachés,
De toi se sert, ô femme, ô reine des péchés,
— De toi, vil animal, — pour pétrir un génie ?

O fangeuse grandeur ! sublime ignominie !

XXVII

SED NON SATIATA

Bizarre déité, brune comme les nuits,
Au parfum mélangé de musc et de havane,
Œuvre de quelque obi, le Faust de la savane,
Sorcière au flanc d'ébène, enfant des noirs minuit

Je préfère au constance, à l'opium, au nuits,
L'élixir de ta bouche où l'amour se pavane;
Quand vers toi mes désirs partent en caravane,
Tes yeux sont la citerne où boivent mes ennuis.

Par ces deux grands yeux noirs, soupiraux de ton âme
O démon sans pitié ! verse-moi moins de flamme;
Je ne suis pas le Styx pour t'embrasser neuf fois,

Hélas ! et je ne puis, Mégère libertine,
Pour briser ton courage et te mettre aux abois,
Dans l'enfer de ton lit devenir Proserpine !

XXVIII

Avec ses vêtements ondoyants et nacrés,
Même quand elle marche on croirait qu'elle danse,
Comme ces longs serpents que les jongleurs sacrés
Au bout de leurs bâtons agitent en cadence.

Comme le sable morne et l'azur des déserts,
Insensibles tous deux à l'humaine souffrance,
Comme les longs réseaux de la houle des mers,
Elle se développe avec indifférence.

Ses yeux polis sont faits de minéraux charmants,
Et dans cette nature étrange et symbolique
Où l'ange inviolé se mêle au sphinx antique,

Où tout n'est qu'or, acier, lumière et diamants,
Resplendit à jamais, comme un astre inutile,
La froide majesté de la femme stérile.

XXIX

LE SERPENT QUI DANSE

Que j'aime voir, chère indolente,
De ton corps si beau,
Comme une étoffe vacillante,
Miroiter la peau !

Sur ta chevelure profonde
Aux âcres parfums,
Mer odorante et vagabonde
Aux flots bleus et bruns,

Comme un navire qui s'éveille
  Au vent du matin,
Mon âme rêveuse appareille
  Pour un ciel lointain.

Tes yeux, où rien ne se révèle
  De doux ni d'amer,
Sont deux bijoux froids où se mêle
  L'or avec le fer.

A te voir marcher en cadence,
  Belle d'abandon,
On dirait un serpent qui danse
  Au bout d'un bâton.

Sous le fardeau de ta paresse
  Ta tête d'enfant
Se balance avec la mollesse
  D'un jeune éléphant,

Et ton corps se penche et s'allonge
  Comme un fin vaisseau
Qui roule bord sur bord et plonge
  Ses vergues dans l'eau.

Comme un flot grossi par la fonte
  Des glaciers grondants,
Quand l'eau de ta bouche remonte
  Au bord de tes dents,

Je crois boire un vin de Bohême,
  Amer et vainqueur,
Un ciel liquide qui parsème
  D'étoiles mon cœur !

XXX

UNE CHAROGNE

Rappelez-vous l'objet que vous vîmes, mon âme,
Ce beau matin d'été si doux :
Au détour d'un sentier une charogne infâme
Sur un lit semé de cailloux,

Les jambes en l'air, comme une femme lubrique,
Brûlante et suant les poisons,
Ouvrait d'une façon nonchalante et cynique
Son ventre plein d'exhalaisons.

Le soleil rayonnait sur cette pourriture,
Comme afin de la cuire à point,
Et de rendre au centuple à la grande Nature
Tout ce qu'ensemble elle avait joint;

Et le ciel regardait la carcasse superbe
Comme une fleur s'épanouir.
La puanteur était si forte, que sur l'herbe
Vous crûtes vous évanouir.

Les mouches bourdonnaient sur ce ventre putride,
D'où sortaient de noirs bataillons
De larves, qui coulaient comme un épais liquide
Le long de ces vivants haillons.

Tout cela descendait, montait comme une vague,
Ou s'élançait en pétillant;
On eût dit que le corps, enflé d'un souffle vague,
Vivait en se multipliant.

Et ce monde rendait une étrange musique,
Comme l'eau courante et le vent,
Ou le grain qu'un vanneur d'un mouvement rhyth-
Agite et tourne dans son van. [mique

Les formes s'effaçaient et n'étaient plus qu'un rêve,
Une ébauche lente à venir,
Sur la toile oubliée, et que l'artiste achève
Seulement par le souvenir.

Derrière les rochers une chienne inquiète
Nous regardait d'un œil fâché,
Épiant le moment de reprendre au squelette
Le morceau qu'elle avait lâché.

— Et pourtant vous serez semblable à cette ordure,
A cette horrible infection,
Étoile de mes yeux, soleil de ma nature,
Vous, mon ange et ma passion !

Oui ! telle que vous serez, ô la reine des grâces,
Après les derniers sacrements,
Quand vous irez, sous l'herbe et les floraisons grasses,
Moisir parmi les ossements.

Alors, ô ma beauté ! dites à la vermine
Qui vous mangera de baisers,
Que j'ai gardé la forme et l'essence divine
De mes amours décomposés !

XXXI

DE PROFUNDIS CLAMAVI

J'implore ta pitié, Toi, l'unique que j'aime,
Du fond du gouffre obscur où mon cœur est tombé.
C'est un univers morne à l'horizon plombé,
Où nagent dans la nuit l'horreur et le blasphème;

Un soleil sans chaleur plane au-dessus six mois,
Et les six autres mois la nuit couvre la terre;
C'est un pays plus nu que la terre polaire;
— Ni bêtes, ni ruisseaux, ni verdure, ni bois !

Or il n'est pas d'horreur au monde qui surpasse
La froide cruauté de ce soleil de glace
Et cette immense nuit semblable au vieux Chaos;

Je jalouse le sort des plus vils animaux
Qui peuvent se plonger dans un sommeil stupide,
Tant l'écheveau du temps lentement se dévide !

XXXII

LE VAMPIRE

Toi qui, comme un coup de couteau,
Dans mon cœur plaintif es entrée;
Toi qui, forte comme un troupeau
De démons, vins, folle et parée,

De mon esprit humilié
Faire ton lit et ton domaine;
— Infame à qui je suis lié
Comme le forçat à la chaîne,

Comme au jeu le joueur têtu,
Comme à la bouteille l'ivrogne,
Comme aux vermines la charogne,
— Maudite, maudite sois-tu !

J'ai prié le glaive rapide
De conquérir ma liberté,
Et j'ai dit au poison perfide
De secourir ma lâcheté.

Hélas ! le poison et le glaive
M'ont pris en dédain et m'ont dit :
" Tu n'es pas digne qu'on t'enlève
A ton esclavage maudit,

Imbécile ! — de son empire
Si nos efforts te délivraient,
Tes baisers ressusciteraient
Le cadavre de ton vampire ! "

XXXIII

LE LÉTHÉ

Viens sur mon cœur, âme cruelle et sourde,
Tigre adoré, monstre aux airs indolents;
Je veux longtemps plonger mes doigts tremblants
Dans l'épaisseur de ta crinière lourde;

Dans tes jupons remplis de ton parfum
Ensevelir ma tête endolorie,
Et respirer, comme une fleur flétrie,
Le doux relent de mon amour défunt.

Je veux dormir ! dormir plutôt que vivre !
Dans un sommeil aussi doux que la mort,
J'étalerai mes baisers sans remord
Sur ton beau corps poli comme le cuivre.

Pour engloutir mes sanglots apaisés
Rien ne me vaut l'abîme de ta couche;
L'oubli puissant habite sur ta bouche,
Et le Léthé coule dans tes baisers.

A mon destin, désormais mon délice,
J'obéirai comme un prédestiné;
Martyr docile, innocent condamné,
Dont la ferveur attise le supplice,

Je sucerai, pour noyer ma rancœur,
Le népenthès et la bonne ciguë
Aux bouts charmants de cette gorge aiguë,
Qui n'a jamais emprisonné de cœur.

XXXIV

Une nuit que j'étais près d'une affreuse Juive,
Comme au long d'un cadavre un cadavre étendu,
Je me pris à songer près de ce corps vendu
A la triste beauté dont mon désir se prive.

Je me représentai sa majesté native,
Son regard de vigueur et de grâces armé,
Ses cheveux qui lui font un casque parfumé,
Et dont le souvenir pour l'amour me ravive.

Car j'eusse avec ferveur baisé ton noble corps,
Et depuis tes pieds frais jusqu'à tes noires tresses
Déroulé le trésor des profondes caresses,

Si, quelque soir, d'un pleur obtenu sans effort
Tu pouvais seulement, ô reine des cruelles !
Obscurcir la splendeur de tes froides prunelles.

XXXV

REMORDS POSTHUME

Lorsque tu dormiras, ma belle ténébreuse,
Au fond d'un monument construit en marbre noir
Et lorsque tu n'auras pour alcôve et manoir
Qu'un caveau pluvieux et qu'une fosse creuse;

Quand la pierre, opprimant ta poitrine peureuse
Et tes flancs qu'assouplit un charmant nonchaloir,
Empêchera ton cœur de battre et de vouloir,
Et tes pieds de courir leur course aventureuse,

Le tombeau, confident de mon rêve infini
(Car le tombeau toujours comprendra le poëte),
Durant ces grandes nuits d'où le somme est banni,

Te dira : " Que vous sert, courtisane imparfaite,
De n'avoir pas connu ce que pleurent les morts ? "
— Et le ver rongera ta peau comme un remords.

XXXVI

LE CHAT

Viens, mon beau chat, sur mon cœur amoureux;
Retiens les griffes de ta patte,
Et laisse-moi plonger dans tes beaux yeux,
Mêlés de métal et d'agate.

Lorsque mes doigts caressent à loisir
Ta tête et ton dos élastique,
Et que ma main s'enivre du plaisir
De palper ton corps électrique,

Je vois ma femme en esprit. Son regard,
Comme le tien, aimable bête,
Profond et froid, coupe et fend comme un dard,

Et, des pieds jusques à la tête,
Un air subtil, un dangereux parfum
Nagent autour de son corps brun.

XXXVII

DUELLUM

Deux guerriers ont couru l'un sur l'autre; leurs armes
Ont éclaboussé l'air de lueurs et de sang.
Ces jeux, ces cliquetis du fer sont les vacarmes
D'une jeunesse en proie à l'amour vagissant.

Les glaives sont brisés ! comme notre jeunesse,
Ma chère ! Mais les dents, les ongles acérés,
Vengent bientôt l'épée et la dague traîtresse.
— O fureur des cœurs mûrs par l'amour ulcérés !

Dans le ravin hanté des chats-pards et des onces
Nos héros, s'étreignant méchamment, ont roulé,
Et leur peau fleurira l'aridité des ronces.

— Ce gouffre, c'est l'enfer, de nos amis peuplé !
Roulons-y sans remords, amazone inhumaine,
Afin d'éterniser l'ardeur de notre haine !

XXXVIII

LE BALCON

Mère des souvenirs, maîtresse des maîtresses,
O toi, tous mes plaisirs ! ô toi, tous mes devoirs !
Tu te rappelleras la beauté des caresses,
La douceur du foyer et le charme des soirs,
Mère des souvenirs, maîtresse des maîtresses !

Les soirs illuminés par l'ardeur du charbon,
Et les soirs au balcon, voilés de vapeurs roses,
Que ton sein m'était doux ! que ton cœur m'était bon !
Nous avons dit souvent d'impérissables choses
Les soirs illuminés par l'ardeur du charbon.

Que les soleils sont beaux dans les chaudes soirées !
Que l'espace est profond ! Que le cœur est puissant !
En me penchant vers toi, reine des adorées,
Je croyais respirer le parfum de ton sang.
Que les soleils sont beaux dans les chaudes soirées !

La nuit s'épaississait ainsi qu'une cloison,
Et mes yeux dans le noir devinaient tes prunelles,
Et je buvais ton souffle, ô douceur ! ô poison !

Et tes pieds s'endormaient dans mes mains fraternelles.
La nuit s'épaississait ainsi qu'une cloison.

Je sais l'art d'évoquer les minutes heureuses,
Et revis mon passé blotti dans tes genoux.
Car à quoi bon chercher tes beautés langoureuses
Ailleurs qu'en ton cher corps et qu'en ton cœur si doux?
Je sais l'art d'évoquer les minutes heureuses !

Ces serments, ces parfums, ces baisers infinis,
Renaîtront-ils d'un gouffre interdit à nos sondes,
Comme montent au ciel les soleils rajeunis
Après s'être lavés au fond des mers profondes ?
— O serments ! ô parfums ! ô baisers infinis !

XXXIX

LE POSSÉDÉ

Le soleil s'est couvert d'un crêpe. Comme lui,
O Lune de ma vie ! emmitoufle-toi d'ombre;
Dors ou fume à ton gré; sois muette, sois sombre,
Et plonge tout entière au gouffre de l'Ennui;

Je t'aime ainsi ! Pourtant, si tu veux aujourd'hui,
Comme un astre éclipsé qui sort de la pénombre,
Te pavaner aux lieux que la Folie encombre,
C'est bien ! Charmant poignard, jaillis de ton étui !

Allume ta prunelle à la flamme des lustres !
Allume le désir dans les regards des rustres !
Tout de toi m'est plaisir, morbide ou pétulant;

Sois ce que tu voudras, nuit noire, rouge aurore;
Il n'est pas une fibre en tout mon corps tremblant
Qui ne crie : *O mon cher Belzébuth, je t'adore !*

XL

UN FANTOME

I

LES TÉNÈBRES

Dans les caveaux d'insondable tristesse
Où le Destin m'a déjà relégué;
Où jamais n'entre un rayon rose et gai;
Où, seul avec la Nuit, maussade hôtesse,

Je suis comme un peintre qu'un Dieu moqueur
Condamne à peindre, hélas ! sur les ténèbres;
Où, cuisinier aux appétits funèbres,
Je fais bouillir et je mange mon cœur,

Par instants brille, et s'allonge et s'étale
Un spectre fait de grâce et de splendeur.
A sa rêveuse allure orientale,

Quand il atteint sa totale grandeur,
Je reconnais ma belle visiteuse :
C'est Elle ! noire et pourtant lumineuse.

II

LE PARFUM

Lecteur, as-tu quelquefois respiré
Avec ivresse et lente gourmandise
Ce grain d'encens qui remplit une église,
Ou d'un sachet le musc invétéré ?

Charme profond, magique, dont nous grise
Dans le présent le passé restauré !
Ainsi l'amant sur un corps adoré
Du souvenir cueille la fleur exquise.

De ses cheveux élastiques et lourds,
Vivant sachet, encensoir de l'alcôve,
Une senteur montait, sauvage et fauve,

Et des habits, mousseline ou velours,
Tout imprégnés de sa jeunesse pure,
Se dégageait un parfum de fourrure.

III

LE CADRE

Comme un beau cadre ajoute à la peinture,
Bien qu'elle soit d'un pinceau très-vanté,
Je ne sais quoi d'étrange et d'enchanté
En l'isolant de l'immense nature,

Ainsi bijoux, meubles, métaux, dorure,
S'adaptaient juste à sa rare beauté;
Rien n'offusquait sa parfaite clarté,
Et tout semblait lui servir de bordure.

Même on eût dit parfois qu'elle croyait
Que tout voulait l'aimer; elle noyait
Sa nudité voluptueusement

Dans les baisers du satin et du linge,
Et, lente ou brusque, à chaque mouvement
Montrait la grâce enfantine du singe.

IV

LE PORTRAIT

La Maladie et la Mort font des cendres
De tout le feu qui pour nous flamboya.
De ces grands yeux si fervents et si tendres,
De cette bouche où mon cœur se noya,

De ces baisers puissants comme un dictame,
De ces transports plus vifs que des rayons,
Que reste-t-il ? C'est affreux, ô mon âme !
Rien qu'un dessin fort pâle, aux trois crayons,

Qui, comme moi, meurt dans la solitude,
Et que le Temps, injurieux vieillard,
Chaque jour frotte avec son aile rude...

Noir assassin de la Vie et de l'Art,
Tu ne tueras jamais dans ma mémoire
Celle qui fut mon plaisir et ma gloire !

XLI

Je te donne ces vers afin que si mon nom
Aborde heureusement aux époques lointaines,
Et fait rêver un soir les cervelles humaines,
Vaisseau favorisé par un grand aquilon,

Ta mémoire, pareille aux fables incertaines,
Fatigue le lecteur ainsi qu'un tympanon,
Et par un fraternel et mystique chaînon
Reste comme pendue à mes rimes hautaines;

Être maudit à qui, de l'abîme profond
Jusqu'au plus haut du ciel, rien, hors moi, ne répond !
— O toi qui, comme une ombre à la trace éphémère,

Foules d'un pied léger et d'un regard serein
Les stupides mortels qui t'ont jugée amère,
Statue aux yeux de jais, grand ange au front d'airain !

XLII

SEMPER EADEM

" D'où vous vient, disiez-vous, cette tristesse étrange,
Montant comme la mer sur le roc noir et nu ? "
— Quand notre cœur a fait une fois sa vendange,
Vivre est un mal. C'est un secret de tous connu,

Une douleur très-simple et non mystérieuse,
Et, comme votre joie, éclatante pour tous.
Cessez donc de chercher, ô belle curieuse !
Et, bien que votre voix soit douce, taisez-vous !

Taisez-vous, ignorante ! âme toujours ravie !
Bouche au rire enfantin ! Plus encor que la Vie,
La Mort nous tient souvent par des liens subtils.

Laissez, laissez mon cœur s'enivrer d'un *mensonge*,
Plonger dans vos beaux yeux comme dans un beau
Et sommeiller longtemps à l'ombre de vos cils ! [songe

XLIII

TOUT ENTIÈRE

Le Démon, dans ma chambre haute,
Ce matin est venu me voir,
Et, tâchant à me prendre en faute,
Me dit : " Je voudrais bien savoir,

Parmi toutes les belles choses
Dont est fait son enchantement,
Parmi les objets noirs ou roses
Qui composent son corps charmant,

Quel est le plus doux. " — O mon âme !
Tu répondis à l'Abhorré :
" Puisqu'en Elle tout est dictame,
Rien ne peut être préféré.

Lorsque tout me ravit, j'ignore
Si quelque chose me séduit.
Elle éblouit comme l'Aurore
Et console comme la Nuit;

Et l'harmonie est trop exquise,
Qui gouverne tout son beau corps,
Pour que l'impuissante analyse
En note les nombreux accords.

O métamorphose mystique
De tous mes sens fondus en un !
Son haleine fait la musique,
Comme sa voix fait le parfum ! "

XLIV

Que diras-tu ce soir, pauvre âme solitaire,
Que diras-tu, mon cœur, cœur autrefois flétri,
A la très-belle, à la très-bonne, à la très-chère,
Dont le regard divin t'a soudain refleuri ?

—Nous mettrons notre orgueil à chanter ses louan-
Rien ne vaut la douceur de son autorité; [ges :
Sa chair spirituelle a le parfum des Anges,
Et son œil nous revêt d'un habit de clarté.

Que ce soit dans la nuit et dans la solitude,
Que ce soit dans la rue et dans la multitude,
Son fantôme dans l'air danse comme un flambeau.

Parfois il parle et dit : " Je suis belle, et j'ordonne
Que pour l'amour de moi vous n'aimiez que le Beau;
Je suis l'Ange gardien, la Muse et la Madone! "

XLV

LE FLAMBEAU VIVANT

Ils marchent devant moi, ces Yeux pleins de lumières,
Qu'un Ange très-savant a sans doute aimantés;
Ils marchent, ces divins frères qui sont mes frères,
Secouant dans mes yeux leurs feux diamantés.

Me sauvant de tout piége et de tout péché grave,
Ils conduisent mes pas dans la route du Beau;
Ils sont mes serviteurs et je suis leur esclave;
Tout mon être obéit à ce vivant flambeau.

Charmants Yeux, vous brillez de la clarté mystique
Qu'ont les cierges brûlant en plein jour; le soleil
Rougit, mais n'éteint pas leur flamme fantastique;

Ils célèbrent la Mort, vous chantez le Réveil;
Vous marchez en chantant le réveil de mon âme,
Astres dont nul soleil ne peut flétrir la flamme !

XLVI

A CELLE QUI EST TROP GAIE

Ta tête, ton geste, ton air
Sont beaux comme un beau paysage;
Le rire joue en ton visage
Comme un vent frais dans un ciel clair.

Le passant chagrin que tu frôles
Est ébloui par la santé
Qui jaillit comme une clarté
De tes bras et de tes épaules.

Les retentissantes couleurs
Dont tu parsèmes tes toilettes
Jettent dans l'esprit des poëtes
L'image d'un ballet de fleurs.

Ces robes folles sont l'emblème
De ton esprit bariolé;
Folle dont je suis affolé,
Je te hais autant que je t'aime !

Quelquefois dans un beau jardin
Où je traînais mon atonie,
J'ai senti comme une ironie,
Le soleil déchirer mon sein;

Et le printemps et la verdure
Ont tant humilié mon cœur,
Que j'ai puni sur une fleur
L'insolence de la Nature.

Ainsi je voudrais, une nuit,
Quand l'heure des voluptés sonne,
Vers les trésors de ta personne,
Comme un lâche, ramper sans bruit,

Pour châtier ta chair joyeuse,
Pour meurtrir ton sein pardonné,
Et faire à ton flanc étonné
Une blessure large et creuse,

Et, vertigineuse douceur !
A travers ces lèvres nouvelles,
Plus éclatantes et plus belles,
T'infuser mon venin, ma sœur !

XLVII

RÉVERSIBILITÉ

Ange plein de gaieté, connaissez-vous l'angoisse,
La honte, les remords, les sanglots, les ennuis,
Et les vagues terreurs de ces affreuses nuits
Qui compriment le cœur comme un papier qu'on froisse?
Ange plein de gaieté, connaissez-vous l'angoisse ?

Ange plein de bonté, connaissez-vous la haine,
Les poings crispés dans l'ombre et les larmes de fiel,
Quand la Vengeance bat son infernal rappel,
Et de nos facultés se fait le capitaine ?
Ange plein de bonté, connaissez-vous la haine ?

Ange plein de santé, connaissez-vous les Fièvres,
Qui, le long des grands murs de l'hospice blafard,
Comme des exilés, s'en vont d'un pied traînard,
Cherchant le soleil rare et remuant les lèvres ?
Ange plein de santé, connaissez-vous les Fièvres ?

Ange plein de beauté, connaissez-vous les rides,
Et la peur de vieillir, et ce hideux tourment
De lire la secrète horreur du dévouement
Dans des yeux où longtemps burent nos yeux avides ?
Ange plein de beauté, connaissez-vous les rides ?

Ange plein de bonheur, de joie et de lumières,
David mourant aurait demandé la santé
Aux émanations de ton corps enchanté;
Mais de toi je n'implore, ange, que tes prières,
Ange plein de bonheur, de joie et de lumières !

XLVIII

CONFESSION

Une fois, une seule, aimable et douce femme,
A mon bras votre bras poli
S'appuya (sur le fond ténébreux de mon âme
Ce souvenir n'est point pâli);

Il était tard; ainsi qu'une médaille neuve
La pleine lune s'étalait,
Et la solennité de la nuit, comme un fleuve,
Sur Paris dormant ruisselait.

Et le long des maisons, sous les portes cochères,
Des chats passaient furtivement,
L'oreille au guet, ou bien, comme des ombres chères,
Nous accompagnaient lentement.

Tout à coup, au milieu de l'intimité libre
Éclose à la pâle clarté,
De vous, riche et sonore instrument où ne vibre
Que la radieuse gaieté,

De vous, claire et joyeuse ainsi qu'une fanfare
Dans le matin étincelant,
Une note plaintive, une note bizarre
S'échappa tout en chancelant

Comme une enfant chétive, horrible, sombre, im-
Dont sa famille rougirait, [monde,
Et qu'elle aurait longtemps, pour la cacher au monde,
Dans un caveau mise au secret.

Pauvre ange, elle chantait, votre note criarde :
" Que rien ici-bas n'est certain,
Et que toujours, avec quelque soin qu'il se farde,
Se trahit l'égoïsme humain;

Que c'est un dur métier que d'être belle femme,
Et que c'est le travail banal
De la danseuse folle et froide qui se pâme
Dans un sourire machinal;

Que bâtir sur les cœurs est une chose sotte;
Que tout craque, amour et beauté,
Jusqu'à ce que l'Oubli les jette dans sa hotte
Pour les rendre à l'Éternité ! "

J'ai souvent évoqué cette lune enchantée,
Ce silence et cette langueur,
Et cette confidence horrible chuchotée
Au confessionnal du cœur.

XLIX

L'AUBE SPIRITUELLE

Quand chez les débauchés l'aube blanche et vermeille
Entre en société de l'Idéal rongeur,
Par l'opération d'un mystère vengeur
Dans la brute assoupie un ange se réveille.

Des Cieux Spirituels l'inaccessible azur,
Pour l'homme terrassé qui rêve encore et souffre,
S'ouvre et s'enfonce avec l'attirance du gouffre.
Ainsi, chère Déesse, Être lucide et pur,

Sur les débris fumeux des stupides orgies
Ton souvenir plus clair, plus rose, plus charmant,
A mes yeux agrandis voltige incessamment.

Le soleil a noirci la flamme des bougies;
Ainsi, toujours vainqueur, ton fantôme est pareil,
Ame resplendissante, à l'immortel soleil !

L

HARMONIE DU SOIR

Voici venir les temps où vibrant sur sa tige
Chaque fleur s'évapore ainsi qu'un encensoir;
Les sons et les parfums tournent dans l'air du soir;
Valse mélancolique et langoureux vertige !

Chaque fleur s'évapore ainsi qu'un encensoir;
Le violon frémit comme un cœur qu'on afflige;
Valse mélancolique et langoureux vertige !
Le ciel est triste et beau comme un grand reposoir.

Le violon frémit comme un cœur qu'on afflige,
Un cœur tendre, qui hait le néant vaste et noir !
Le ciel est triste et beau comme un grand reposoir;
Le soleil s'est noyé dans son sang qui se fige.

Un cœur tendre qui hait le néant vaste et noir,
Du passé lumineux recueille tout vestige !
Le soleil s'est noyé dans son sang qui se fige...
Ton souvenir en moi luit comme un ostensoir !

LI

LE FLACON

Il est de forts parfums pour qui toute matière
Est poreuse. On dirait qu'ils pénètrent le verre.
En ouvrant un coffret venu de l'Orient
Dont la serrure grince et rechigne en criant,

Ou dans une maison déserte quelque armoire
Pleine de l'âcre odeur des temps, poudreuse et noire,
Parfois on trouve un vieux flacon qui se souvient,
D'où jaillit toute vive une âme qui revient.

Mille pensers dormaient, chrysalides funèbres,
Frémissant doucement dans les lourdes ténèbres,
Qui dégagent leur aile et prennent leur essor,
Teintés d'azur, glacés de rose, lamés d'or.

Voilà le souvenir enivrant qui voltige
Dans l'air troublé; les yeux se ferment; le Vertige
Saisit l'âme vaincue et la pousse à deux mains
Vers un gouffre obscurci de miasmes humains;

Il la terrasse au bord d'un gouffre séculaire,
Où, Lazare odorant déchirant son suaire,
Se meut dans son réveil le cadavre spectral
D'un viel amour ranci, charmant et sépulcral.

Ainsi, quand je serai perdu dans la mémoire
Des hommes, dans le coin d'une sinistre armoire
Quand on m'aura jeté, vieux flacon désolé,
Décrépit, poudreux, sale, abject, visqueux, fêlé,

Je serai ton cercueil, aimable pestilence !
Le témoin de ta force et de ta virulence,
Cher poison préparé par les anges ! liqueur
Qui me ronge, ô la vie et la mort de mon cœur !

LII

LE POISON

Le vin sait revêtir le plus sordide bouge
D'un luxe miraculeux,
Et fait surgir plus d'un portique fabuleux
Dans l'or de sa vapeur rouge,
Comme un soleil couchant dans un ciel nébuleux.

L'opium agrandit ce qui n'a pas de bornes,
Allonge l'illimité,
Approfondit le temps, creuse la volupté,
Et de plaisirs noirs et mornes
Remplit l'âme au-delà de sa capacité.

Tout cela ne vaut pas le poison qui découle
De tes yeux, de tes yeux verts,
Lacs où mon âme tremble et se voit à l'envers...
Mes songes viennent en foule
Pour se désaltérer à ces gouffres amers.

Tout cela ne vaut pas le terrible prodige
De ta salive qui mord,
Qui plonge dans l'oubli mon âme sans remord,
Et, charriant le vertige,
La roule défaillante aux rives de la mort !

LIII

CIEL BROUILLÉ

On dirait ton regard d'une vapeur couvert;
Ton œil mystérieux (est-il bleu, gris ou vert ?)
Alternativement tendre, rêveur, cruel,
Réfléchit l'indolence et la pâleur du ciel.

Tu rappelles ces jours blancs, tièdes et voilés,
Qui font se fondre en pleurs les cœurs ensorcelés,
Quand, agités d'un mal inconnu qui les tord,
Les nerfs trop éveillés raillent l'esprit qui dort.

Tu ressembles parfois à ces beaux horizons
Qu'allument les soleils des brumeuses saisons...
Comme tu resplendis, paysage mouillé
Qu'enflamment les rayons tombant d'un ciel brouillé !

O femme dangereuse, ô séduisants climats !
Adorerai-je aussi ta neige et vos frimas,
Et saurai-je tirer de l'implacable hiver
Des plaisirs plus aigus que la glace et le fer ?

LIV

LE CHAT

I

Dans ma cervelle se promène,
Ainsi qu'en son appartement,
Un beau chat, fort, doux et charmant.
Quand il miaule, on l'entend à peine,

Tant son timbre est tendre et discret;
Mais que sa voix s'apaise ou gronde,
Elle est toujours riche et profonde.
C'est là son charme et son secret.

Cette voix qui perle et qui filtre
Dans mon fonds le plus ténébreux,
Me remplit comme un vers nombreux
Et me réjouit comme un philtre.

Elle endort les plus cruels maux
Et contient toutes les extases;
Pour dire les plus longues phrases,
Elle n'a pas besoin de mots.

Non, il n'est pas d'archet qui morde
Sur mon cœur, parfait instrument,
Et fasse plus royalement
Chanter sa plus vibrante corde,

Que ta voix, chat mystérieux,
Chat séraphique, chat étrange,
En qui tout est, comme en un ange,
Aussi subtil qu'harmonieux !

II

De sa fourrure blonde et brune
Sort un parfum si doux, qu'un soir
J'en fus embaumé, pour l'avoir
Caressée une fois, rien qu'une.

C'est l'esprit familier du lieu;
Il juge, il préside, il inspire
Toutes choses dans son empire;
Peut-être est-il fée, est-il dieu ?

Quand mes yeux, vers ce chat que j'aime
Tirés comme par un aimant,
Se retournent docilement
Et que je regarde en moi-même,

Je vois avec étonnement
Le feu de ses prunelles pâles,
Clairs fanaux, vivantes opales,
Qui me contemplent fixement.

LV

LE BEAU NAVIRE

Je veux te raconter, ô molle enchanteresse !
Les diverses beautés qui parent ta jeunesse;
        Je veux te peindre ta beauté,
Où l'enfance s'allie à la maturité.

Quand tu vas balayant l'air de ta jupe large,
Tu fais l'effet d'un beau vaisseau qui prend le large,
        Chargé de toile, et va roulant
Suivant un rhythme doux, et paresseux, et lent.

Sur ton cou large et rond, sur tes épaules grasses,
Ta tête se pavane avec d'étranges grâces;
        D'un air placide et triomphant
Tu passes ton chemin, majestueuse enfant.

Je veux te raconter, ô molle enchanteresse !
Les diverses beautés qui parent ta jeunesse;
        Je veux te peindre ta beauté,
Où l'enfance s'allie à la maturité.

Ta gorge qui s'avance et qui pousse la moire,
Ta gorge triomphante est une belle armoire
        Dont les panneaux bombés et clairs
Comme les boucliers accrochent des éclairs;

Boucliers provocants, armés de pointes roses !
Armoire à doux secrets, pleine de bonnes choses,
        De vins, de parfums, de liqueurs
Qui feraient délirer les cerveaux et les cœurs !

Quand tu vas balayant l'air de ta jupe large,
Tu fais l'effet d'un beau vaisseau qui prend le large,
        Chargé de toile, et va roulant
Suivant un rhythme doux, et paresseux, et lent.

Tes nobles jambes, sous les volants qu'elles chassent,
Tourmentent les désirs obscurs et les agacent,
        Comme deux sorcières qui font
Tourner un philtre noir dans un vase profond.

Tes bras, qui se joueraient des précoces hercules,
Sont des boas luisants les solides émules,
        Faits pour serrer obstinément,
Comme pour l'imprimer dans ton cœur, ton amant.

Sur ton cou large et rond, sur tes épaules grasses,
Ta tête se pavane avec d'étranges grâces;
        D'un air placide et triomphant
Tu passes ton chemin, majestueuse enfant.

LVI

L'INVITATION AU VOYAGE

Mon enfant, ma sœur,
Songe à la douceur
D'aller là-bas vivre ensemble !
Aimer à loisir,
Aimer et mourir
Au pays qui te ressemble !
Les soleils mouillés
De ces ciels brouillés
Pour mon esprit ont les charmes
Si mystérieux
De tes traîtres yeux,
Brillant à travers leurs larmes.

Là, tout n'est qu'ordre et beauté,
Luxe, calme et volupté.

Des meubles luisants,
Polis par les ans,
Décoreraient notre chambre;
Les plus rares fleurs
Mêlant leurs odeurs
Aux vagues senteurs de l'ambre,
Les riches plafonds,
Les miroirs profonds,
La splendeur orientale,
Tout y parlerait
A l'âme en secret
Sa douce langue natale.

Là, tout n'est qu'ordre et beauté,
Luxe, calme et volupté.

Vois sur ces canaux
Dormir ces vaisseaux
Dont l'humeur est vagabonde;
C'est pour assouvir
Ton moindre désir
Qu'ils viennent du bout du monde.
— Les soleils couchants
Revêtent les champs,
Les canaux, la ville entière,
D'hyacinthe et d'or;
Le monde s'endort
Dans une chaude lumière.

Là, tout n'est qu'ordre et beauté,
Luxe, calme et volupté.

LVII

L'IRRÉPARABLE

Pouvons-nous étouffer le vieux, le long Remords,
Qui vit, s'agite et se tortille,
Et se nourrit de nous comme le ver des morts,
Comme du chêne la chenille ?
Pouvons-nous étouffer l'implacable Remords ?

Dans quel philtre, dans quel vin, dans quelle tisane,
Noierons-nous ce vieil ennemi,
Destructeur et gourmand comme la courtisane,
Patient comme la fourmi ?
Dans quel philtre ? — dans quel vin ? — dans quelle
[tisane ?

Dis-le, belle sorcière, oh ! dis, si tu le sais,
A cet esprit comblé d'angoisse
Et pareil au mourant qu'écrasent les blessés,
Que le sabot du cheval froisse,
Dis-le, belle sorcière, oh ! dis, si tu le sais,

A cet agonisant que le loup déjà flaire
Et que surveille le corbeau,
A ce soldat brisé ! s'il faut qu'il désespère
D'avoir sa croix et son tombeau;
Ce pauvre agonisant que déjà le loup flaire !

Peut-on illuminer un ciel bourbeux et noir ?
Peut-on déchirer des ténèbres
Plus denses que la poix, sans matin et sans soir,
Sans astres, sans éclairs funèbres ?
Peut-on illuminer un ciel bourbeux et noir ?

L'Espérance qui brille aux carreaux de l'Auberge
Est soufflée, est morte à jamais !
Sans lune et sans rayons, trouver où l'on héberge
Les martyrs d'un chemin mauvais !
Le Diable a tout éteint aux carreaux de l'Auberge !

Adorable sorcière, aimes-tu les damnés ?
Dis, connais-tu l'irrémissible ?
Connais-tu le Remords, aux traits empoisonnés,
A qui notre cœur sert de cible ?
Adorable sorcière, aimes-tu les damnés ?

L'Irréparable ronge, avec sa dent maudite
Notre âme, piteux monument,
Et souvent il attaque, ainsi que le termite,
Par la base le bâtiment.
L'Irréparable ronge avec sa dent maudite !

— J'ai vu parfois, au fond d'un théâtre banal
Qu'enflammait l'orchestre sonore,
Une fée allumer dans un ciel infernal
Une miraculeuse aurore;
J'ai vu parfois au fond d'un théâtre banal

Un être, qui n'était que lumière, or et gaze,
Terrasser l'énorme Satan;
Mais mon cœur, que jamais ne visite l'extase,
Est un théâtre où l'on attend
Toujours, toujours en vain, l'Être aux ailes de gaze !

LVIII

CAUSERIE

Vous êtes un beau ciel d'automne, clair et rose !
Mais la tristesse en moi monte comme la mer,
Et laisse, en refluant, sur ma lèvre morose
Le souvenir cuisant de son limon amer.

— Ta main se glisse en vain sur mon sein qui se pâme;
Ce qu'elle cherche, amie, est un lieu saccagé
Par la griffe et la dent féroce de la femme.
Ne cherchez plus mon cœur; les bêtes l'ont mangé.

Mon cœur est un palais flétri par la cohue;
On s'y soûle, on s'y tue, on s'y prend aux cheveux !
— Un parfum nage autour de votre gorge nue !...

O Beauté, dur fléau des âmes, tu le veux !
Avec tes yeux de feu, brillants comme des fêtes,
Calcine ces lambeaux qu'ont épargnés les bêtes !

LIX

CHANT D'AUTOMNE

I

Bientôt nous plongerons dans les froides ténèbres;
Adieu, vive clarté de nos étés trop courts !
J'entends déjà tomber avec des chocs funèbres
Le bois retentissant sur le pavé des cours.

Tout l'hiver va rentrer dans mon être : colère,
Haine, frissons, horreur, labeur dur et forcé,
Et, comme le soleil dans son enfer polaire,
Mon cœur ne sera plus qu'un bloc rouge et glacé.

J'écoute en frémissant chaque bûche qui tombe;
L'échafaud qu'on bâtit n'a pas d'écho plus sourd.
Mon esprit est pareil à la tour qui succombe
Sous les coups du bélier infatigable et lourd.

Il me semble, bercé par ce choc monotone,
Qu'on cloue en grande hâte un cercueil quelque part.
Pour qui ? — C'était hier l'été; voici l'automne !
Ce bruit mystérieux sonne comme un départ.

II

J'aime de vos longs yeux la lumière verdâtre,
Douce beauté, mais tout aujourd'hui m'est amer,
Et rien, ni votre amour, ni le boudoir, ni l'âtre,
Ne me vaut le soleil rayonnant sur la mer.

Et pourtant aimez-moi, tendre cœur ! soyez mère,
Même pour un ingrat, même pour un méchant;
Amante ou sœur, soyez la douceur éphémère
D'un glorieux automne ou d'un soleil couchant.

Courte tâche ! La tombe attend; elle est avide !
Ah ! laissez-moi, mon front posé sur vos genoux,
Goûter, en regrettant l'été blanc et torride,
De l'arrière-saison le rayon jaune et doux !

LX

A UNE MADONE

EX-VOTO DANS LE GOUT ESPAGNOL

Je veux bâtir pour toi, Madone, ma maîtresse,
Un autel souterrain au fond de ma détresse,
Et creuser dans le coin le plus noir de mon cœur,
Loin du désir mondain et du regard moqueur,
Une niche, d'azur et d'or tout émaillée,
Où tu te dresseras, Statue émerveillée.
Avec mes Vers polis, treillis d'un pur métal
Savamment constellé de rimes de cristal,
Je ferai pour ta tête une énorme Couronne;
Et dans ma Jalousie, ô mortelle Madone,
Je saurai te tailler un Manteau, de façon
Barbare, roide et lourd, et doublé de soupçon,
Qui, comme une guérite, enfermera tes charmes;
Non de Perles brodé, mais de toutes mes Larmes !
Ta Robe, ce sera mon Désir, frémissant,
Onduleux, mon Désir qui monte et qui descend,
Aux pointes se balance, aux vallons se repose,

Et revêt d'un baiser tout ton corps blanc et rose.
Je te ferai de mon Respect de beaux Souliers
De satin, par tes pieds divins humiliés,
Qui, les emprisonnant dans une molle étreinte,
Comme un moule fidèle en garderont l'empreinte.
Si je ne puis, malgré tout mon art diligent,
Pour Marchepied tailler une Lune d'argent,
Je mettrai le Serpent qui me mord les entrailles
Sous tes talons, afin que tu foules et railles,
Reine victorieuse et féconde en rachats,
Ce monstre tout gonflé de haine et de crachats.
Tu verras mes Pensers, rangés comme les Cierges
Devant l'autel fleuri de la Reine des Vierges,
Étoilant de reflets le plafond peint en bleu,
Te regarder toujours avec des yeux de feu;
Et comme tout en moi te chérit et t'admire,
Tout se fera Benjoin, Encens, Oliban, Myrrhe,
Et sans cesse vers toi, sommet blanc et neigeux,
En Vapeurs montera mon Esprit orageux.

Enfin, pour compléter ton rôle de Marie,
Et pour mêler l'amour avec la barbarie,
Volupté noire ! des sept Péchés capitaux,
Bourreau plein de remords, je ferai sept Couteaux
Bien affilés, et, comme un jongleur insensible,
Prenant le plus profond de ton amour pour cible,
Je les planterai tous dans ton Cœur pantelant,
Dans ton Cœur sanglotant, dans ton Cœur ruisselant !

LXI

CHANSON D'APRÈS-MIDI

Quoique tes sourcils méchants
Te donnent un air étrange
Qui n'est pas celui d'un ange,
Sorcière aux yeux alléchants,

Je t'adore ô ma frivole,
Ma terrible passion !
Avec la dévotion
Du prêtre pour son idole.

Le désert et la forêt
Embaument tes tresses rudes:
Ta tête a les attitudes
De l'énigme et du secret.

Sur ta chair le parfum rôde
Comme autour d'un encensoir;
Tu charmes comme le soir,
Nymphe ténébreuse et chaude.

Ah ! les philtres les plus forts
Ne valent pas ta paresse,
Et tu connais la caresse
Qui fait revivre les morts !

Tes hanches sont amoureuses
De ton dos et de tes seins,
Et tu ravis les coussins
Par tes poses langoureuses

Quelquefois, pour apaiser
Ta rage mystérieuse,
Tu prodigues, sérieuse,
La morsure et le baiser;

Tu me déchires, ma brune,
Avec un rire moqueur,
Et puis tu mets sur mon cœur
Ton œil doux comme la lune.

Sous tes souliers de satin,
Sous tes charmants pieds de soie,
Moi, je mets ma grande joie,
Mon génie et mon destin,

Mon âme par toi guérie,
Par toi, lumière et couleur !
Explosion de chaleur
Dans ma noire Sibérie !

LXII

SISINA

Imaginez Diane en galant équipage,
Parcourant les forêts ou battant les halliers,
Cheveux et gorge au vent, s'enivrant de tapage,
Superbe et défiant les meilleurs cavaliers !

Avez-vous vu Théroigne, amante du carnage,
Excitant à l'assaut un peuple sans souliers,
La joue et l'œil en feu, jouant son personnage,
Et montant, sabre au poing, les royaux escaliers ?

Telle la Sisina ! Mais la douce guerrière
A l'âme charitable autant que meurtrière;
Son courage, affolé de poudre et de tambours,

Devant les suppliants sait mettre bas les armes,
Et son cœur, ravagé par la flamme, a toujours,
Pour qui s'en montre digne, un réservoir de larmes.

LXIII

FRANCISCÆ MEÆ LAUDES

Novis te cantabo chordis,
O novelletum quod ludis
In solitudine cordis.

Esto sertis implicata,
O femina delicata
Per quam solvuntur peccata !

Sicut beneficum Lethe,
Hauriam oscula de te,
Quæ imbuta es magnete.

Quum vitiorum tempestas
Turbabat omnes semitas,
Apparuisti, Deitas,

Velut stella salutaris
In naufragiis amaris...
Suspendam cor tuis aris !

Piscina plena virtutis,
Fons æternæ juventutis,
Labris vocem redde mutis !

Quod erat spurcum, cremasti;
Quod rudius, exæquasti;
Quod debile, confirmasti.

In fame mea taberna,
In nocte mea lucerna,
Recte me semper guberna.

Adde nunc vires viribus,
Dulce balneum suavibus
Unguentatum odoribus !

Meos circa lumbos mica,
O castitatis lorica,
Aqua tincta seraphica;

Patera gemmis corusca,
Panis salsus, mollis esca,
Divinum vinum, Francisca !

LXIV

A UNE DAME CRÉOLE

Au pays parfumé que le soleil caresse,
J'ai connu, sous un dais d'arbres tout empourprés
Et de palmiers d'où pleut sur les yeux la paresse,
Une dame créole aux charmes ignorés.

Son teint est pâle et chaud; la brune enchanteresse
A dans le cou des airs noblement maniérés;
Grande et svelte en marchant comme une chasseresse,
Son sourire est tranquille et ses yeux assurés.

Si vous alliez, Madame, au vrai pays de gloire,
Sur les bords de la Seine ou de la verte Loire,
Belle digne d'orner les antiques manoirs,

Vous feriez, à l'abri des ombreuses retraites,
Germer mille sonnets dans le cœur des poëtes,
Que vos grands yeux rendraient plus soumis que vos
[noirs.

LXV

MŒSTA ET ERRABUNDA

Dis-moi, ton cœur parfois s'envole-t-il, Agathe,
Loin du noir océan de l'immonde cité,
Vers un autre océan où la splendeur éclate,
Bleu, clair, profond, ainsi que la virginité ?
Dis-moi, ton cœur parfois s'envole-t-il, Agathe ?

La mer, la vaste mer, console nos labeurs !
Quel démon a doté la mer, rauque chanteuse
Qu'accompagne l'immense orgue des vents gron-
De cette fonction sublime de berceuse ? [deurs,
La mer, la vaste mer, console nos labeurs !

Emporte-moi, wagon ! enlève-moi, frégate !
Loin, loin ! ici la boue est faite de nos pleurs !
— Est-il vrai que parfois le triste cœur d'Agathe
Dise : Loin des remords, des crimes, des douleurs,
Emporte-moi, wagon, enlève-moi, frégate ?

Comme vous êtes loin, paradis parfumé,
Où sous un clair azur tout n'est qu'amour et joie,
Où tout ce que l'on aime est digne d'être aimé,
Où dans la volupté pure le cœur se noie !
Comme vous êtes loin, paradis parfumé !

Mais le vert paradis des amours enfantines,
Les courses, les chansons, les baisers, les bouquets,
Les violons vibrant derrière les collines,
Avec les brocs de vin, le soir, dans les bosquets,
— Mais le vert paradis des amours enfantines,

L'innocent paradis, plein de plaisirs furtifs,
Est-il déjà plus loin que l'Inde et que la Chine ?
Peut-on le rappeler avec des cris plaintifs,
Et l'animer encor d'une voix argentine,
L'innocent paradis plein de plaisirs furtifs ?

LXVI

LE REVENANT

Comme les anges à l'œil fauve,
Je reviendrai dans ton alcôve
Et vers toi glisserai sans bruit
Avec les ombres de la nuit;

Et je te donnerai, ma brune,
Des baisers froids comme la lune
Et des caresses de serpent
Autour d'une fosse rampant.

Quand viendra le matin livide,
Tu trouveras ma place vide,
Où jusqu'au soir il fera froid.

Comme d'autres par la tendresse,
Sur ta vie et sur ta jeunesse,
Moi, je veux régner par l'effroi.

LXVII

SONNET D'AUTOMNE

Ils me disent, tes yeux, clairs comme le cristal :
" Pour toi, bizarre amant, quel est donc mon mérite?"
— Sois charmante et tais-toi ! Mon cœur, que tout
Excepté la candeur de l'antique animal, [irrite,

Ne veut pas te montrer son secret infernal,
Berceuse dont la main aux longs sommeils m'invite,
Ni sa noire légende avec la flamme écrite.
Je hais la passion et l'esprit me fait mal !

Aimons-nous doucement. L'Amour dans sa guérite,
Ténébreux, embusqué, bande son arc fatal.
Je connais les engins de son vieil arsenal :

Crime, horreur et folie ! — O pâle marguerite !
Comme moi n'es-tu pas un soleil automnal,
O ma si blanche, ô ma si froide Marguerite ?

LXVIII

TRISTESSES DE LA LUNE

Ce soir, la lune rêve avec plus de paresse;
Ainsi qu'une beauté, sur de nombreux coussins,
Qui d'une main discrète et légère caresse
Avant de s'endormir le contour de ses seins,

Sur le dos satiné des molles avalanches,
Mourante, elle se livre aux longues pâmoisons,
Et promène ses yeux sur les visions blanches
Qui montent dans l'azur comme des floraisons.

Quand parfois sur ce globe, en sa langueur oisive,
Elle laisse filer une larme furtive,
Un poëte pieux, ennemi du sommeil,

Dans le creux de sa main prend cette larme pâle,
Aux reflets irisés comme un fragment d'opale,
Et la met dans son cœur loin des yeux du soleil.

LXIX

LES CHATS

Les amoureux fervents et les savants austères
Aiment également, dans leur mûre saison,
Les chats puissants et doux, orgueil de la maison,
Qui comme eux sont frileux et comme eux sédentaires.

Amis de la science et de la volupté,
Ils cherchent le silence et l'horreur des ténèbres;
L'Érèbe les eût pris pour ses coursiers funèbres,
S'ils pouvaient au servage incliner leur fierté.

Ils prennent en songeant les nobles attitudes
Des grands sphinx allongés au fond des solitudes,
Qui semblent s'endormir dans un rêve sans fin;

Leurs reins féconds sont pleins d'étincelles magiques,
Et des parcelles d'or, ainsi qu'un sable fin,
Étoilent vaguement leurs prunelles mystiques.

LXX

LES HIBOUX

Sous les ifs noirs qui les abritent,
Les hiboux se tiennent rangés,
Ainsi que les dieux étrangers,
Dardant leur œil rouge. Ils méditent.

Sans remuer ils se tiendront
Jusqu'à l'heure mélancolique
Où, poussant le soleil oblique,
Les ténèbres s'établiront.

Leur attitude au sage enseigne
Qu'il faut en ce monde qu'il craigne
Le tumulte et le mouvement;

L'homme ivre d'une ombre qui passe
Porte toujours le châtiment
D'avoir voulu changer de place.

LXXI

LA PIPE

Je suis la pipe d'un auteur,
On voit, à contempler ma mine
D'Abyssinienne ou de Cafrine,
Que mon maître est un grand fumeur.

Quand il est comblé de douleur,
Je fume comme la chaumine
Où se prépare la cuisine
Pour le retour du laboureur.

J'enlace et je berce son âme
Dans le réseau mobile et bleu
Qui monte de ma bouche en feu,

Et je roule un puissant dictame
Qui charme son cœur et guérit
De ses fatigues son esprit.

LXXII

LA MUSIQUE

La musique souvent me prend comme une mer !
Vers ma pâle étoile,
Sous un plafond de brume ou dans un vaste éther,
Je mets à la voile;

La poitrine en avant et les poumons gonflés
Comme de la toile,
J'escalade le dos des flots amoncelés
Que la nuit me voile;

Je sens vibrer en moi toutes les passions
D'un vaisseau qui souffre;
Le bon vent, la tempête et ses convulsions

Sur l'immense gouffre
Me bercent. D'autres fois, calme plat, grand miroir
De mon désespoir !

LXXIII

SÉPULTURE

Si par une nuit lourde et sombre
Un bon chrétien, par charité,
Derrière quelque vieux décombre
Enterre votre corps vanté.

A l'heure où les chastes étoiles
Ferment leurs yeux appesantis,
L'araignée y fera ses toiles,
Et la vipère ses petits;

Vous entendrez toute l'année
Sur votre tête condamnée
Les cris lamentables des loups

Et des sorcières faméliques,
Les ébats des vieillards lubriques
Et les complots des noirs filous.

LXXIV

UNE GRAVURE FANTASTIQUE

Ce spectre singulier n'a pour toute toilette,
Grotesquement campé sur son front de squelette,
Qu'un diadème affreux sentant le carnaval.
Sans éperons, sans fouet, il essouffle un cheval,
Fantôme comme lui, rosse apocalyptique,
Qui bave des naseaux comme un épileptique.
Au travers de l'espace ils s'enfoncent tous deux,

Et foulent l'infini d'un sabot hasardeux.
Le cavalier promène un sabre qui flamboie
Sur les foules sans nom que sa monture broie,
Et parcourt, comme un prince inspectant sa maison,
Le cimetière immense et froid, sans horizon,
Où gisent, aux lueurs d'un soleil blanc et terne,
Les peuples de l'histoire ancienne et moderne.

LXXV

LE MORT JOYEUX

Dans une terre grasse et pleine d'escargots
Je veux creuser moi-même une fosse profonde,
Où je puisse à loisir étaler mes vieux os
Et dormir dans l'oubli comme un requin dans l'onde.

Je hais les testaments et je hais les tombeaux;
Plutôt que d'implorer une larme du monde,
Vivant, j'aimerais mieux inviter les corbeaux
A saigner tous les bouts de ma carcasse immonde.

O vers ! noirs compagnons sans oreille et sans yeux,
Voyez venir à vous un mort libre et joyeux;
Philosophes viveurs, fils de la pourriture,

A travers ma ruine allez donc sans remords,
Et dites-moi s'il est encor quelque torture
Pour ce vieux corps sans âme et mort parmi les morts !

LXXVI

LE TONNEAU DE LA HAINE

La Haine est le tonneau des pâles Danaïdes;
La Vengeance éperdue aux bras rouges et forts
A beau précipiter dans ses ténèbres vides
De grands seaux pleins du sang et des larmes des morts,

Le Démon fait des trous secrets à ces abîmes,
Par où fuiraient mille ans de sueurs et d'efforts,
Quand même elle saurait ranimer ses victimes,
Et pour les pressurer ressusciter leurs corps.

La Haine est un ivrogne au fond d'une taverne,
Qui sent toujours la soif naître de la liqueur
Et se multiplier comme l'hydre de Lerne.

— Mais les buveurs heureux connaissent leur vain-
Et la Haine est vouée à ce sort lamentable [queur,
De ne pouvoir jamais s'endormir sous la table.

LXXVII

LA CLOCHE FÊLÉE

Il est amer et doux, pendant les nuits d'hiver,
D'écouter, près du feu qui palpite et qui fume,
Les souvenirs lointains lentement s'élever
Au bruit des carillons qui chantent dans la brume.

Bienheureuse la cloche au gosier vigoureux
Qui, malgré sa vieillesse, alerte et bien portante,
Jette fidèlement son cri religieux,
Ainsi qu'un vieux soldat qui veille sous la tente !

Moi, mon âme est fêlée, et lorsqu'en ses ennuis
Elle veut de ses chants peupler l'air froid des nuits,
Il arrive souvent que sa voix affaiblie

Semble le râle épais d'un blessé qu'on oublie
Au bord d'un lac de sang, sous un grand tas de morts,
Et qui meurt, sans bouger, dans d'immenses efforts.

LXXVIII

SPLEEN

Pluviôse, irrité contre la ville entière,
De son urne à grands flots verse un froid ténébreux
Aux pâles habitants du voisin cimetière
Et la mortalité sur les faubourgs brumeux.

Mon chat sur le carreau cherchant une litière
Agite sans repos son corps maigre et galeux;
L'âme d'un vieux poëte erre dans la gouttière
Avec la triste voix d'un fantôme frileux.

Le bourdon se lamente, et la bûche enfumée
Accompagne en fausset la pendule enrhumée,
Cependant qu'en un jeu plein de sales parfums,

Héritage fatal d'une vieille hydropique,
Le beau valet de cœur et la dame de pique
Causent sinistrement de leurs amours défunts.

LXXIX

SPLEEN

J'ai plus de souvenirs que si j'avais mille ans.

Un gros meuble à tiroirs encombré de bilans,
De vers, de billets doux, de procès, de romances,
Avec de lourds cheveux roulés dans des quittances,
Cache moins de secrets que mon triste cerveau.
C'est une pyramide, un immense caveau,
Qui contient plus de morts que la fosse commune.
— Je suis un cimetière abhorré de la lune,
Où comme des remords se traînent de longs vers
Qui s'acharnent toujours sur mes morts les plus chers.
Je suis un vieux boudoir plein de roses fanées,
Où gît tout un fouillis de modes surannées,
Où les pastels plaintifs et les pâles Boucher,
Seuls, respirent l'odeur d'un flacon débouché.

Rien n'égale en longueur les boiteuses journées,
Quand sous les lourds flocons des neigeuses années,
L'ennui, fruit de la morne incuriosité,
Prend les proportions de l'immortalité.
— Désormais tu n'es plus, ô matière vivante !
Qu'un granit entouré d'une vague épouvante,
Assoupi dans le fond d'un Saharah brumeux;
Un vieux sphinx ignoré du monde insoucieux,
Oublié sur la carte, et dont l'humeur farouche
Ne chante qu'aux rayons du soleil qui se couche.

LXXX

SPLEEN

Je suis comme le roi d'un pays pluvieux,
Riche, mais impuissant, jeune et pourtant très-vieux,
Qui, de ses précepteurs méprisant les courbettes,
S'ennuie avec ses chiens comme avec d'autres bêtes.
Rien ne peut l'égayer, ni gibier, ni faucon,
Ni son peuple mourant en face du balcon.
Du bouffon favori la grotesque ballade
Ne distrait plus le front de ce cruel malade;
Son lit fleurdelisé se transforme en tombeau,
Et les dames d'atour, pour qui tout prince est beau,
Ne savent plus trouver d'impudique toilette
Pour tirer un souris de ce jeune squelette.
Le savant qui lui fait de l'or n'a jamais pu
De son être extirper l'élément corrompu,
Et dans ces bains de sang qui des Romains nous viennent,
Et dont sur leurs vieux jours les puissants se souviennent,
Il n'a su réchauffer ce cadavre hébété
Où coule au lieu de sang l'eau verte du Léthé.

LXXXI

SPLEEN

Quand le ciel bas et lourd pèse comme un couvercle
Sur l'esprit gémissant en proie aux longs ennuis,
Et que de l'horizon embrassant tout le cercle
Il nous verse un jour noir plus triste que les nuits;

Quand la terre est changée en un cachot humide,
Où l'Espérance, comme une chauve-souris,
S'en va battant les murs de son aile timide
Et se cognant la tête à des plafonds pourris;

Quand la pluie étalant ses immenses traînées
D'une vaste prison imite les barreaux,
Et qu'un peuple muet d'infâmes araignées
Vient tendre ses filets au fond de nos cerveaux,

Des cloches tout à coup sautent avec furie
Et lancent vers le ciel un affreux hurlement,
Ainsi que des esprits errants et sans patrie
Qui se mettent à geindre opiniâtrément.

— Et de longs corbillards, sans tambours ni musique,
Défilent lentement dans mon âme; l'Espoir,
Vaincu, pleure, et l'Angoisse atroce, despotique,
Sur mon crâne incliné plante son drapeau noir.

LXXXII

OBSESSION

Grands bois, vous m'effrayez comme des cathédrales;
Vous hurlez comme l'orgue; et dans nos cœurs maudits,
Chambres d'éternel deuil où vibrent de vieux râles,
Répondent les échos de vos *De profundis*.

Je te hais, Océan ! tes bonds et tes tumultes,
Mon esprit les retrouve en lui; ce rire amer
De l'homme vaincu, plein de sanglots et d'insultes,
Je l'entends dans le rire énorme de la mer.

Comme tu me plairais, ô nuit ! sans ces étoiles
Dont la lumière parle un langage connu !
Car je cherche le vide, et le noir, et le nu !

Mais les ténèbres sont elles-mêmes des toiles
Où vivent, jaillissant de mon œil par milliers,
Des êtres disparus aux regards familiers.

LXXXIII

LE GOÛT DU NÉANT

Morne esprit, autrefois amoureux de la lutte,
L'Espoir, dont l'éperon attisait ton ardeur,
Ne veut plus t'enfourcher ! Couche-toi sans pudeur,
Vieux cheval dont le pied à chaque obstacle butte.

Résigne-toi, mon cœur; dors ton sommeil de brute.

Esprit vaincu, fourbu ! Pour toi, vieux maraudeur,
L'amour n'a plus de goût, non plus que la dispute;
Adieu donc, chants du cuivre et soupirs de la flûte !
Plaisirs, ne tentez plus un cœur sombre et boudeur !

Le Printemps adorable a perdu son odeur !

Et le Temps m'engloutit minute par minute,
Comme la neige immense un corps pris de roideur;
Je contemple d'en haut le globe en sa rondeur,
Et je n'y cherche plus l'abri d'une cahute.

Avalanche, veux-tu m'emporter dans ta chute ?

LXXXIV

ALCHIMIE DE LA DOULEUR

L'un t'éclaire avec son ardeur,
L'autre en toi met son deuil, Nature !
Ce qui dit à l'un : Sépulture !
Dit à l'autre : Vie et splendeur !

Hermès inconnu qui m'assistes
Et qui toujours m'intimidas,
Tu me rends l'égal de Midas,
Le plus triste des alchimistes;

Par toi je change l'or en fer
Et le paradis en enfer;
Dans le suaire des nuages

Je découvre un cadavre cher,
Et sur les célestes rivages
Je bâtis de grands sarcophages.

LXXXV

HORREUR SYMPATHIQUE

— Dans ce ciel bizarre et livide,
Tourmenté comme ton destin,
Quels pensers dans ton âme vide
Descendent ? réponds, libertin.

— Insatiablement avide
De l'obscur et de l'incertain,
Je ne geindrai pas comme Ovide
Chassé du paradis latin.

Cieux déchirés comme des grèves,
En vous se mire mon orgueil;
Vos vastes nuages en deuil

Sont les corbillards de mes rêves,
Et vos lueurs sont le reflet
De l'Enfer où mon cœur se plaît.

LXXXVI

L'HÉAUTONTIMOROUMÉNOS

A J. G. F.

Je te frapperai sans colère
Et sans haine, comme un boucher,
Comme Moïse le rocher !
Et je ferai de ta paupière,

Pour abreuver mon Saharah,
Jaillir les eaux de la souffrance.
Mon désir gonflé d'espérance
Sur tes pleurs salés nagera

Comme un vaisseau qui prend le large,
Et dans mon cœur qu'ils soûleront
Tes chers sanglots retentiront
Comme un tambour qui bat la charge !

Ne suis-je pas un faux accord
Dans la divine symphonie,
Grâce à la vorace Ironie
Qui me secoue et qui me mord ?

Elle est dans ma voix, la criarde !
C'est tout mon sang, ce poison noir !
Je suis le sinistre miroir
Où la mégère se regarde!

Je suis la plaie et le couteau !
Je suis le soufflet et la joue !
Je suis les membres et la roue,
Et la victime et le bourreau !

Je suis de mon cœur le vampire,
— Un de ces grands abandonnés
Au rire éternel condamnés,
Et qui ne peuvent plus sourire !

LXXXVII

L'IRRÉMÉDIABLE

I

Une Idée, une Forme, un Être
Parti de l'azur et tombé
Dans un Styx bourbeux et plombé
Où nul œil du Ciel ne pénètre;

Un Ange, imprudent voyageur
Qu'a tenté l'amour du difforme,
Au fond d'un cauchemar énorme
Se débattant comme un nageur,

Et luttant, angoisses funèbres !
Contre un gigantesque remous
Qui va chantant comme les fous
Et pirouettant dans les ténèbres;

Un malheureux ensorcelé
Dans ses tâtonnements futiles,
Pour fuir d'un lieu plein de reptiles,
Cherchant la lumière et la clé;

Un damné descendant sans lampe,
Au bord d'un gouffre dont l'odeur
Trahit l'humide profondeur,
D'éternels escaliers sans rampe,

Où veillent des monstres visqueux
Dont les larges yeux de phosphore
Font une nuit plus noire encore
Et ne rendent visibles qu'eux;

Un navire pris dans le pôle,
Comme en un piége de cristal,
Cherchant par quel détroit fatal
Il est tombé dans cette geôle;

— Emblèmes nets, tableau parfait
D'une fortune irrémédiable,
Qui donne à penser que le Diable
Fait toujours bien tout ce qu'il fait !

II

Tête-à-tête sombre et limpide
Qu'un cœur devenu son miroir !
Puits de Vérité, clair et noir,
Où tremble une étoile livide,

Un phare ironique, infernal,
Flambeau des grâces sataniques,
Soulagement et gloires uniques,
— La conscience dans le Mal !

LXXXVIII

L'HORLOGE

Horloge ! dieu sinistre, effrayant, impassible,
Dont le doigt nous menace et nous dit : "*Souviens-toi !*
Les vibrantes Douleurs dans ton cœur plein d'effroi
Se planteront bientôt comme dans une cible;

Le Plaisir vaporeux fuira vers l'horizon
Ainsi qu'une sylphide au fond de la coulisse;
Chaque instant te dévore un morceau du délice
A chaque homme accordé pour toute sa saison.

Trois mille six cents fois par heure, la Seconde
Chuchote : *Souviens-toi !* — Rapide, avec sa voix
D'insecte, Maintenant dit : Je suis Autrefois,
Et j'ai pompé ta vie avec ma trompe immonde !

Remember ! Souviens-toi ! prodigue ! *Esto memor !*
(Mon gosier de métal parle toutes les langues.)
Les minutes, mortel folâtre, sont des gangues
Qu'il ne faut pas lâcher sans en extraire l'or !

Souviens-toi que le Temps est un joueur avide
Qui gagne sans tricher, à tout coup ! c'est la loi.
Le jour décroît; la nuit augmente; *souviens-toi !*
Le gouffre a toujours soif; la clepsydre se vide.

Tantôt sonnera l'heure où le divin Hasard,
Où l'auguste Vertu, ton épouse encor vierge,
Où le Repentir même (oh ! la dernière auberge !),
Où tout te dira : Meurs, vieux lâche ! il est trop tard ! »

TABLEAUX PARISIENS

LXXXIX

PAYSAGE

Je veux, pour composer chastement mes églogues,
Coucher auprès du ciel, comme les astrologues,
Et, voisin des clochers, écouter en rêvant
Leurs hymnes solennels emportés par le vent.
Les deux mains au menton, du haut de ma mansarde,
Je verrai l'atelier qui chante et qui bavarde;
Les tuyaux, les clochers, ces mâts de la cité,
Et les grands ciels qui font rêver d'éternité.

Il est doux, à travers les brumes, de voir naître
L'étoile dans l'azur, la lampe à la fenêtre,
Les fleuves de charbon monter au firmament
Et la lune verser son pâle enchantement.
Je verrai les printemps, les étés, les automnes,
Et quand viendra l'hiver aux neiges monotones,
Je fermerai partout portières et volets
Pour bâtir dans la nuit mes féeriques palais.
Alors je rêverai des horizons bleuâtres,
Des jardins, des jets d'eau pleurant dans les albâtres,
Des baisers, des oiseaux chantant soir et matin,
Et tout ce que l'Idylle a de plus enfantin.
L'Émeute, tempêtant vainement à ma vitre,
Ne fera pas lever mon front de mon pupitre;
Car je serai plongé dans cette volupté
D'évoquer le Printemps avec ma volonté,
De tirer un soleil de mon cœur, et de faire
De mes pensers brûlants une tiède atmosphère.

XC

LE SOLEIL

Le long du vieux faubourg, où pendent aux masures
Les persiennes, abri des secrètes luxures,
Quand le soleil cruel frappe à traits redoublés
Sur la ville et les champs, sur les toits et les blés,
Je vais m'exercer seul à ma fantasque escrime,
Flairant dans tous les coins les hasards de la rime,
Trébuchant sur les mots comme sur les pavés,
Heurtant parfois des vers depuis longtemps rêvés.

Ce père nourricier, ennemi des chloroses,
Éveille dans les champs les vers comme les roses;
Il fait s'évaporer les soucis vers le ciel,
Et remplit les cerveaux et les ruches de miel.
C'est lui qui rajeunit les porteurs de béquilles
Et les rend gais et doux comme des jeunes filles,
Et commande aux moissons de croître et de mûrir
Dans le cœur immortel qui toujours veut fleurir !

Quand, ainsi qu'un poëte, il descend dans les villes,
Il ennoblit le sort des choses les plus viles,
Et s'introduit en roi, sans bruit et sans valets,
Dans tous les hôpitaux et dans tous les palais.

XCI

A UNE MENDIANTE ROUSSE

Blanche fille aux cheveux roux,
Dont la robe par ses trous
Laisse voir la pauvreté
Et la beauté,

Pour moi, poëte chétif,
Ton jeune corps maladif,
Plein de taches de rousseur,
A sa douceur.

Tu portes plus galamment
Qu'une reine de roman
Ses cothurnes de velours
Tes sabots lourds.

Au lieu d'un haillon trop court,
Qu'un superbe habit de cour
Traîne à plis bruyants et longs
Sur tes talons;

En place de bas troués,
Que pour les yeux des roués
Sur ta jambe un poignard d'or
Reluise encor;

Que des nœuds mal attachés
Dévoilent pour nos péchés
Tes deux beaux seins, radieux
Comme des yeux;

Que pour te déshabiller
Tes bras se fassent prier
Et chassent à coups mutins
Les doigts lutins;

Perles de la plus belle eau,
Sonnets de maître Belleau
Par tes galants mis aux fers
Sans cesse offerts,

Valetaille de rimeurs
Te dédiant leurs primeurs
Et contemplant ton soulier
Sous l'escalier,

Maint page épris du hasard,
Maint seigneur et maint Ronsard
Épieraient pour le déduit
Ton frais réduit !

Tu compterais dans tes lits
Plus de baisers que de lis
Et rangerais sous tes lois
Plus d'un Valois !

— Cependant tu vas gueusant
Quelque vieux débris gisant
Au seuil de quelque Véfour
De carrefour;

Tu vas lorgnant en dessous
Des bijoux de vingt-neuf sous
Dont je ne puis, oh ! pardon !
Te faire don.

Va donc, sans autre ornement,
Parfum, perles, diamant,
Que ta maigre nudité,
O ma beauté !

XCII

LE CYGNE

A Victor Hugo.

I

Andromaque, je pense à vous ! Ce petit fleuve,
Pauvre et triste miroir où jadis resplendit
L'immense majesté de vos douleurs de veuve,
Ce Simoïs menteur qui par vos pleurs grandit,

A fécondé soudain ma mémoire fertile,
Comme je traversais le nouveau Carrousel.
Le vieux Paris n'est plus (la forme d'une ville
Change plus vite, hélas ! que le cœur d'un mortel);

Je ne vois qu'en esprit tout ce camp de baraques,
Ces tas de chapiteaux ébauchés et de fûts,
Les herbes, les gros blocs verdis par l'eau des flaques,
Et, brillant aux carreaux, le bric-à-brac confus.

Là s'étalait jadis une ménagerie;
Là je vis, un matin, à l'heure où sous les cieux
Froids et clairs le Travail s'éveille, où la voirie
Pousse un sombre ouragan dans l'air silencieux,

Un cygne qui s'était évadé de sa cage,
Et, de ses pieds palmés frottant le pavé sec,
Sur le sol raboteux traînait son blanc plumage.
Près d'un ruisseau sans eau la bête ouvrant le bec

Baignait nerveusement ses ailes dans la poudre,
Et disait, le cœur plein de son beau lac natal :
“ Eau, quand donc pleuvras-tu ? quand tonneras-tu,
Je vois ce malheureux, mythe étrange et fatal, [foudre ?”

Vers le ciel quelquefois, comme l'homme d'Ovide,
Vers le ciel ironique et crullement bleu,
Sur son cou convulsif tendant sa tête avide,
Comme s'il adressait des reproches à Dieu !

II

Paris change ! mais rien dans ma mélancolie
N'a bougé ! palais neufs, échafaudages, blocs,
Vieux faubourgs, tout pour moi devient allégorie,
Et mes chers souvenirs sont plus lourds que des rocs.

Aussi devant ce Louvre une image m'opprime :
Je pense à mon grand cygne, avec ses gestes fous,
Comme les exilés, ridicule et sublime,
Et rongé d'un désir sans trêve ! et puis à vous,

Andromaque, des bras d'un grand époux tombée,
Vil bétail, sous la main du superbe Pyrrhus,
Auprès d'un tombeau vide en extase courbée;
Veuve d'Hector, hélas ! et femme d'Hélénus !

Je pense à la négresse, amaigrie et phthisique,
Piétinant dans la boue, et cherchant, l'œil hagard,
Les cocotiers absents de la superbe Afrique
Derrière la muraille immense du brouillard;

A quiconque a perdu ce qui ne se retrouve
Jamais, jamais ! à ceux qui s'abreuvent de pleurs
Et tettent la Douleur comme une bonne louve !
Aux maigres orphelins séchant comme des fleurs !

Ainsi dans la forêt où mon esprit s'exile
Un vieux Souvenir sonne à plein souffle du cor !
Je pense aux matelots oubliés dans une île,
Aux captifs, aux vaincus !... à bien d'autres encor !

XCIII

LES SEPT VIEILLARDS

A Victor Hugo.

Fourmillante cité, cité pleine de rêves,
Où le spectre, en plein jour, raccroche le passant !
Les mystères partout coulent comme des séves
Dans les canaux étroits du colosse puissant.

Un matin, cependant que dans la triste rue
Les maisons, dont la brume allongeait la hauteur,
Simulaient les deux quais d'une rivière accrue,
Et que, décor semblable à l'âme de l'acteur,

Un brouillard sale et jaune inondait tout l'espace,
Je suivais, roidissant mes nerfs comme un héros
Et discutant avec mon âme déjà lasse,
Le faubourg secoué par les lourds tombereaux.

Tout à coup, un vieillard dont les guenilles jaunes
Imitaient la couleur de ce ciel pluvieux,
Et dont l'aspect aurait fait pleuvoir les aumônes,
Sans la méchanceté qui luisait dans ses yeux,

M'apparut. On eût dit sa prunelle trempée
Dans le fiel; son regard aiguisait les frimas,
Et sa barbe à longs poils, roide comme une épée,
Se projetait, pareille à celle de Judas.

Il n'était pas voûté, mais cassé, son échine
Faisant avec sa jambe un parfait angle droit,
Si bien que son bâton, parachevant sa mine,
Lui donnait la tournure et le pas maladroit

D'un quadrupède infirme ou d'un juif à trois pattes.
Dans la neige et la boue il allait s'empêtrant,
Comme s'il écrasait des morts sous ses savates,
Hostile à l'univers plutôt qu'indifférent.

Son pareil le suivait : barbe, œil, dos, bâton, loques,
Nul trait ne distinguait, du même enfer venu,
Ce jumeau centenaire, et ces spectres baroques
Marchaient du même pas vers un but inconnu.

A quel complot infâme étais-je donc en butte,
Ou quel méchant hasard ainsi m'humiliait ?
Car je comptai sept fois, de minute en minute,
Ce sinistre vieillard qui se multipliait !

Que celui-là qui rit de mon inquiétude,
Et qui n'est pas saisi d'un frisson fraternel,
Songe bien que malgré tant de décrépitude
Ces sept monstres hideux avaient l'air éternel !

Aurais-je, sans mourir, contemplé le huitième,
Sosie inexorable, ironique et fatal,
Dégoûtant Phénix, fils et père de lui-même ?
— Mais je tournai le dos au cortége infernal.

Exaspéré comme un ivrogne qui voit double,
Je rentrai, je fermai ma porte, épouvanté,
Malade et morfondu, l'esprit fiévreux et trouble,
Blessé par le mystère et par l'absurdité !

Vainement ma raison voulait prendre la barre;
La tempête en jouant déroutait ses efforts,
Et mon âme dansait, dansait, vieille gabarre
Sans mâts, sur une mer monstrueuse et sans bords !

XCIV

LES PETITES VIEILLES

A Victor Hugo.

I

Dans les plis sinueux des vieilles capitales,
Où tout, même l'horreur, tourne aux enchantements,
Je guette, obéissant à mes humeurs fatales,
Des êtres singuliers, décrépits et charmants.

Ces monstres disloqués furent jadis des femmes,
Éponine ou Laïs ! Monstres brisés, bossus
Ou tordus, aimons-les ! ce sont encor des âmes.
Sous des jupons troués ou sous de froids tissus

Ils rampent, flagellés par les bises iniques,
Frémissant au fracas roulant des omnibus,
Et serrant sur leur flanc, ainsi que des reliques,
Un petit sac brodé de fleurs ou de rébus;

Ils trottent, tous pareils à des marionnettes;
Se traînent, comme font les animaux blessés,
Ou dansent, sans vouloir danser, pauvres sonnettes
Où se pend un Démon sans pitié ! Tout cassés

Qu'ils sont, ils ont des yeux perçants comme une vrille,
Luisants comme ces trous où l'eau dort dans la nuit;
Ils ont les yeux divins de la petite fille
Qui s'étonne et qui rit à tout ce qui reluit.

— Avez-vous observé que maints cercueils de vieilles
Sont presque aussi petits que celui d'un enfant ?
La Mort savante met dans ces bières pareilles
Un symbole d'un goût bizarre et captivant,

Et lorsque j'entrevois un fantôme débile
Traversant de Paris le fourmillant tableau,
Il me semble toujours que cet être fragile
S'en va tout doucement vers un nouveau berceau;

A moins que, méditant sur la géométrie,
Je ne cherche, à l'aspect de ces membres discords,
Combien de fois il faut que l'ouvrier varie
La forme de la boîte où l'on met tous ces corps.

— Ces yeux sont des puits faits d'un million de larmes,
Des creusets qu'un métal refroidi pailleta...
Ces yeux mystérieux ont d'invincibles charmes
Pour celui que l'austère infortune allaita !

II

De Frascati défunt Vestale enamourée;
Prêtresse de Thalie, hélas ! dont le souffleur
Enterré sait le nom; célèbre évaporée
Que Tivoli jadis ombragea dans sa fleur,

Toutes m'enivrent ! mais parmi ces êtres frêles
Il en est qui, faisant de la douleur un miel,
Ont dit au Dévouement qui leur prêtait ses ailes :
Hippogriffe puissant, mène-moi jusqu'au ciel !

L'une, par sa patrie au malheur exercée,
L'autre, que son époux surchargea de douleurs,
L'autre, par son enfant Madone transpercée,
Toutes auraient pu faire un fleuve avec leurs pleurs !

III

Ah ! que j'en ai suivi de ces petites vieilles !
Une, entre autres, à l'heure où le soleil tombant
Ensanglante le ciel de blessures vermeilles,
Pensive, s'asseyait à l'écart sur un banc,

Pour entendre un de ces concerts, riches de cuivre,
Dont les soldats parfois inondent nos jardins,
Et qui, dans ces soirs d'or où l'on se sent revivre,
Versent quelque héroïsme au cœur des citadins.

Celle-là, droite encor, fière et sentant la règle,
Humait avidement ce chant vif et guerrier;
Son œil parfois s'ouvrait comme l'œil d'un vieil aigle;
Son front de marbre avait l'air fait pour le laurier !

IV

Telles vous cheminez, stoïques et sans plaintes,
A travers le chaos des vivantes cités,
Mères au cœur saignant, courtisanes ou saintes,
Dont autrefois les noms par tous étaient cités.

Vous qui fûtes la grâce ou qui fûtes la gloire,
Nul ne vous reconnaît ! un ivrogne incivil
Vous insulte en passant d'un amour dérisoire;
Sur vos talons gambade un enfant lâche et vil.

Honteuses d'exister, ombres ratatinées,
Peureuses, le dos bas, vous côtoyez les murs;
Et nul ne vous salue, étranges destinées !
Débris d'humanité pour l'éternité mûrs !

Mais moi, moi qui de loin tendrement vous surveille,
L'œil inquiet fixé sur vos pas incertains,
Tout comme si j'étais votre père, ô merveille !
Je goûte à votre insu des plaisirs clandestins :

Je vois s'épanouir vos passions novices;
Sombres ou lumineux, je vis vos jours perdus;
Mon cœur multiplié jouit de tous vos vices !
Mon âme resplendit de toutes vos vertus !

Ruines ! ma famille ! ô cerveaux congénères !
Je vous fais chaque soir un solennel adieu !
Où serez-vous demain, Èves octogénaires,
Sur qui pèse la griffe effroyable de Dieu ?

XCV

LES AVEUGLES

Contemple-les, mon âme; ils sont vraiment affreux !
Pareils aux mannequins; vaguement ridicules;
Terribles, singuliers, comme les somnambules;
Dardant on ne sait où leurs globes ténébreux.

Leurs yeux, d'où la divine étincelle est partie,
Comme s'ils regardaient au loin, restent levés
Au ciel; on ne les voit jamais vers les pavés
Pencher rêveusement leur tête appesantie.

Ils traversent ainsi le noir illimité,
Ce frère du silence éternel. O cité !
Pendant qu'autour de nous tu chantes, ris et beugles,

Éprise du plaisir jusqu'à l'atrocité,
Vois ! je me traîne aussi ! mais, plus qu'eux hébété,
Je dis : Que cherchent-ils au Ciel, tous ces aveugles ?

XCVI

A UNE PASSANTE

La rue assourdissante autour de moi hurlait.
Longue, mince, en grand deuil, douleur majestueuse,
Une femme passa, d'une main fastueuse
Soulevant, balançant le feston et l'ourlet;

Agile et noble, avec sa jambe de statue.
Moi, je buvais, crispé comme un extravagant,
Dans son œil, ciel livide où germe l'ouragan,
La douceur qui fascine et le plaisir qui tue.

Un éclair... puis la nuit ! — Fugitive beauté
Dont le regard m'a fait soudainement renaître,
Ne te verrai-je plus que dans l'éternité ?

Ailleurs, bien loin d'ici ! trop tard ! *jamais* peut-être !
Car j'ignore où tu fuis, tu ne sais où je vais,
O toi que j'eusse aimée, ô toi qui le savais !

XCVII

LE SQUELETTE LABOUREUR

I

Dans les planches d'anatomie
Qui traînent sur ces quais poudreux
Où maint livre cadavéreux
Dort comme une antique momie,

Dessins auxquels la gravité
Et le savoir d'un vieil artiste,
Bien que le sujet en soit triste,
Ont communiqué la Beauté,

On voit, ce qui rend plus complètes
Ces mystérieuses horreurs,
Bêchant comme des laboureurs,
Des Écorchés et des Squelettes.

II

De ce terrain que vous fouillez,
Manants résignés et funèbres,
De tout l'effort de vos vertèbres,
Ou de vos muscles dépouillés,

Dites, quelle moisson étrange,
Forçats arrachés au charnier,
Tirez-vous, et de quel fermier
Avez-vous à remplir la grange ?

Voulez-vous (d'un destin trop dur
Épouvantable et clair emblème !)
Montrer que dans la fosse même
Le sommeil promis n'est pas sûr;

Qu'envers nous le Néant est traître;
Que tout, même la Mort, nous ment,
Et que sempiternellement,
Hélas ! il nous faudra peut-être

Dans quelque pays inconnu
Écorcher la terre revêche
Et pousser une lourde bêche
Sous notre pied sanglant et nu ?

XCVIII

LE CRÉPUSCULE DU SOIR

Voici le soir charmant, ami du criminel;
Il vient comme un complice, à pas de loup; le ciel
Se ferme lentement comme une grande alcôve,
Et l'homme impatient se change en bête fauve.

O soir, aimable soir, désiré par celui
Dont les bras, sans mentir, peuvent dire : Aujourd'hui
Nous avons travaillé ! — C'est le soir qui soulage
Les esprits que dévore une douleur sauvage,
Le savant obstiné dont le front s'alourdit,
Et l'ouvrier courbé qui regagne son lit.
Cependant des démons malsains dans l'atmosphère
S'éveillent lourdement, comme des gens d'affaire,
Et cognent en volant les volets et l'auvent.
A travers les lueurs que tourmente le vent

La Prostitution s'allume dans les rues;
Comme une fourmilière elle ouvre ses issues;
Partout elle se fraye un occulte chemin,
Ainsi que l'ennemi qui tente un coup de main;
Elle remue au sein de la cité de fange
Comme un ver qui dérobe à l'Homme ce qu'il mange.
On entend çà et là les cuisines siffler,
Les théâtres glapir, les orchestres ronfler;
Les tables d'hôte, dont le jeu fait les délices,
S'emplissent de catins et d'escrocs, leurs complices,
Et les voleurs, qui n'ont ni trêve ni merci,
Vont bientôt commencer leur travail, eux aussi,
Et forcer doucement les portes et les caisses
Pour vivre quelques jours et vêtir leurs maîtresses.

Recueille-toi, mon âme, en ce grave moment,
Et ferme ton oreille à ce rugissement.
C'est l'heure où les douleurs des malades s'aigrissent!
La sombre Nuit les prend à la gorge; ils finissent
Leur destinée et vont vers le gouffre commun;
L'hôpital se remplit de leurs soupirs. — Plus d'un
Ne viendra plus chercher la soupe parfumée,
Au coin du feu, le soir, auprès d'une âme aimée.

Encore la plupart n'ont-ils jamais connu
La douceur du foyer et n'ont jamais vécu !

XCIX

LE JEU

Dans des fauteuils fanés des courtisanes vieilles,
Pâles, le sourcil peint, l'œil câlin et fatal,
Minaudant, et faisant de leurs maigres oreilles
Tomber un cliquetis de pierre et de métal;

Autour des verts tapis des visages sans lèvre,
Des lèvres sans couleur, des mâchoires sans dent,
Et des doigts convulsés d'une infernale fièvre,
Fouillant la poche vide ou le sein palpitant;

Sous de sales plafonds un rang de pâles lustres
Et d'énormes quinquets projetant leurs lueurs
Sur des fronts ténébreux de poëtes illustres
Qui viennent gaspiller leurs sanglantes sueurs;

Voilà le noir tableau qu'en un rêve nocturne
Je vis se dérouler sous mon œil clairvoyant.
Moi-même, dans un coin de l'antre taciturne,
Je me vis accoudé, froid, muet, enviant,

Enviant de ces gens la passion tenace,
De ces vieilles putains la funèbre gaieté,
Et tous gaillardement trafiquant à ma face,
L'un de son vieil honneur, l'autre de sa beauté !

Et mon cœur s'effraya d'envier maint pauvre homme
Courant avec ferveur à l'abîme béant,
Et qui, soûl de son sang, préférerait en somme
La douleur à la mort et l'enfer au néant !

C

DANSE MACABRE

A Ernest Christophe.

Fière, autant qu'un vivant, de sa noble stature,
Avec son gros bouquet, son mouchoir et ses gants,
Elle a la nonchalance et la désinvolture
D'une coquette maigre aux airs extravagants.

Vit-on jamais au bal une taille plus mince ?
Sa robe exagérée, en sa royale ampleur,
S'écroule abondamment sur un pied sec que pince
Un soulier pomponné, joli comme une fleur.

La ruche qui se joue au bord des clavicules,
Comme un ruisseau lascif qui se frotte au rocher,
Défend pudiquement des lazzi ridicules
Les funèbres appas qu'elle tient à cacher.

Ses yeux profonds sont faits de vide et de ténèbres,
Et son crâne, de fleurs artistement coiffé,
Oscille mollement sur ses frêles vertèbres.
O charme d'un néant follement attifé !

Aucuns t'appelleront une caricature,
Qui ne comprennent pas, amants ivres de chair,
L'élégance sans nom de l'humaine armature.
Tu réponds, grand squelette, à mon goût le plus cher !

Viens-tu troubler, avec ta puissante grimace,
La fête de la Vie ? ou quelque vieux désir,
Éperonnant encor ta vivante carcasse,
Te pousse-t-il, crédule, au sabbat du Plaisir ?

Au chant des violons, aux flammes des bougies,
Espères-tu chasser ton cauchemar moqueur,
Et viens-tu demander au torrent des orgies
De rafraîchir l'enfer allumé dans ton cœur ?

Inépuisable puits de sottise et de fautes !
De l'antique douleur éternel alambic !
A travers le treillis recourbé de tes côtes
Je vois, errant encor, l'insatiable aspic.

Pour dire vrai, je crains que ta coquetterie
Ne trouve pas un prix digne de ses efforts;
Qui, de ces cœurs mortels, entend la raillerie ?
Les charmes de l'horreur n'enivrent que les forts !

Le gouffre de tes yeux, plein d'horribles pensées,
Exhale le vertige, et les danseurs prudents
Ne contempleront pas sans d'amères nausées
Le sourire éternel de tes trente-deux dents.

Pourtant, qui n'a serré dans ses bras un squelette,
Et qui ne s'est nourri des choses du tombeau ?
Qu'importe le parfum, l'habit ou la toilette ?
Qui fait le dégoûté montre qu'il se croit beau.

Bayadère sans nez, irrésistible gouge,
Dis donc à ces danseurs qui font les offusqués :
"Fiers mignons, malgré l'art des poudres et du rouge,
Vous sentez tous la mort ! O squelettes musqués,

Antinoüs flétris, dandys à face glabre,
Cadavres vernissés, lovelaces chenus,
Le branle universel de la danse macabre
Vous entraîne en des lieux qui ne sont pas connus !

Des quais froids de la Seine aux bords brûlants du
Le troupeau mortel saute et se pâme, sans voir [Gange,
Dans un trou du plafond la trompette de l'Ange
Sinistrement béante ainsi qu'un tromblon noir.

En tout climat, sous tout soleil, la Mort t'admire
En tes contorsions, risible Humanité,
Et souvent, comme toi, se parfumant de myrrhe,
Mêle son ironie à ton insanité ! "

CI

L'AMOUR DU MENSONGE

Quand je te vois passer, ô ma chère indolente,
Au chant des instruments qui se brise au plafond
Suspendant ton allure harmonieuse et lente,
Et promenant l'ennui de ton regard profond;

Quand je contemple, aux feux du gaz qui le colore,
Ton front pâle, embelli par un morbide attrait,
Où les torches du soir allument une aurore,
Et tes yeux attirants comme ceux d'un portrait,

Je me dis : Qu'elle est belle ! et bizarrement fraîche !
Le souvenir massif, royale et lourde tour,
La couronne, et son cœur, meurtri comme une pêche,
Est mûr, comme son corps, pour le savant amour.

Es-tu le fruit d'automne aux saveurs souveraines ?
Es-tu vase funèbre attendant quelques pleurs,
Parfum qui fait rêver aux oasis lointaines,
Oreiller caressant, ou corbeille de fleurs ?

Je sais qu'il est des yeux, des plus mélancoliques,
Qui ne recèlent point de secrets précieux;
Beaux écrins sans joyaux, médaillons sans reliques,
Plus vides, plus profonds que vous-mêmes, ô Cieux !

Mais ne suffit-il pas que tu sois l'apparence,
Pour réjouir un cœur qui fuit la vérité ?
Qu'importe ta bêtise ou ton indifférence ?
Masque ou décor, salut ! J'adore ta beauté.

CII

Je n'ai pas oublié, voisine de la ville,
Notre blanche maison, petite mais tranquille;
Sa Pomone de plâtre et sa vieille Vénus
Dans un bosquet chétif cachant leurs membres nus,
Et le soleil, le soir, ruisselant et superbe,
Qui, derrière la vitre où se brisait sa gerbe,
Semblait, grand œil ouvert dans le ciel curieux,
Contempler nos dîners longs et silencieux,
Répandant largement ses beaux reflet de cierge
Sur la nappe frugale et les rideaux de serge.

CIII

La servante au grand cœur dont vous étiez jalouse,
Et qui dort son sommeil sous une humble pelouse,
Nous devrions pourtant lui porter quelques fleurs.
Les morts, les pauvres morts, ont de grandes douleurs,
Et quand Octobre souffle, émondeur des vieux arbres,
Son vent mélancolique à l'entour de leurs marbres,
Certe, ils doivent trouver les vivants bien ingrats,
A dormir, comme ils font, chaudement dans leurs draps,
Tandis que, dévorés de noires songeries,
Sans compagnon de lit, sans bonnes causeries,
Vieux squelettes gelés travaillés par le ver,
Ils sentent s'égoutter les neiges de l'hiver
Et le siècle couler, sans qu'amis ni famille
Remplacent les lambeaux qui pendent à leur grille.

Lorsque la bûche siffle et chante, si le soir,

Calme, dans le fauteuil, je la voyais s'asseoir,
Si, par une nuit bleue et froide de décembre,
Je la trouvais tapie en un coin de ma chambre,
Grave, et venant du fond de son lit éternel
Couver l'enfant grandi de son œil maternel,
Que pourrais-je répondre à cette âme pieuse,
Voyant tomber des pleurs de sa paupière creuse ?

CIV

BRUMES ET PLUIES

O fins d'automne, hivers, printemps trempés de boue,
Endormeuses saisons ! je vous aime et vous loue
D'envelopper ainsi mon cœur et mon cerveau
D'un linceul vaporeux et d'un vague tombeau.

Dans cette grande plaine où l'autan froid se joue,
Où par les longues nuits la girouette s'enroue,
Mon âme mieux qu'au temps du tiède renouveau
Ouvrira largement ses ailes de corbeau.

Rien n'est plus doux au cœur plein de choses funèbres,
Et sur qui dès longtemps descendent les frimas,
O blafardes saisons, reines de nos climats,

Que l'aspect permanent de vos pâles ténèbres,
— Si ce n'est, par un soir sans lune, deux à deux,
D'endormir la douleur sur un lit hasardeux.

CV

RÊVE PARISIEN

A Constantin Guys.

I

De ce terrible paysage,
Tel que jamais mortel n'en vit,
Ce matin encore l'image,
Vague et lointaine, me ravit.

Le sommeil est plein de miracles !
Par un caprice singulier,
J'avais banni de ces spectacles
Le végétal irrégulier,

Et, peintre fier de mon génie,
Je savourais dans mon tableau
L'enivrante monotonie
Du métal, du marbre et de l'eau.

Babel d'escaliers et d'arcades,
C'était un palais infini,
Plein de bassins et de cascades
Tombant dans l'or mat ou bruni;

Et des cataractes pesantes,
Comme des rideaux de cristal,
Se suspendaient, éblouissantes,
A des murailles de métal.

Non d'arbres, mais de colonnades
Les étangs dormants s'entouraient,
Où de gigantesques naïades,
Comme des femmes, se miraient.

Des nappes d'eau s'épanchaient, bleues,
Entre des quais roses et verts,
Pendant des millions de lieues,
Vers les confins de l'univers;

C'étaient des pierres inouïes
Et des flots magiques; c'étaient
D'immenses glaces éblouies
Par tout ce qu'elles reflétaient !

Insouciants et taciturnes,
Des Ganges, dans le firmament,
Versaient le trésor de leurs urnes
Dans des gouffres de diamant.

Architecte de mes féeries,
Je faisais, à ma volonté,
Sous un tunnel de pierreries
Passer un océan dompté;

Et tout, même la couleur noire,
Semblait fourbi, clair, irisé;
Le liquide enchâssait sa gloire
Dans le rayon cristallisé.

Nul astre d'ailleurs, nuls vestiges
De soleil, même au bas du ciel,
Pour illuminer ces prodiges,
Qui brillaient d'un feu personnel !

Et sur ces mouvantes merveilles
Planait (terrible nouveauté !
Tout pour l'œil, rien pour les oreilles !)
Un silence d'éternité.

II

En rouvrant mes yeux pleins de flamme
J'ai vu l'horreur de mon taudis,
Et senti, rentrant dans mon âme,
La pointe des soucis maudits;

La pendule aux accents funèbres
Sonnait brutalement midi,
Et le ciel versait des ténèbres
Sur le triste monde engourdi.

CVI

LE CRÉPUSCULE DU MATIN

La diane chantait dans les cours des casernes,
Et le vent du matin soufflait sur les lanternes.

C'était l'heure où l'essaim des rêves malfaisants
Tord sur leurs oreillers les bruns adolescents;
Où, comme un œil sanglant qui palpite et qui bouge,
La lampe sur le jour fait une tache rouge;
Où l'âme, sous le poids du corps revêche et lourd,
Imite les combats de la lampe et du jour.
Comme un visage en pleurs que les brises essuient,
L'air est plein du frisson des choses qui s'enfuient,
Et l'homme est las d'écrire et la femme d'aimer.

Les maisons çà et là commençaient à fumer.
Les femmes de plaisir, la paupière livide,
Bouche ouverte, dormaient de leur sommeil stupide;
Les pauvresses, traînant leurs seins maigres et froids,
Soufflaient sur leurs tisons et soufflaient sur leurs doigts.

C'était l'heure où parmi le froid et la lésine
S'aggravent les douleurs des femmes en gésine;
Comme un sanglot coupé par un sang écumeux
Le chant du coq au loin déchirait l'air brumeux;
Une mer de brouillards baignait les édifices,
Et les agonisants dans le fond des hospices
Poussaient leur dernier râle en hoquets inégaux.
Les débauchés rentraient, brisés par leurs travaux.

L'aurore grelottante en robe rose et verte
S'avançait lentement sur la Seine déserte,
Et le sombre Paris, en se frottant les yeux,
Empoignait ses outils, vieillard laborieux.

LE VIN

CVII

L'AME DU VIN

Un soir, l'âme du vin chantait dans les bouteilles :
" Homme, vers toi je pousse, ô cher déshérité,
Sous ma prison de verre et mes cires vermeilles,
Un chant plein de lumière et de fraternité !

Je sais combien il faut, sur la colline en flamme,.
De peine, de sueur et de soleil cuisant
Pour engendrer ma vie et pour me donner l'âme;
Mais je ne serai point ingrat ni malfaisant,

Car j'éprouve une joie immense quand je tombe
Dans le gosier d'un homme usé par ses travaux,
Et sa chaude poitrine est une douce tombe
Où je me plais bien mieux que dans mes froids caveaux.

Entends-tu retentir les refrains des dimanches
Et l'espoir qui gazouille en mon sein palpitant ?
Les coudes sur la table et retroussant tes manches,
Tu me glorifieras et tu seras content;

J'allumerai les yeux de ta femme ravie;
A ton fils je rendrai sa force et ses couleurs
Et serai pour ce frêle athlète de la vie
L'huile qui raffermit les muscles des lutteurs.

En toi je tomberai, végétale ambroisie,
Grain précieux jeté par l'éternel Semeur,
Pour que de notre amour naisse la poésie
Qui jaillira vers Dieu comme une rare fleur ! "

CVIII

LE VIN DES CHIFFONNIERS

Souvent, à la clarté rouge d'un réverbère
Dont le vent bat la flamme et tourmente le verre,
Au cœur d'un vieux faubourg, labyrinthe fangeux
Où l'humanité grouille en ferments orageux,

On voit un chiffonnier qui vient, hochant la tête,
Buttant, et se cognant aux murs comme un poëte,
Et, sans prendre souci des mouchards, ses sujets,
Épanche tout son cœur en glorieux projets.

Il prête des serments, dicte des lois sublimes,
Terrasse les méchants, relève les victimes,
Et sous le firmament comme un dais suspendu
S'enivre des splendeurs de sa propre vertu.

Oui, ces gens harcelés de chagrins de ménage,
Moulus par le travail et tourmentés par l'âge,
Éreintés et pliant sous un tas de débris,
Vomissement confus de l'énorme Paris,

Reviennent, parfumés d'une odeur de futailles,
Suivis de compagnons, blanchis dans les batailles,
Dont la moustache pend comme les vieux drapeaux.
Les bannières, les fleurs et les arcs triomphaux

Se dressent devant eux, solennelle magie !
Et dans l'étourdissante et lumineuse orgie
Des clairons, du soleil, des cris et du tambour,
Ils apportent la gloire au peuple ivre d'amour !

C'est ainsi qu'à travers l'Humanité frivole
Le vin roule de l'or, éblouissant Pactole;
Par le gosier de l'homme il chante ses exploits
Et règne par ses dons ainsi que les vrais rois.

Pour noyer la rancœur et bercer l'indolence
De tous ces vieux maudits qui meurent en silence,
Dieu, touché de remords, avait fait le sommeil;
L'Homme ajouta le Vin, fils sacré du Soleil !

CIX

LE VIN DE L'ASSASSIN

Ma femme est morte, je suis libre !
Je puis donc boire tout mon soûl.
Lorsque je rentrais sans un sou,
Ses cris me déchiraient la fibre.

Autant qu'un roi je suis heureux;
L'air est pur, le ciel admirable...
Nous avions un été semblable
Lorsque j'en devins amoureux !

L'horrible soif qui me déchire
Aurait besoin pour s'assouvir
D'autant de vin qu'en peut tenir
Son tombeau; — ce n'est pas peu dire :

Je l'ai jetée au fond d'un puits,
Et j'ai même poussé sur elle
Tous les pavés de la margelle.
— Je l'oublierai si je le puis !

Au nom des serments de tendresse,
Dont rien ne peut nous délier,
Et pour nous réconcilier
Comme au beau temps de notre ivresse,

J'implorai d'elle un rendez-vous,
Le soir, sur une route obscure.
Elle y vint ! — folle créature !
Nous sommes tous plus ou moins fous !

Elle était encore jolie,
Quoique bien fatiguée ! et moi,
Je l'aimais trop ! voilà pourquoi
Je lui dis : Sors de cette vie !

Nul ne peut me comprendre. Un seul
Parmi ces ivrognes stupides
Songea-t-il dans ses nuits morbides
A faire du vin un linceul ?

Cette crapule invulnérable
Comme les machines de fer
Jamais, ni l'été ni l'hiver,
N'a connu l'amour véritable,

Avec ses noirs enchantements,
Son cortége infernal d'alarmes,
Ses fioles de poison, ses larmes,
Ses bruits de chaîne et d'ossements !

— Me voilà libre et solitaire !
Je serai ce soir ivre mort;
Alors, sans peur et sans remord,
Je me coucherai sur la terre,

Et je dormirai comme un chien !
Le chariot aux lourdes roues
Chargé de pierres et de boues,
Le wagon enragé peut bien

Écraser ma tête coupable
Ou me couper par le milieu,
Je m'en moque comme de Dieu,
Du Diable ou de la Sainte-Table !

CX

LE VIN DU SOLITAIRE

Le regard singulier d'une femme galante
Qui se glisse vers nous comme le rayon blanc
Que la lune onduleuse envoie au lac tremblant,
Quand elle y veut baigner sa beauté nonchalante;

Le dernier sac d'écus dans les doigts d'un joueur;
Un baiser libertin de la maigre Adeline;
Les sons d'une musique énervante et câline,
Semblable au cri lointain de l'humaine douleur,

Tout cela ne vaut pas, ô bouteille profonde,
Les baumes pénétrants que ta panse féconde
Garde au cœur altéré du poëte pieux;

Tu lui verses l'espoir, la jeunesse et la vie,
— Et l'orgueil, ce trésor de toute gueuserie,
Qui nous rend triomphants et semblables aux Dieux !

CXI

LE VIN DES AMANTS

Aujourd'hui l'espace est splendide !
Sans mors, sans éperons, sans bride,
Partons à cheval sur le vin
Pour un ciel féerique et divin !

Comme deux anges que torture
Une implacable calenture,
Dans le bleu cristal du matin
Suivons le mirage lointain !

Mollement balancés sur l'aile
Du tourbillon intelligent,
Dans un délire parallèle,

Ma sœur, côte à côte nageant,
Nous fuirons sans repos ni trêves
Vers le paradis de mes rêves !

FLEURS DU MAL

CXII

LA DESTRUCTION

Sans cesse à mes côtés s'agite le Démon;
Il nage autour de moi comme un air impalpable;
Je l'avale et le sens qui brûle mon poumon
Et l'emplit d'un désir éternel et coupable.

Parfois il prend, sachant mon grand amour de l'Art,
La forme de la plus séduisante des femmes,
Et, sous de spécieux prétextes de cafard,
Accoutume ma lèvre à des philtres infâmes.

Il me conduit ainsi, loin du regard de Dieu,
Haletant et brisé de fatigue, au milieu
Des plaines de l'Ennui, profondes et désertes,

Et jette dans mes yeux pleins de confusion
Des vêtements souillés, des blessures ouvertes,
Et l'appareil sanglant de la Destruction !

CXIII

UNE MARTYRE

DESSIN D'UN MAITRE INCONNU

Au milieu des flacons, des étoffes lamées
        Et des meubles voluptueux,
Des marbres, des tableaux, des robes parfumées
        Qui traînent à plis somptueux,

Dans une chambre tiède où, comme en une serre,
L'air est dangereux et fatal,
Où des bouquets mourants dans leurs cercueils de
Exhalent leur soupir final, [verre

Un cadavre sans tête épanche, comme un fleuve,
Sur l'oreiller désaltéré
Un sang rouge et vivant, dont la toile s'abreuve
Avec l'avidité d'un pré.

Semblable aux visions pâles qu'enfante l'ombre
Et qui nous enchaînent les yeux,
La tête, avec l'amas de sa crinière sombre
Et de ses bijoux précieux,

Sur la table de nuit, comme une renoncule,
Repose; et, vide de pensers,
Un regard vague et blanc comme le crépuscule
S'échappe des yeux révulsés.

Sur le lit, le tronc nu sans scrupules étale
Dans le plus complet abandon
La secrète splendeur et la beauté fatale
Dont la nature lui fit don;

Un bas rosâtre, orné de coins d'or, à la jambe,
Comme un souvenir est resté;
La jarretière, ainsi qu'un œil secret qui flambe,
Darde un regard diamanté.

Le singulier aspect de cette solitude
Et d'un grand portrait langoureux,
Aux yeux provocateurs comme son attitude,
Révèle un amour ténébreux,

Une coupable joie et des fêtes étranges
Pleines de baisers infernaux,
Dont se réjouissait l'essaim de mauvais anges
Nageant dans les plis des rideaux;

Et cependant, à voir la maigreur élégante
De l'épaule au contour heurté,
La hanche un peu pointue et la taille fringante
Ainsi qu'un reptile irrité,

Elle est bien jeune encor ! — Son âme exaspérée
Et ses sens par l'ennui mordus
S'étaient-ils entr'ouverts à la meute altérée
Des désirs errants et perdus ?

L'homme vindicatif que tu n'as pu, vivante,
Malgré tant d'amour, assouvir,
Combla-t-il sur ta chair inerte et complaisante
L'immensité de son désir ?

Réponds, cadavre impur ! et par tes tresses roides
Te soulevant d'un bras fiévreux,
Dis-moi, tête effrayante, a-t-il sur tes dents froides
Collé les suprêmes adieux ?

— Loin du monde railleur, loin de la foule impure,
Loin des magistrats curieux,
Dors en paix, dors en paix, étrange créature,
Dans ton tombeau mystérieux;

Ton époux court le monde, et ta forme immortelle
Veille près de lui quand il dort;
Autant que toi sans doute il te sera fidèle,
Et constant jusques à la mort.

CXIV

LESBOS

Mère des jeux latins et des voluptés grecques,
Lesbos, où les baisers, languissants ou joyeux,
Chauds comme les soleils, frais comme les pastèques,
Font l'ornement des nuits et des jours glorieux;
Mère des jeux latins et des voluptés grecques,

Lesbos, où les baisers sont comme les cascades
Qui se jettent sans peur dans les gouffres sans fonds,
Et courent, sanglotant et gloussant par saccades,
Orageux et secrets, fourmillants et profonds;
Lesbos, où les baisers sont comme les cascades !

Lesbos, où les Phrynés l'une l'autre s'attirent,
Où jamais un soupir ne resta sans écho,
A l'égal de Paphos les étoiles t'admirent,
Et Vénus à bon droit peut jalouser Sapho !
Lesbos, où les Phrynés l'une l'autre s'attirent,

Lesbos, terre des nuits chaudes et langoureuses,
Qui font qu'à leurs miroirs, stérile volupté !
Les filles aux yeux creux, de leurs corps amoureuses,
Caressent les fruits mûrs de leur nubilité;
Lesbos, terre des nuits chaudes et langoureuses,

Laisse du vieux Platon se froncer l'œil austère;
Tu tires ton pardon de l'excès des baisers,
Reine du doux empire, aimable et noble terre,
Et des raffinements toujours inépuisés.
Laisse du vieux Platon se froncer l'œil austère.

Tu tires ton pardon de l'éternel martyre,
Infligé sans relâche aux cœurs ambitieux,
Qu'attire loin de nous le radieux sourire
Entrevu vaguement au bord des autres cieux !
Tu tires ton pardon de l'éternel martyre !

Qui des Dieux osera, Lesbos, être ton juge
Et condamner ton front pâli dans les travaux,
Si ses balances d'or n'ont pesé le déluge
De larmes qu'à la mer ont versé tes ruisseaux ?
Qui des Dieux osera, Lesbos, être ton juge !

Que nous veulent les lois du juste et de l'injuste ?
Vierges au cœur sublime, honneur de l'archipel,
Votre religion comme une autre est auguste,
Et l'amour se rira de l'Enfer et du Ciel !
Que nous veulent les lois du juste et de l'injuste ?

Car Lesbos entre tous m'a choisi sur la terre
Pour chanter le secret de ses vierges en fleurs,
Et je fus dès l'enfance admis au noir mystère
Des rires effrénés mêlés aux sombres pleurs;
Car Lesbos entre tous m'a choisi sur la terre.

Et depuis lors je veille au sommet de Leucate,
Comme une sentinelle à l'œil perçant et sûr,
Qui guette nuit et jour brick, tartane ou frégate,
Dont les formes au loin frissonnent dans l'azur;
Et depuis lors je veille au sommet de Leucate

Pour savoir si la mer est indulgente et bonne,
Et parmi les sanglots dont le roc retentit
Un soir ramènera vers Lesbos, qui pardonne,
Le cadavre adoré de Sapho, qui partit,
Pour savoir si la mer est indulgente et bonne !

De la mâle Sapho, l'amante et le poëte,
Plus belle que Vénus par ses mornes pâleurs !
— L'œil d'azur est vaincu par l'œil noir que tachète
Le cercle ténébreux tracé par les douleurs
De la mâle Sapho, l'amante et le poëte !

— Plus belle que Vénus se dressant sur le monde
Et versant les trésors de sa sérénité
Et le rayonnement de sa jeunesse blonde
Sur le vieil Océan de sa fille enchanté;
Plus belle que Vénus se dressant sur le monde !

— De Sapho qui mourut le jour de son blasphème,
Quand, insultant le rite et le culte inventé,
Elle fit son beau corps la pâture suprême
D'un brutal dont l'orgueil punit l'impiété
De celle qui mourut le jour de son blasphème.

Et c'est depuis ce temps que Lesbos se lamente,
Et malgré les honneurs que lui rend l'univers,
S'enivre chaque nuit du cri de la tourmente
Que poussent vers les cieux ses rivages déserts !
Et c'est depuis ce temps que Lesbos se lamente !

CXV

FEMMES DAMNÉES

Delphine et Hippolyte

A la pâle clarté des lampes languissantes,
Sur de profonds coussins tout imprégnés d'odeur,
Hippolyte rêvait aux caresses puissantes
Qui levaient le rideau de sa jeune candeur.

Elle cherchait, d'un œil troublé par la tempête,
De sa naïveté le ciel déjà lointain,
Ainsi qu'un voyageur qui retourne la tête
Vers les horizons bleus dépassés le matin.

De ses yeux amortis les paresseuses larmes,
L'air brisé, la stupeur, la morne volupté,
Ses bras vaincus, jetés comme de vaines armes,
Tout servait, tout parait sa fragile beauté.

Étendue à ses pieds, calme et pleine de joie,
Delphine la couvait avec des yeux ardents,
Comme un animal fort qui surveille une proie,
Après l'avoir d'abord marquée avec les dents.

Beauté forte à genoux devant la beauté frêle,
Superbe, elle humait voluptueusement
Le vin de son triomphe, et s'allongeait vers elle,
Comme pour recueillir un doux remerciement.

Elle cherchait dans l'œil de sa pâle victime
Le cantique muet que chante le plaisir,
Et cette gratitude infinie et sublime
Qui sort de la paupière ainsi qu'un long soupir.

— " Hippolyte, cher cœur, que dis-tu de ces choses ?
Comprends-tu maintenant qu'il ne faut pas offrir
L'holocauste sacré de tes premières roses
Aux souffles violents qui pourraient les flétrir ?

Mes baisers sont légers comme ces éphémères
Qui caressent le soir les grands lacs transparents,
Et ceux de ton amant creuseront leurs ornières
Comme des chariots ou des socs déchirants;

Ils passeront sur toi comme un lourd attelage
De chevaux et de bœufs aux sabots sans pitié...
Hippolyte, ô ma sœur ! tourne donc ton visage,
Toi, mon âme et mon cœur, mon tout et ma moitié,

Tourne vers moi tes yeux pleins d'azur et d'étoiles !
Pour un de ces regards charmants, baume divin,
Des plaisirs plus obscurs je lèverai les voiles
Et je t'endormirai dans un rêve sans fin ! "

Mais Hippolyte alors, levant sa jeune tête :
— " Je ne suis point ingrate et ne me repens pas,
Ma Delphine, je souffre et je suis inquiète,
Comme après un nocturne et terrible repas.

Je sens fondre sur moi de lourdes épouvantes
Et de noirs bataillons de fantômes épars,
Qui veulent me conduire en des routes mouvantes
Qu'un horizon sanglant ferme de toutes parts.

Avons-nous donc commis une action étrange ?
Explique, si tu peux, mon trouble et mon effroi :
Je frissonne de peur quand tu me dis : " Mon ange !"
Et cependant je sens ma bouche aller vers toi.

Ne me regarde pas ainsi, toi, ma pensée !
Toi que j'aime à jamais, ma sœur d'élection,
Quand même tu serais une embûche dressée
Et le commencement de ma perdition ! "

Delphine, secouant sa crinière tragique,
Et comme trépignant sur le trépied de fer,
L'œil fatal, répondit d'une voix despotique :
— " Qui donc devant l'amour ose parler d'enfer ?

Maudit soit à jamais le rêveur inutile
Qui voulut le premier, dans sa stupidité,
S'éprenant d'un problème insoluble et stérile,
Aux choses de l'amour mêler l'honnêteté !

Celui qui veut unir dans un accord mystique
L'ombre avec la chaleur, la nuit avec le jour,
Ne chauffera jamais son corps paralytique
A ce rouge soleil que l'on nomme l'amour !

Va, si tu veux, chercher un fiancé stupide;
Cours offrir un cœur vierge à ses cruels baisers;
Et pleine de remords et d'horreur, et livide,
Tu me rapporteras tes seins stigmatisés...

On ne peut ici-bas contenter qu'un seul maître ! "
Mais l'enfant, épanchant une immense douleur,
Cria soudain : — " Je sens s'élargir dans mon être
Un abîme béant; cet abîme est mon cœur !

Brûlant comme un volcan, profond comme le vide !
Rien ne rassasiera ce monstre gémissant
Et ne rafraîchira la soif de l'Euménide
Qui, la torche à la main, le brûle jusqu'au sang.

Que nos rideaux fermés nous séparent du monde,
Et que la lassitude amène le repos !
Je veux m'anéantir dans ta gorge profonde
Et trouver sur ton sein la fraîcheur des tombeaux ! "

— Descendez, descendez, lamentables victimes,
Descendez le chemin de l'enfer éternel !
Plongez au plus profond du gouffre où tous les crimes,
Flagellés par un vent qui ne vient pas du ciel,

Bouillonnent pêle-mêle avec un bruit d'orage.
Ombres folles, courez au but de vos désirs;
Jamais vous ne pourrez assouvir votre rage,
Et votre châtiment naîtra de vos plaisirs.

Jamais un rayon frais n'éclaira vos cavernes;
Par les fentes des murs des miasmes fiévreux
Filtrent en s'enflammant ainsi que des lanternes
Et pénètrent vos corps de leurs parfums affreux.

L'âpre stérilité de votre jouissance
Altère votre soif et roidit votre peau,
Et le vent furibond de la concupiscence
Fait claquer votre chair ainsi qu'un vieux drapeau.

Loin des peuples vivants, errantes condamnées,
A travers les déserts courez comme les loups;
Faites votre destin, âmes désordonnées,
Et fuyez l'infini que vous portez en vous !

CXVI

FEMMES DAMNÉES

Comme un bétail pensif sur le sable couchées,
Elles tournent leurs yeux vers l'horizon des mers,
Et leurs pieds se cherchant et leurs mains rapprochées
Ont de douces langueurs et des frissons amers

Les unes, cœurs épris de longues confidences,
Dans le fond des bosquets où jasent les ruisseaux,
Vont épelant l'amour des craintives enfances
Et creusent le bois vert des jeunes arbrisseaux;

D'autres, comme des sœurs, marchent lentes et graves
A travers les rochers pleins d'apparitions,
Où saint Antoine a vu surgir comme des laves
Les seins nus et pourprés de ses tentations;

Il en est, aux lueurs des résines croulantes,
Qui dans le creux muet des vieux antres païens
T'appellent au secours de leurs fièvres hurlantes,
O Bacchus, endormeur des remords anciens !

Et d'autres, dont la gorge aime les scapulaires
Qui, recélant un fouet sous leurs longs vêtements,
Mêlent, dans le bois sombre et les nuits solitaires,
L'écume du plaisir aux larmes des tourments.

O vierges, ô démons, ô monstres, ô martyres,
De la réalité grands esprits contempteurs,
Chercheuses d'infini, dévotes et satyres,
Tantôt pleines de cris, tantôt pleines de pleurs,

Vous que dans votre enfer mon âme a poursuivies,
Pauvres sœurs, je vous aime autant que je vous plains,
Pour vos mornes douleurs, vos soifs inassouvies,
Et les urnes d'amour dont vos grands cœurs sont pleins !

CXVII

LES DEUX BONNES SŒURS

La Débauche et la Mort sont deux aimables filles,
Prodigues de baisers et riches de santé,
Dont le flanc toujours vierge et drapé de guenilles
Sous l'éternel labeur n'a jamais enfanté.

Au poëte sinistre, ennemi des familles,
Favori de l'enfer, courtisan mal renté,
Tombeaux et lupanars montrent sous leurs charmilles
Un lit que le remords n'a jamais fréquenté.

Et la bière et l'alcôve en blasphèmes fécondes
Nous offrent tour à tour, comme deux bonnes sœurs,
De terribles plaisirs et d'affreuses douceurs.

Quand veux-tu m'enterrer, Débauche aux bras immondes ?
O Mort, quand viendras-tu, sa rivale en attraits,
Sur ses myrtes infects enter tes noirs cyprès ?

CXVIII

LA FONTAINE DE SANG

Il me semble parfois que mon sang coule à flots,
Ainsi qu'une fontaine aux rhythmiques sanglots.
Je l'entends bien qui coule avec un long murmure,
Mais je me hâte en vain pour trouver la blessure.

A travers la cité, comme dans un champ clos,
Il s'en va, transformant les pavés en îlots,
Désaltérant la soif de chaque créature,
Et partout colorant en rouge la nature.

J'ai demandé souvent à des vins captieux
D'endormir pour un jour la terreur qui me mine;
Le vin rend l'œil plus clair et l'oreille plus fine !

J'ai cherché dans l'amour un sommeil oublieux;
Mais l'amour n'est pour moi qu'un matelas d'aiguilles
Fait pour donner à boire à ces cruelles filles !

CXIX

ALLÉGORIE

C'est une femme belle et de riche encolure,
Qui laisse dans son vin traîner sa chevelure.
Les griffes de l'amour, les poisons du tripot,
Tout glisse et tout s'émousse au granit de sa peau.
Elle rit à la Mort et nargue la Débauche,
Ces monstres dont la main, qui toujours gratte et fauche,
Dans ses jeux destructeurs a pourtant respecté
De ce corps ferme et droit la rude majesté.
Elle marche en déesse et repose en sultane;
Elle a dans le plaisir la foi mahométane,
Et dans ses bras ouverts, que remplissent ses seins,
Elle appelle des yeux la race des humains.
Elle croit, elle sait, cette vierge inféconde
Et pourtant nécessaire à la marche du monde,
Que la beauté du corps est un sublime don
Qui de toute infamie arrache le pardon.
Elle ignore l'Enfer comme le Purgatoire,
Et quand l'heure viendra d'entrer dans la Nuit noire,
Elle regardera la face de la Mort,
Ainsi qu'un nouveau-né, — sans haine et sans remord.

CXX

LA BÉATRICE

Dans des terrains cendreux, calcinés, sans verdure,
Comme je me plaignais un jour à la nature,
Et que de ma pensée, en vaguant au hasard,
J'aiguisais lentement sur mon cœur le poignard,

Je vis en plein midi descendre sur ma tête
Un nuage funèbre et gros d'une tempête,
Qui portait un troupeau de démons vicieux,
Semblables à des nains cruels et curieux.
A me considérer froidement ils se mirent,
Et, comme des passants sur un fou qu'ils admirent,
Je les entendis rire et chuchoter entre eux,
En échangeant maint signe et maint clignement d'yeux :

— " Contemplons à loisir cette caricature
Et cette ombre d'Hamlet imitant sa posture,
Le regard indécis et les cheveux au vent.
N'est-ce pas grand'pitié de voir ce bon vivant,
Ce gueux, cet histrion en vacances, ce drôle,
Parce qu'il sait jouer artistement son rôle,
Vouloir intéresser au chant de ses douleurs
Les aigles, les grillons, les ruisseaux et les fleurs,
Et même à nous, auteurs de ces vieilles rubriques,
Réciter en hurlant ses tirades publiques ? "

J'aurais pu (mon orgueil aussi haut que les monts
Domine la nuée et le cri des démons)
Détourner simplement ma tête souveraine,
Si je n'eusse pas vu parmi leur troupe obscène,
Crime qui n'a pas fait chanceler le soleil !
La reine de mon cœur au regard nonpareil,
Qui riait avec eux de ma sombre détresse
Et leur versait parfois quelque sale caresse.

CXXI

LES MÉTAMORPHOSES DU VAMPIRE

La femme cependant, de sa bouche de fraise,
En se tordant ainsi qu'un serpent sur la braise,
Et pétrissant ses seins sur le fer de son busc,
Laissait couler ces mots tout imprégnés de musc :
— " Moi, j'ai la lèvre humide, et je sais la science
De perdre au fond d'un lit l'antique conscience.
Je sèche tous les pleurs sur mes seins triomphants,
Et fais rire les vieux du rire des enfants.
Je remplace, pour qui me voit nue et sans voiles,
La lune, le soleil, le ciel et les étoiles !
Je suis, mon cher savant, si docte aux voluptés,
Lorsque j'étouffe un homme en mes bras redoutés,
Ou lorsque j'abandonne aux morsures mon buste,
Timide et libertine, et fragile et robuste,
Que sur ces matelas qui se pâment d'émoi,
Les anges impuissants se damneraient pour moi ! "

Quand elle eut de mes os sucé toute la moelle,
Et que languissamment je me tournai vers elle
Pour lui rendre un baiser d'amour, je ne vis plus
Qu'une outre aux flancs gluants, toute pleine de pus !
Je fermai les deux yeux, dans ma froide épouvante,
Et quand je les rouvris à la clarté vivante,
A mes côtés, au lieu du mannequin puissant
Qui semblait avoir fait provision de sang,
Tremblaient confusément des débris de squelette,
Qui d'eux-mêmes rendaient le cri d'une girouette
Ou d'une enseigne, au bout d'une tringle de fer,
Que balance le vent pendant les nuits d'hiver.

CXXII

UN VOYAGE A CYTHÈRE

Mon cœur, comme un oiseau, voltigeait tout joyeux
Et planait librement à l'entour des cordages;
Le navire roulait sous un ciel sans nuages,
Comme un ange enivré d'un soleil radieux.

Quelle est cette île triste et noire ? — C'est Cythère,
Nous dit-ton, un pays fameux dans les chansons,
Eldorado banal de tous les vieux garçons.
Regardez, après tout, c'est une pauvre terre.

— Ile des doux secrets et des fêtes du cœur !
De l'antique Vénus le superbe fantôme
Au-dessus de tes mers plane comme un arome,
Et charge les esprits d'amour et de langueur.

Belle île aux myrtes verts, pleine de fleurs écloses,
Vénérée à jamais par toute nation,
Où les soupirs des cœurs en adoration
Roulent comme l'encens sur un jardin de roses

Ou le roucoulement éternel d'un ramier !
— Cythère n'était plus qu'un terrain des plus maigres,
Un désert rocailleux troublé par des cris aigres.
J'entrevoyais pourtant un objet singulier !

Ce n'était pas un temple aux ombres bocagères,
Où la jeune prêtresse, amoureuse des fleurs,
Allait, le corps brûlé de secrètes chaleurs,
Entre-bâillant sa robe aux brises passagères;

Mais voilà qu'en rasant la côte d'assez près
Pour troubler les oiseaux avec nos voiles blanches,
Nous vîmes que c'était un gibet à trois branches,
Du ciel se détachant en noir, comme un cyprès.

De féroces oiseaux perchés sur leur pâture
Détruisaient avec rage un pendu déjà mûr,
Chacun plantant, comme un outil, son bec impur
Dans tous les coins saignants de cette pourriture;

Les yeux étaient deux trous, et du ventre effondré
Les intestins pesants lui coulaient sur les cuisses,
Et ses bourreaux, gorgés de hideuses délices,
L'avaient à coups de bec absolument châtré.

Sous les pieds, un troupeau de jaloux quadrupèdes,
Le museau relevé, tournoyait et rôdait;
Une plus grande bête au milieu s'agitait
Comme un exécuteur entouré de ses aides.

Habitant de Cythère, enfant d'un ciel si beau,
Silencieusement tu souffrais ces insultes
En expiation de tes infâmes cultes
Et des péchés qui t'ont interdit le tombeau.

Ridicule pendu, tes douleurs sont les miennes !
Je sentis, à l'aspect de tes membres flottants,
Comme un vomissement, remonter vers mes dents
Le long fleuve de fiel des douleurs anciennes;

Devant toi, pauvre diable au souvenir si cher,
J'ai senti tous les becs et toutes les mâchoires
Des corbeaux lancinants et des panthères noires
Qui jadis aimaient tant à triturer ma chair.

— Le ciel était charmant, la mer était unie;
Pour moi tout était noir et sanglant désormais,
Hélas ! et j'avais, comme en un suaire épais,
Le cœur enseveli dans cette allégorie.

Dans ton île, ô Vénus ! je n'ai trouvé debout
Qu'un gibet symbolique où pendait mon image...
— Ah ! Seigneur ! donnez-moi la force et le courage
De contempler mon cœur et mon corps sans dégoût !

CXXIII

L'AMOUR ET LE CRANE

VIEUX CUL-DE-LAMPE

L'amour est assis sur le crâne
De l'Humanité,
Et sur ce trône le profane,
Au rire effronté,

Souffle gaiement des bulles rondes
Qui montent dans l'air,
Comme pour rejoindre les mondes
Au fond de l'éther.

Le globe lumineux et frêle
Prend un grand essor,
Crève et crache son âme grêle
Comme un songe d'or.

J'entends le crâne à chaque bulle
Prier et gémir :
" Ce jeu féroce et ridicule,
Quand doit-il finir ?

Car ce que ta bouche cruelle
Éparpille en l'air,
Monstre assassin, c'est ma cervelle,
Mon sang et ma chair ! "

RÉVOLTE

CXXIV

LE RENIEMENT DE SAINT PIERRE

Qu'est-ce que Dieu fait donc de ce flot d'anathèmes
Qui monte tous les jours vers ses chers Séraphins ?
Comme un tyran gorgé de viande et de vins,
Il s'endort au doux bruit de nos affreux blasphèmes.

Les sanglots des martyrs et des suppliciés
Sont une symphonie enivrante sans doute,
Puisque, malgré le sang que leur volupté coûte,
Les cieux ne s'en sont point encore rassasiés !

— Ah ! Jésus, souviens-toi du Jardin des Olives !
Dans ta simplicité tu priais à genoux
Celui qui dans son ciel riait au bruit des clous
Que d'ignobles bourreaux plantaient dans tes chairs
[vives.
Lorsque tu vis cracher sur ta divinité
La crapule du corps de garde et des cuisines,
Et lorsque tu sentis s'enfoncer les épines
Dans ton crâne où vivait l'immense Humanité;

Quand de ton corps brisé la pesanteur horrible
Allongeait tes deux bras distendus, que ton sang
Et ta sueur coulaient de ton front pâlissant,
Quand tu fus devant tous posé comme une cible,

Rêvais-tu de ces jours si brillants et si beaux
Où tu vins pour remplir l'éternelle promesse,
Où tu foulais, monté sur une douce ânesse,
Des chemins tout jonchés de fleurs et de rameaux,

Où, le cœur tout gonflé d'espoir et de vaillance,
Tu fouettais tous ces vils marchands à tour de bras
Où tu fus maître enfin ? Le remords n'a-t-il pas
Pénétré dans ton flanc plus avant que la lance ?

— Certes, je sortirai, quant à moi, satisfait
D'un monde où l'action n'est pas la sœur du rêve;
Puissé-je user du glaive et périr par le glaive !
Saint Pierre a renié Jésus... il a bien fait !

CXXV

ABEL ET CAÏN

I

Race d'Abel, dors, bois et mange;
Dieu te sourit complaisamment.

Race de Caïn, dans la fange
Rampe et meurs misérablement.

Race d'Abel, ton sacrifice
Flatte le nez du Séraphin !

Race de Caïn, ton supplice
Aura-t-il jamais une fin ?

Race d'Abel, vois tes semailles
Et ton bétail venir à bien;

Race de Caïn, tes entrailles
Hurlent la faim comme un vieux chien.

Race d'Abel, chauffe ton ventre
A ton foyer patriarcal;

Race de Caïn, dans ton antre
Tremble de froid, pauvre chacal !

Race d'Abel, aime et pullule !
Ton or fait aussi des petits.

Race de Caïn, cœur qui brûle,
Prends garde à ces grands appétits.

Race d'Abel, tu crois et broutes
Comme les punaises des bois !

Race de Caïn, sur les routes
Traîne ta famille aux abois.

II

Ah ! race d'Abel, ta charogne
Engraissera le sol fumant !

Race de Caïn, ta besogne
N'est pas faite suffisamment;

Race d'Abel, voici ta honte :
Le fer est vaincu par l'épieu !

Race de Caïn, au ciel monte
Et sur la terre jette Dieu !

CXXVI

LES LITANIES DE SATAN

O toi, le plus savant et le plus beau des Anges,
Dieu trahi par le sort et privé de louanges,

O Satan, prends pitié de ma longue misère !

O Prince de l'exil, à qui l'on a fait tort,
Et qui, vaincu, toujours te redresses plus fort,

O Satan, prends pitié de ma longue misère !

Toi qui sais tout, grand roi des choses souterraines,
Guérisseur familier des angoisses humaines,

O Satan, prends pitié de ma longue misère !

Toi qui, même aux lépreux, aux parias maudits,
Enseignes par l'amour le goût du Paradis,

O Satan, prends pitié de ma longue misère !

O toi qui de la Mort, ta vieille et forte amante,
Engendras l'Espérance, — une folle charmante !

O Satan, prends pitié de ma longue misère !

Toi qui fais au proscrit ce regard calme et haut
Qui damne tout un peuple autour d'un échafaud,

O Satan, prends pitié de ma longue misère !

Toi qui sais en quels coins des terres envieuses
Le Dieu jaloux cacha les pierres précieuses,

O Satan, prends pitié de ma longue misère !

Toi dont l'œil clair connaît les profonds arsenaux
Où dort enseveli le peuple des métaux,

O Satan, prends pitié de ma longue misère !

Toi dont la large main cache les précipices
Au somnambule errant au bord des édifices,

O Satan, prends pitié de ma longue misère !

Toi qui, magiquement, assouplis les vieux os
De l'ivrogne attardé foulé par les chevaux,

O Satan, prends pitié de ma longue misère !

Toi qui, pour consoler l'homme frêle qui souffre,
Nous appris à mêler le salpêtre et le soufre,

O Satan, prends pitié de ma longue misère !

Toi qui poses ta marque, ô complice subtil,
Sur le front du Crésus impitoyable et vil,

O Satan, prends pitié de ma longue misère !

Toi qui mets dans les yeux et dans le cœur des filles
Le culte de la plaie et l'amour des guenilles,

O Satan, prends pitié de ma longue misère !

Bâton des exilés, lampe des inventeurs,
Confesseur des pendus et des conspirateurs,

O Satan, prends pitié de ma longue misère !

Père adoptif de ceux qu'en sa noire colère
Du paradis terrestre a chassés Dieu le Père,

O Satan, prends pitié de ma longue misère !

PRIÈRE

Gloire et louange à toi, Satan, dans les hauteurs
Du Ciel, où tu régnas, et dans les profondeurs
De l'Enfer, où, vaincu, tu rêves en silence !
Fais que mon âme un jour, sous l'Arbre de Science,
Près de toi se repose, à l'heure où sur ton front
Comme un Temple nouveau ses rameaux s'épandront !

LA MORT

CXXVII

LA MORT DES AMANTS

Nous aurons des lits pleins d'odeurs légères,
Des divans profonds comme des tombeaux,
Et d'étranges fleurs sur des étagères,
Écloses pour nous sous des cieux plus beaux.

Usant à l'envi leurs chaleurs dernières,
Nos deux cœurs seront deux vastes flambeaux,
Qui réfléchiront leurs doubles lumières
Dans nos deux esprits, ces miroirs jumeaux.

Un soir fait de rose et de bleu mystique,
Nous échangerons un éclair unique,
Comme un long sanglot, tout chargé d'adieux;

Et plus tard un Ange, entr'ouvrant les portes,
Viendra ranimer, fidèle et joyeux,
Les miroirs ternis et les flammes mortes.

CXXVIII

LA MORT DES PAUVRES

C'est la mort qui console, hélas ! et qui fait vivre;
C'est le but de la vie, et c'est le seul espoir
Qui, comme un élixir, nous monte et nous enivre,
Et nous donne le cœur de marcher jusqu'au soir;

A travers la tempête, et la neige, et le givre,
C'est la clarté vibrante à notre horizon noir;
C'est l'auberge fameuse inscrite sur le livre,
Où l'on pourra manger, et dormir, et s'asseoir;

C'est un Ange qui tient dans ses doigts magnétiques
Le sommeil et le don des rêves extatiques,
Et qui refait le lit des gens pauvres et nus;

C'est la gloire des Dieux, c'est le grenier mystique,
C'est la bourse du pauvre et sa patrie antique,
C'est le portique ouvert sur les Cieux inconnus !

CXXIX

LA MORT DES ARTISTES

Combien faut-il de fois secouer mes grelots
Et baiser ton front bas, morne caricature ?
Pour piquer dans le but, de mystique nature,
Combien, ô mon carquois, perdre de javelots ?

Nous userons notre âme en de subtils complots,
Et nous démolirons mainte lourde armature,
Avant de contempler la grande Créature
Dont l'infernal désir nous remplit de sanglots !

Il en est qui jamais n'ont connu leur Idole,
Et ces sculpteurs damnés et marqués d'un affront,
Qui vont se martelant la poitrine et le front,

N'ont qu'un espoir, étrange et sombre Capitole !
C'est que la Mort, planant comme un soleil nouveau,
Fera s'épanouir les fleurs de leur cerveau !

CXXX

LA FIN DE LA JOURNÉE

Sous une lumière blafarde
Court, danse et se tord sans raison
La Vie, impudente et criarde.
Aussi, sitôt qu'à l'horizon

La nuit voluptueuse monte,
Apaisant tout, même la faim,
Effaçant tout, même la honte,
Le Poëte se dit : " Enfin !

Mon esprit, comme mes vertèbres,
Invoque ardemment le repos;
Le cœur plein de songes funèbres,

Je vais me coucher sur le dos
Et me rouler dans vos rideaux,
O rafraîchissantes ténèbres ! "

CXXXI

LE RÊVE D'UN CURIEUX

A F. N.

Connais-tu, comme moi, la douleur savoureuse,
Et de toi fais-tu dire : " Oh ! l'homme singulier ! "
— J'allais mourir. C'était dans mon âme amoureuse,
Désir mêlé d'horreur, un mal particulier;

Angoisse et vif espoir, sans humeur factieuse.
Plus allait se vidant le fatal sablier,
Plus ma torture était âpre et délicieuse;
Tout mon cœur s'arrachait au monde familier.

J'étais comme l'enfant avide du spectacle,
Haïssant le rideau comme on hait un obstacle...
Enfin la vérité froide se révéla :

J'étais mort sans surprise, et la terrible aurore
M'enveloppait. — Eh quoi ! n'est-ce donc que cela ?
La toile était levée et j'attendais encore.

CXXXII

LE VOYAGE

A Maxime du Camp.

I

Pour l'enfant, amoureux de cartes et d'estampes,
L'univers est égal à son vaste appétit.
Ah ! que le monde est grand à la clarté des lampes !
Aux yeux du souvenir que le monde est petit !

Un matin nous partons, le cerveau plein de flamme,
Le cœur gros de rancune et de désirs amers,
Et nous allons, suivant le rhythme de la lame,
Berçant notre infini sur le fini des mers :

Les uns, joyeux de fuir une patrie infâme;
D'autres, l'horreur de leurs berceaux, et quelques-uns,
Astrologues noyés dans les yeux d'une femme,
La Circé tyrannique aux dangereux parfums.

Pour n'être pas changés en bêtes, ils s'enivrent
D'espace et de lumière et de cieux embrasés;
La glace qui les mord, les soleils qui les cuivrent,
Effacent lentement la marque des baisers.

Mais les vrais voyageurs sont ceux-là seuls qui partent
Pour partir; cœurs légers, semblables aux ballons,
De leur fatalité jamais ils ne s'écartent,
Et, sans savoir pourquoi, disent toujours : Allons !

Ceux-là dont les désirs ont la forme des nues,
Et qui rêvent, ainsi qu'un conscrit le canon,
De vastes voluptés, changeantes, inconnues,
Et dont l'esprit humain n'a jamais su le nom !

II

Nous imitons, horreur ! la toupie et la boule
Dans leur valse et leurs bonds; même dans nos sommeils
La Curiosité nous tourmente et nous roule,
Comme un Ange cruel qui fouette des soleils.

Singulière fortune où le but se déplace,
Et, n'étant nulle part, peut être n'importe où !
Où l'Homme, dont jamais l'espérance n'est lasse,
Pour trouver le repos court toujours comme un fou !

Notre âme est un trois-mâts cherchant son Icarie;
Une voix retentit sur le pont : " Ouvre l'œil ! "
Une voix de la hune, ardente et folle, crie :
" Amour... gloire... bonheur ! " Enfer ! c'est un écueil !

Chaque îlot signalé par l'homme de vigie
Est un Eldorado promis par le Destin;
L'Imagination qui dresse son orgie
Ne trouve qu'un récif aux clartés du matin.

O le pauvre amoureux des pays chimériques !
Faut-il le mettre aux fers, le jeter à la mer,
Ce matelot ivrogne, inventeur d'Amériques
Dont le mirage rend le gouffre plus amer ?

Tel le vieux vagabond, piétinant dans la boue,
Rêve, le nez en l'air, de brillants paradis;
Son œil ensorcelé découvre une Capoue
Partout où la chandelle illumine un taudis.

III

Étonnants voyageurs ! quelles nobles histoires
Nous lisons dans vos yeux profonds comme les mers !
Montrez-nous les écrins de vos riches mémoires,
Ces bijoux merveilleux, faits d'astres et d'éthers.

Nous voulons voyager sans vapeur et sans voile !
Faites, pour égayer l'ennui de nos prisons,
Passer sur nos esprits, tendus comme une toile,
Vos souvenirs avec leurs cadres d'horizons.

Dites, qu'avez-vous vu ?

IV

“ Nous avons vu des astres
Et des flots; nous avons vu des sables aussi;
Et, malgré bien des chocs et d'imprévus désastres,
Nous nous sommes souvent ennuyés, comme ici.

La gloire du soleil sur la mer violette,
La gloire des cités dans le soleil couchant,
Allumaient dans nos cœurs une ardeur inquiète
De plonger dans un ciel au reflet alléchant.

Les plus riches cités, les plus grands paysages,
Jamais ne contenaient l'attrait mystérieux
De ceux que le hasard fait avec les nuages.
Et toujours le désir nous rendait soucieux !

— La jouissance ajoute au désir de la force.
Désir, vieil arbre à qui le plaisir sert d'engrais,
Cependant que grossit et durcit ton écorce,
Tes branches veulent voir le soleil de plus près !

Grandiras-tu toujours, grand arbre plus vivace
Que le cyprès ? — Pourtant nous avons, avec soin,
Cueilli quelques croquis pour votre album vorace,
Frères qui trouvez beau tout ce qui vient de loin !

Nous avons salué des idoles à trompe;
Des trônes constellés de joyaux lumineux;
Des palais ouvragés dont la féerique pompe
Serait pour vos banquiers un rêve ruineux;

Des costumes qui sont pour les yeux une ivresse;
Des femmes dont les dents et les ongles sont teints,
Et des jongleurs savants que le serpent caresse. "

V

Et puis, et puis encore ?

VI

" O cerveaux enfantins !

Pour ne pas oublier la chose capitale,
Nous avons vu partout, et sans l'avoir cherché,
Du haut jusques en bas de l'échelle fatale,
Le spectacle ennuyeux de l'immortel péché :

La femme, esclave vile, orgueilleuse et stupide,
Sans rire s'adorant et s'aimant sans dégoût;
L'homme, tyran goulu, paillard, dur et cupide,
Esclave de l'esclave et ruisseau dans l'égout;

Le bourreau qui jouit, le martyr qui sanglote;
La fête qu'assaisonne et parfume le sang;
Le poison du pouvoir énervant le despote,
Et le peuple amoureux du fouet abrutissant;

Plusieurs religions semblables à la nôtre,
Toutes escaladant le ciel; la Sainteté,
Comme en un lit de plume un délicat se vautre,
Dans les clous et le crin cherchant la volupté;

L'Humanité bavarde, ivre de son génie,
Et, folle maintenant comme elle était jadis,
Criant à Dieu, dans sa furibonde agonie :
" O mon semblable, ô mon maître, je te maudis ! "

Et les moins sots, hardis amants de la Démence,
Fuyant le grand troupeau parqué par le Destin,
Et se réfugiant dans l'opium immense !
— Tel est du globe entier l'éternel bulletin. "

VII

Amer savoir, celui qu'on tire du voyage !
Le monde, monotone et petit, aujourd'hui,
Hier, demain, toujours, nous fait voir notre image :
Une oasis d'horreur dans un désert d'ennui !

Faut-il partir ? rester ? Si tu peux rester, reste;
Pars, s'il le faut. L'un court, et l'autre se tapit
Pour tromper l'ennemi vigilant et funeste,
Le Temps ! Il est, hélas ! des coureurs sans répit,

Comme le Juif errant et comme les apôtres,
A qui rien ne suffit, ni wagon ni vaisseau,
Pour fuir ce rétiaire infâme; il en est d'autres
Qui savent le tuer sans quitter leur berceau.

Lorsque enfin il mettra le pied sur notre échine,
Nous pourrons espérer et crier : En avant !
De même qu'autrefois nous partions pour la Chine,
Les yeux fixés au large et les cheveux au vent,

Nous nous embarquerons sur la mer des Ténèbres
Avec le cœur joyeux d'un jeune passager.
Entendez-vous ces voix, charmantes et funèbres,
Qui chantent : " Par ici ! vous qui voulez manger

Le Lotus parfumé ! c'est ici qu'on vendange
Les fruits miraculeux dont votre cœur a faim;
Venez vous enivrer de la douceur étrange
De cette après-midi qui n'a jamais de fin ? "

A l'accent familier nous devinons le spectre;
Nos Pylades là-bas tendent leurs bras vers nous.
" Pour rafraîchir ton cœur nage vers ton Électre ! "
Dit celle dont jadis nous baisions les genoux.

VIII

O Mort, vieux capitaine, il est temps ! levons l'ancre.
Ce pays nous ennuie, ô Mort ! Appareillons !
Si le ciel et la mer sont noirs comme de l'encre,
Nos cœurs que tu connais sont remplis de rayons !

Verse-nous ton poison pour qu'il nous réconforte !
Nous voulons, tant ce feu nous brûle le cerveau,
Plonger au fond du gouffre, Enfer ou Ciel, qu'importe ?
Au fond de l'Inconnu pour trouver du *nouveau !*

SUPPLÉMENT
AUX FLEURS DU MAL

I

ÉPIGRAPHE POUR UN LIVRE CONDAMNÉ

Lecteur paisible et bucolique,
Sobre et naïf homme de bien,
Jette ce livre saturnien,
Orgiaque et mélancolique.

Si tu n'as fait ta rhétorique
Chez Satan, le rusé doyen,
Jette ! tu n'y comprendrais rien,
Ou tu me croirais hystérique.

Mais si, sans se laisser charmer,
Ton œil sait plonger dans les gouffres,
Lis-moi, pour apprendre à m'aimer;

Ame curieuse qui souffres
Et vas cherchant ton paradis,
Plains-moi... Sinon je te maudis !

II

LA VOIX

Mon berceau s'adossait à la bibliothèque,
Babel sombre, où roman, science, fabliau,
Tout, la cendre latine et la poussière grecque,
Se mêlaient. J'étais haut comme un in-folio.
Deux voix me parlaient. L'une, insidieuse et ferme,
Disait : " La Terre est un gâteau plein de douceur;
Je puis (et ton plaisir serait alors sans terme !)
Te faire un appétit d'une égale grosseur. "
Et l'autre : " Viens ! oh ! viens voyager dans les rêves,
Au delà du possible, au delà du connu ! "
Et celle-là chantait comme le vent des grèves,
Fantôme vagissant, on ne sait d'où venu,
Qui caresse l'oreille et cependant l'effraie.
Je te répondis : " Oui ! douce voix ! " C'est d'alors
Que date ce qu'on peut, hélas ! nommer ma plaie
Et ma fatalité. Derrière les décors
De l'existence immense, au plus noir de l'abîme,
Je vois distinctement des mondes singuliers,
Et, de ma clairvoyance extatique victime,
Je traîne des serpents qui mordent mes souliers.
Et c'est depuis ce temps que pareil aux prophètes,
J'aime si tendrement le désert et la mer;
Que je ris dans les deuils et pleure dans les fêtes,
Et trouve un goût suave au vin le plus amer;
Que je prends très-souvent les faits pour des mensonges,
Et que, les yeux au ciel, je tombe dans des trous.
Mais la Voix me console et dit : " Garde tes songes :
Les sages n'en ont pas d'aussi beaux que les fous !"

III

L'EXAMEN DE MINUIT

La pendule, sonnant minuit,
Ironiquement nous engage
A nous rappeler quel usage
Nous fîmes du jour qui s'enfuit :
— Aujourd'hui, date fatidique,
Vendredi, treize, nous avons,
Malgré tout ce que nous savons,
Mené le train d'un hérétique;

Nous avons blasphémé Jésus,
Des Dieux le plus incontestable !
Comme un parasite à la table
De quelque monstrueux Crésus,
Nous avons, pour plaire à la brute,
Digne vassale des Démons,
Insulté ce que nous aimons,
Et flatté ce qui nous rebute;

Contristé, servile bourreau,
Le faible qu'à tort on méprise;
Salué l'énorme Bêtise,
La Bêtise au front de taureau;
Baisé la stupide Matière
Avec grande dévotion,
Et de la putréfaction
Béni la blafarde lumière.

Enfin, nous avons, pour noyer
Le vertige dans le délire,
Nous, prêtre orgueilleux de la Lyre,
Dont la gloire est de déployer
L'ivresse des choses funèbres,
Bu sans soif et mangé sans faim !...
— Vite soufflons la lampe, afin
De nous cacher dans les ténèbres !

IV

L'AVERTISSEUR

Tout homme digne de ce nom
A dans le cœur un Serpent jaune,
Installé comme sur un trône,
Qui, s'il dit : " Je veux ! " répond : " Non ! "

Plonge tes yeux dans les yeux fixes
Des Satyresses ou des Nixes,
La Dent dit : " Pense à ton devoir ! "

Fais des enfants, plante des arbres,
Polis des vers, sculpte des marbres,
La Dent dit : " Vivras-tu ce soir ? "

Quoi qu'il ébauche ou qu'il espère,
L'homme ne vit pas un moment
Sans subir l'avertissement
De l'insupportable Vipère.

V

LE REBELLE

Un Ange furieux fond du ciel comme un aigle,
Du mécréant saisit à plein poing les cheveux,
Et dit, le secouant : “ Tu connaîtras la règle !
(Car je suis ton bon Ange, entends-tu ?) Je le veux !

Sache qu'il faut aimer, sans faire la grimace,
Le pauvre, le méchant, le tortu, l'hébété,
Pour que tu puisses faire à Jésus, quand il passe,
Un tapis triomphal avec ta charité.

Tel est l'Amour ! Avant que ton cœur ne se blase,
A la gloire de Dieu rallume ton extase;
C'est la Volupté vraie aux durables appas ! ”

Et l'Ange, châtiant autant, ma foi ! qu'il aime,
De ses poings de géant torture l'anathème;
Mais le damné répond toujours : “ Je ne veux pas ! ”

VI

LE GOUFFRE

Pascal avait son gouffre, avec lui se mouvant.
— Hélas ! tout est abîme, — action, désir, rêve,
Parole ! et sur mon poil qui tout droit se relève
Maintes fois de la Peur je sens passer le vent.

En haut, en bas, partout, la profondeur, la grève,
Le silence, l'espace affreux et captivant...
Sur le fond de mes nuits Dieu de son doigt savant
Dessine un cauchemar multiforme et sans trêve.

J'ai peur du sommeil comme on a peur d'un grand trou,
Tout plein de vague horreur, menant on ne sait où;
Je ne vois qu'infini par toutes les fenêtres,

Et mon esprit, toujours du vertige hanté,
Jalouse du néant l'insensibilité.
— Ah ! ne jamais sortir des Nombres et des Êtres !

VII

LES PLAINTES D'UN ICARE

Les amants des prostituées
Sont heureux, dispos et repus;
Quant à moi, mes bras sont rompus
Pour avoir étreint des nuées.

C'est grâce aux astres nonpareils,
Qui tout au fond du ciel flamboient,
Que mes yeux consumés ne voient
Que des souvenirs de soleils.

En vain j'ai voulu de l'espace
Trouver la fin et le milieu;
Sous je ne sais quel œil de feu
Je sens mon aile qui se casse;

Et brûlé par l'amour du beau,
Je n'aurai pas l'honneur sublime
De donner mon nom à l'abîme
Qui me servira de tombeau.

VIII

LE COUVERCLE

En quelque lieu qu'il aille, ou sur mer ou sur terre,
Sous un climat de flamme ou sous un soleil blanc,
Serviteur de Jésus, courtisan de Cythère,
Mendiant ténébreux ou Crésus rutilant,

Citadin, campagnard, vagabond, sédentaire,
Que son petit cerveau soit actif ou soit lent,
Partout l'homme subit la terreur du mystère,
Et ne regarde en haut qu'avec un œil tremblant.

En haut, le Ciel ! ce mur de caveau qui l'étouffe,
Plafond illuminé par un opéra bouffe
Où chaque histrion foule un sol ensanglanté;

Terreur du libertin, espoir du fol ermite :
Le Ciel ! couvercle noir de la grande marmite
Où bout l'imperceptible et vaste Humanité.

IX

LA PRIÈRE D'UN PAÏEN

Ah ! ne ralentis pas tes flammes;
Réchauffe mon cœur engourdi,
Volupté, torture des âmes !
Diva ! supplicem exaudi !

Déesse dans l'air répandue,
Flamme dans notre souterrain !
Exauce une âme morfondue,
Qui te consacre un chant d'airain.

Volupté, sois toujours ma reine !
Prends le masque d'une sirène
Faite de chair et de velours,

Ou verse-moi tes sommeils lourds
Dans le vin informe et mystique,
Volupté, fantôme élastique !

X

LA LUNE OFFENSÉE

O Lune qu'adoraient discrètement nos pères,
Du haut des pays bleus où, radieux sérail,
Les astres vont te suivre en pimpant attirail,
Ma vieille Cynthia, lampe de nos repaires,

Vois-tu les amoureux, sur leurs grabats prospères,
De leur bouche en dormant montrer le frais émail ?
Le poëte buter du front sur son travail ?
Ou sous les gazons secs s'accoupler les vipères ?

Sous ton domino jaune, et d'un pied clandestin,
Vas-tu, comme jadis, du soir jusqu'au matin,
Baiser d'Endymion les grâces surannées ?

— " Je vois ta mère, enfant de ce siècle appauvri,
Qui vers son miroir penche un lourd amas d'années,
Et plâtre artistement le sein qui t'a nourri ! "

XI

LA RANÇON

L'homme a, pour payer sa rançon,
Deux champs au tuf profond et riche,
Qu'il faut qu'il remue et défriche
Avec le fer de la raison;

Pour obtenir la moindre rose,
Pour extorquer quelques épis,
Des pleurs salés de son front gris
Sans cesse il faut qu'il les arrose.

L'un est l'Art, et l'autre l'Amour.
— Pour rendre le juge propice,
Lorsque de la stricte justice
Paraîtra le terrible jour,

Il faudra lui montrer des granges
Pleines de moissons, et des fleurs
Dont les formes et les couleurs
Gagnent le suffrage des Anges.

XII

L'IMPRÉVU

Harpagon qui veillait son père agonisant,
Se dit, rêveur, devant ces lèvres déjà blanches :
" Nous avons au grenier un nombre suffisant,
Ce me semble, de vieilles planches ? "

Célimène roucoule et dit : " Mon cœur est bon,
Et naturellement, Dieu m'a faite très-belle. "
— Son cœur ! cœur racorni, fumé comme un jambon,
Recuit à la flamme éternelle !

Un gazetier fumeux, qui se croit un flambeau,
Dit au pauvre, qu'il a noyé dans les ténèbres :
" Où donc l'aperçois-tu, ce créateur du Beau,
Ce redresseur que tu célèbres ? "

Mieux que tous, je connais certain voluptueux
Qui bâille nuit et jour, et se lamente et pleure,
Répétant, l'impuissant et le fat : " Oui, je veux
Être vertueux, dans une heure ! "

L'Horloge à son tour, dit à voix basse : " Il est mûr,
Le damné ! J'avertis en vain la chair infecte.
L'homme est aveugle, sourd, fragile comme un mur
Qu'habite et que ronge un insecte ! "

Et puis, quelqu'un paraît que tous avaient nié,
Et qui leur dit, railleur et fier : " Dans mon ciboire,
Vous avez, que je crois, assez communié
A la joyeuse Messe noire ?

Chacun de vous m'a fait un temple dans son cœur;
Vous avez, en secret, baisé ma fesse immonde !
Reconnaissez Satan à son rire vainqueur,
Énorme et laid comme le monde !

Avez-vous donc pu croire, hypocrites surpris,
Qu'on se moque du maître, et qu'avec lui l'on triche,
Et qu'il soit naturel de recevoir deux prix,
D'aller au Ciel et d'être riche ?

Il faut que le gibier paye le vieux chasseur
Qui se morfond longtemps à l'affût de la proie.
Je vais vous emporter à travers l'épaisseur,
Compagnons de ma triste joie,

A travers l'épaisseur de la terre et du roc,
A travers les amas confus de votre cendre,
Dans un palais aussi grand que moi, d'un seul bloc
Et qui n'est pas de pierre tendre;

Car il est fait avec l'universel Péché,
Et contient mon orgueil, ma douleur et ma gloire ! "
— Cependant, tout en haut de l'univers juché,
Un ange sonne la victoire

De ceux dont le cœur dit : " Que béni soit son fouet,
Seigneur ! que la Douleur, ô Père, soit bénie !
Mon âme dans tes mains n'est pas un vain jouet,
Et ta prudence est infinie. "

Le son de la trompette est si délicieux,
Dans ces soirs solennels de célestes vendanges,
Qu'il s'infiltre comme une extase dans tous ceux
Dont elle chante les louanges.

XIII

BIEN LOIN D'ICI

C'est ici la case sacrée
Où cette fille très-parée,
Tranquille et toujours préparée,

D'une main éventant ses seins,
Et son coude dans les coussins,
Écoute pleurer les bassins :

C'est la chambre de Dorothée.
— La brise et l'eau chantent au loin
Leur chanson de sanglots heurtée
Pour bercer cette enfant gâtée.

De haut en bas, avec grand soin,
Sa peau délicate est frottée
D'huile odorante et de benjoin.
— Des fleurs se pâment dans un coin.

XIV

RECUEILLEMENT

Sois sage, ô ma Douleur, et tiens-toi plus tranquille.
Tu réclamais le Soir; il descend; le voici :
Une atmosphère obscure enveloppe la ville,
Aux uns portant la paix, aux autres le souci.

Pendant que des mortels la multitude vile,
Sous le fouet du Plaisir, ce bourreau sans merci,
Va cueillir des remords dans la fête servile,
Ma Douleur, donne-moi la main; viens par ici,

Loin d'eux. Vois se pencher les défuntes Années,
Sur les balcons du ciel, en robes surannées;
Surgir du fond des eaux le Regret souriant;

Le Soleil moribond s'endormir sous une arche,
Et, comme un long linceul traînant à l'Orient,
Entends, ma chère, entends la douce Nuit qui marche.

XV

MADRIGAL TRISTE

I

Que m'importe que tu sois sage ?
Sois belle ! et sois triste ! Les pleurs
Ajoutent un charme au visage,
Comme le fleuve au paysage;
L'orage rajeunit les fleurs.

Je t'aime surtout quand la joie
S'enfuit de ton front terrassé;
Quand ton cœur dans l'horreur se noie;
Quand sur ton présent se déploie
Le nuage affreux du passé.

Je t'aime quand ton grand œil verse
Une eau chaude comme le sang;
Quand, malgré ma main qui te berce,
Ton angoisse, trop lourde, perce
Comme un râle d'agonisant.

J'aspire, volupté divine !
Hymne profond, délicieux !
Tous les sanglots de ta poitrine,
Et crois que ton cœur s'illumine
Des perles que versent tes yeux !

II

Je sais que ton cœur, qui regorge
De vieux amours déracinés,
Flamboie encor comme une forge,
Et que tu couves sous ta gorge
Un peu de l'orgueil des damnés;

Mais tant, ma chère, que tes rêves
N'auront pas reflété l'Enfer,
Et qu'en un cauchemar sans trêves,
Songeant de poisons et de glaives,
Éprise de poudre et de fer,

N'ouvrant à chacun qu'avec crainte,
Déchiffrant le malheur partout,
Te convulsant quand l'heure tinte,
Tu n'auras pas senti l'étreinte
De l'irrésistible Dégoût,

Tu ne pourras, esclave reine
Qui ne m'aimes qu'avec effroi,
Dans l'horreur de la nuit malsaine
Me dire, l'âme de cris pleine :
" Je suis ton égale, ô mon Roi ! "

XVI

LE JET D'EAU

Tes beaux yeux sont las, pauvre amante !
Reste longtemps, sans les rouvrir,
Dans cette pose nonchalante
Où t'a surprise le plaisir.
Dans la cour le jet d'eau qui jase
Et ne se tait ni nuit ni jour,
Entretient doucement l'extase
Où ce soir m'a plongé l'amour.

La gerbe épanouie
En mille fleurs,
Où Phœbé réjouie
Met ses couleurs,
Tombe comme une pluie
De larges pleurs.

Ainsi ton âme qu'incendie
L'éclair brûlant des voluptés
S'élance, rapide et hardie,
Vers les vastes cieux enchantés.
Puis, elle s'épanche, mourante,
En un flot de triste langueur,
Qui par une invisible pente
Descend jusqu'au fond de mon cœur.

La gerbe épanouie
En mille fleurs,
Où Phœbé réjouie
Met ses couleurs,
Tombe comme une pluie
De larges pleurs.

O toi, que la nuit rend si belle,
Qu'il m'est doux, penché vers tes seins,
D'écouter la plainte éternelle
Qui sanglote dans les bassins !
Lune, eau sonore, nuit bénie,
Arbres qui frissonnez autour,
Votre pure mélancolie
Est le miroir de mon amour.

La gerbe épanouie
En mille fleurs,
Où Phœbé réjouie
Met ses couleurs,
Tombe comme une pluie
De larges pleurs.

XVII

A UNE MALABARAISE

Tes pieds sont aussi fins que tes mains et ta hanche
Est large à faire envie à la plus belle blanche;
A l'artiste pensif ton corps est doux et cher;
Tes grands yeux de velours sont plus noirs que ta chair.
Aux pays chauds et bleus où ton Dieu t'a fait naître,
Ta tâche est d'allumer la pipe de ton maître,
De pourvoir les flacons d'eaux fraîches et d'odeurs,
De chasser loin du lit les moustiques rôdeurs,
Et, dès que le matin fait chanter les platanes,
D'acheter au bazar ananas et bananes.
Tout le jour, où tu veux, tu mènes tes pieds nus,
Et fredonnes tout bas de vieux airs inconnus;

Et quand descend le soir au manteau d'écarlate,
Tu poses doucement ton corps sur úne natte,
Où tes rêves flottants sont pleins de colibris,
Et toujours, comme toi, gracieux et fleuris.

Pourquoi, l'heureuse enfant, veux-tu voir notre France,
Ce pays trop peuplé que fauche la souffrance,
Et, confiant ta vie aux bras forts des marins,
Faire de grands adieux à tes chers tamarins ?
Toi, vêtue à moitié de mousselines frêles,
Frissonnante là-bas sous la neige et les grêles,
Comme tu pleurerais tes loisirs doux et francs,
Si, le corset brutal emprisonnant tes flancs,
Il te fallait glaner ton souper dans nos fanges
Et vendre le parfum de tes charmes étranges,
L'œil pensif, et suivant, dans nos sales brouillards,
Des cocotiers absents les fantômes épars !

XVIII

LES YEUX DE BERTHE

Vous pouvez mépriser les yeux les plus célèbres,
Beaux yeux de mon enfant, par où filtre et s'enfuit
Je ne sais quoi de bon, de doux comme la Nuit !
Beaux yeux, versez sur moi vos charmantes ténèbres !

Grands yeux de mon enfant, arcanes adorés,
Vous ressemblez beaucoup à ces grottes magiques
Où, derrière l'amas des ombres léthargiques,
Scintillent vaguement des trésors ignorés !

Mon enfant a des yeux obscurs, profonds et vastes,
Comme toi, Nuit immense, éclairés comme toi !
Leurs feux sont ces pensers d'Amour, mêlés de Foi,
Qui pétillent au fond, voluptueux ou chastes.

XIX

HYMNE

A la très-chère, à la très-belle
Qui remplit mon cœur de clarté,
A l'ange, à l'idole immortelle,
Salut en l'immortalité !

Elle se répand dans ma vie
Comme un air imprégné de sel,
Et dans mon âme inassouvie
Verse le goût de l'éternel.

Sachet toujours frais qui parfume
L'atmosphère d'un cher réduit,
Encensoir oublié qui fume
En secret à travers la nuit,

Comment, amour incorruptible,
T'exprimer avec vérité ?
Grain de musc qui gis, invisible,
Au fond de mon éternité !

A la très-bonne, à la très-belle
Qui fait ma joie et ma santé,
A l'ange, à l'idole immortelle,
Salut en l'immortalité !

XX

LE COUCHER DU SOLEIL ROMANTIQUE

Que le soleil est beau quand tout frais il se lève,
Comme une explosion nous lançant son bonjour !
— Bienheureux celui-là qui peut avec amour
Saluer son coucher plus glorieux qu'un rêve !

Je me souviens ! J'ai vu tout, fleur, source, sillon,
Se pâmer sous son œil comme un cœur qui palpite...
— Courons vers l'horizon, il est tard, courons vite,
Pour attraper au moins un oblique rayon !

Mais je poursuis en vain le Dieu qui se retire;
L'irrésistible Nuit établit son empire,
Noire, humide, funeste et pleine de frissons;

Une odeur de tombeau dans les ténèbres nage,
Et mon pied peureux froisse, au bord du marécage,
Des crapauds imprévus et de froids limaçons.

XXI

A THÉODORE DE BANVILLE

1842

Vous avez empoigné les crins de la Déesse
Avec un tel poignet, qu'on vous eût pris, à voir
Et cet air de maîtrise et ce beau nonchaloir,
Pour un jeune ruffian terrassant sa maîtresse.

L'œil clair et plein du feu de la précocité,
Vous avez prélassé votre orgueil d'architecte
Dans des constructions dont l'audace correcte
Fait voir quelle sera votre maturité.

Poëte, notre sang nous fuit par chaque pore;
Est-ce que par hasard la robe de Centaure,
Qui changeait toute veine en funèbre ruisseau,

Était teinte trois fois dans les laves subtiles
De ces vindicatifs et monstrueux reptiles
Que le petit Hercule étranglait au berceau ?

XXII

VERS POUR LE PORTRAIT DE M. HONORÉ DAUMIER

Celui dont nous t'offrons l'image,
Et dont l'art, subtil entre tous,
Nous enseigne à rire de nous,
Celui-là, lecteur, est un sage.

C'est un satirique, un moqueur;
Mais l'énergie avec laquelle
Il peint le Mal et sa séquelle,
Prouve la beauté de son cœur.

Son rire n'est pas la grimace
De Melmoth ou de Méphisto
Sous la torche de l'Alecto
Qui les brûle, mais qui nous glace,

Leur rire, hélas ! de la gaieté
N'est que la douloureuse charge;
Le sien rayonne, franc et large,
Comme un signe de sa bonté !

XXIII

LOLA DE VALENCE

Entre tant de beautés que partout on peut voir,
Je comprends bien, amis, que le désir balance;
Mais on voit scintiller en Lola de Valence
Le charme inattendu d'un bijou rose et noir.

XXIV

SUR *LE TASSE EN PRISON*

D'EUGÈNE DELACROIX

Le poëte au cachot, débraillé, maladif,
Roulant un manuscrit sous son pied convulsif,
Mesure d'un regard que la terreur enflamme
L'escalier de vertige où s'abîme son âme.

Les rires enivrants dont s'emplit la prison
Vers l'étrange et l'absurde invitent sa raison;
Le Doute l'environne, et la Peur ridicule,
Hideuse et multiforme, autour de lui circule.

Ce génie enfermé dans un taudis malsain,
Ces grimaces, ces cris, ces spectres dont l'essaim
Tourbillonne, ameuté derrière son oreille,

Ce rêveur que l'horreur de son logis réveille,
Voilà bien ton emblème, Ame aux songes obscurs,
Que le Réel étouffe entre ses quatre murs !

XXV

LES PROMESSES D'UN VISAGE

J'aime, ô pâle beauté, tes sourcils surbaissés,
D'où semblent couler des ténèbres;
Tes yeux, quoique très-noirs, m'inspirent des pensers
Qui ne sont pas du tout funèbres.

Tes yeux, qui sont d'accord avec tes noirs cheveux,
Avec ta crinière élastique,
Tes yeux, languissamment, me disent : " Si tu veux,
Amant de la muse plastique,

Suivre l'espoir qu'en toi nous avons excité,
Et tous les goûts que tu professes,
Tu pourras constater notre véracité
Depuis le nombril jusqu'aux fesses;

Tu trouveras, au bout de deux beaux seins bien lourds,
    Deux larges médailles de bronze,
Et sous un ventre uni, doux comme du velours,
    Bistré comme la peau d'un bonze,

Une riche toison qui, vraiment, est la sœur
    De cette énorme chevelure,
Souple et frisée, et qui t'égale en épaisseur,
    Nuit sans étoiles, Nuit obscure ! "

XXVI

LE MONSTRE

OU

LE PARANYMPHE

D'UNE NYMPHE MACABRE

I

Tu n'es certes pas, ma très-chère,
Ce que Veuillot nomme un tendron.
Le jeu, l'amour, la bonne chère,
Bouillonnent en toi, vieux chaudron !
Tu n'es plus fraîche, ma très-chère,

Ma vieille infante ! Et cependant
Tes caravanes insensées
T'ont donné ce lustre abondant
Des choses qui sont très-usées,
Mais qui séduisent cependant.

Je ne trouve pas monotone
La verdeur de tes quarante ans;
Je préfère tes fruits, Automne,
Aux fleurs banales du Printemps !
Non ! tu n'es jamais monotone !

Ta carcasse a des agréments
Et des grâces particulières;
Je trouve d'étranges piments
Dans le creux de tes deux salières;
Ta carcasse a des agréments !

Nargue les amants ridicules
Du melon et du giraumont !
Je préfère tes clavicules
A celles du roi Salomon,
Et je plains ces gens ridicules !

Tes cheveux, comme un casque bleu,
Ombragent ton front de guerrière,
Qui ne pense et rougit que peu,
Et puis se sauvent par derrière
Comme les crins d'un casque bleu.

Tes yeux qui semblent de la boue,
Où scintille quelque fanal,
Ravivés au fard de ta joue,
Lancent un éclair infernal !
Tes yeux sont noirs comme la boue !

Par sa luxure et son dédain
Ta lèvre amère nous provoque;
Cette lèvre, c'est un Éden
Qui nous attire et qui nous choque.
Quelle luxure ! et quel dédain !

Ta jambe musculeuse et sèche
Sait gravir au haut des volcans,
Et malgré la neige et la dèche
Danser les plus fougueux cancans.
Ta jambe est musculeuse et sèche;

Ta peau brûlante et sans douceur,
Comme celle des vieux gendarmes,
Ne connaît pas plus la sueur
Que ton œil ne connaît les larmes.
(Et pourtant elle a sa douceur !)

II

Sotte, tu t'en vas droit au Diable !
Volontiers, j'irais avec toi
Si cette vitesse effroyable
Ne me causait pas quelque émoi.
Va-t'en donc, toute seule, au Diable !

Mon rein, mon poumon, mon jarret
Ne me laissent plus rendre hommage
A ce Seigneur, comme il faudrait.
" Hélas ! c'est vraiment bien dommage ! "
Disent mon rein et mon jarret.

Oh ! très-sincèrement je souffre
De ne pas aller aux sabbats,
Pour voir, quand il pète du soufre,
Comment tu lui baises son cas !
Oh ! très-sincèrement je souffre !

Je suis diablement affligé
De ne pas être ta torchère,
Et de te demander congé,
Flambeau d'enfer ! Juge, ma chère,
Combien je dois être affligé,

Puisque depuis longtemps je t'aime,
Étant très-logique ! En effet,
Voulant du Mal chercher la crème
Et n'aimer qu'un monstre parfait,
Vraiment oui ! vieux monstre, je t'aime !

XXVII

SUR LES DÉBUTS D'AMINA BOSCHETTI

AU THÉATRE DE LA MONNAIE, A BRUXELLES

Amina bondit, — fuit, — puis voltige et sourit;
Le Welche dit : " Tout ça, pour moi, c'est du prâcrit;
Je ne connais, en fait de nymphes bocagères,
Que celles de *Montagne-aux-Herbes-potagères.* "

Du bout de son pied fin et de son œil qui rit,
Amina verse à flots le délire et l'esprit;
Le Welche dit : " Fuyez, délices mensongères !
Mon épouse n'a pas ces allures légères. "

Vous ignorez, sylphide au jarret triomphant,
Qui voulez enseigner la walse à l'éléphant,
Au hibou la gaieté, le rire à la cigogne,

Que sur la grâce en feu le Welche dit : " Haro ! "
Et que, le doux Bacchus lui versant du bourgogne,
Le monstre répondrait : " J'aime mieux le faro ! "

XXVIII

A M. EUGÈNE FROMENTIN

A PROPOS D'UN IMPORTUN

QUI SE DISAIT SON AMI

Il me dit qu'il était très-riche,
Mais qu'il craignait le choléra;
— Que de son or il était chiche,
Mais qu'il goûtait fort l'Opéra;

— Qu'il raffolait de la nature,
Ayant connu monsieur Corot;
— Qu'il n'avait pas encor voiture,
Mais que cela viendrait bientôt;

— Qu'il aimait le marbre et la brique,
Les bois noirs et les bois dorés;
— Qu'il possédait dans sa fabrique
Trois contre-maîtres décorés;

— Qu'il avait, sans compter le reste,
Vingt mille actions sur le *Nord;*
— Qu'il avait trouvé, pour un zeste,
Des encadrements d'Oppenord;

— Qu'il donnerait (fût-ce à Luzarches !)
Dans le bric-à-bras jusqu'au cou,
Et qu'au Marché des Patriarches
Il avait fait plus d'un bon coup;

Qu'il n'aimait pas beaucoup sa femme,
Ni sa mère; — mais qu'il croyait
A l'immortalité de l'âme,
Et qu'il avait lu Niboyet !

— Qu'il penchait pour l'amour physique,
Et qu'à Rome, séjour d'ennui,
Une femme, d'ailleurs phthisique,
Était morte d'amour pour lui.

Pendant trois heures et demie,
Ce bavard, venu de Tournai,
M'a dégoisé toute sa vie;
J'en ai le cerveau consterné.

S'il fallait décrire ma peine,
Ce serait à n'en plus finir;
Je me disais, domptant ma haine :
“ Au moins, si je pouvais dormir ! ”

Comme un qui n'est pas à son aise,
Et qui n'ose pas s'en aller,
Je frottais de mon cul ma chaise,
Rêvant de le faire empaler.

Ce monstre se nomme Bastogne;
Il fuyait devant le fléau.
Moi, je fuirai jusqu'en Gascogne,
Ou j'irai me jeter à l'eau,

Si dans ce Paris, qu'il redoute,
Quand chacun sera retourné,
Je trouve encore sur ma route
Ce fléau, natif de Tournai.

XXIX

UN CABARET FOLATRE

SUR LA ROUTE DE BRUXELLES A UCCLE

Vous qui raffolez des squelettes
Et des emblèmes détestés,
Pour épicer les voluptés,
(Fût-ce de simples omelettes !)

Vieux Pharaon, ô Monselet !
Devant cette enseigne imprévue,
J'ai rêvé de vous : *A la vue*
Du Cimetière, Estaminet.

XXX

LE CALUMET DE PAIX*

(Imité de Longfellow)

I

Or Gitche Manito, le Maître de la Vie,
Le Puissant, descendit dans la verte prairie,
Dans l'immense prairie aux coteaux montueux;
Et là, sur les rochers de la Rouge Carrière,
Dominant tout l'espace et baigné de lumière,
Il se tenait debout, vaste et majestueux.

Alors il convoqua les peuples innombrables,
Plus nombreux que ne sont les herbes et les sables.
Avec sa main terrible il rompit un morceau
Du rocher, dont il fit une pipe superbe.
Puis, au bord du ruisseau, dans une énorme gerbe,
Pour s'en faire un tuyau, choisit un long roseau.

Pour la bourrer il prit au saule son écorce;
Et lui, le Tout-Puissant, Créateur de la Force,
Debout, il alluma, comme un divin fanal,
La Pipe de la Paix. Debout sur la Carrière
Il fumait, droit, superbe, et baigné de lumière.
Or pour les nations c'était le grand signal.

* Baudelaire's *Le Calumet de paix* is a partial translation of *The Song of Hiawatha,* undertaken in 1860 at the request of an American musician, Robert Stoepel, who had composed a symphony based on Longfellow's poem.

Et lentement montait la divine fumée
Dans l'air doux du matin, onduleuse, embaumée.
Et d'abord ce ne fut qu'un sillon ténébreux;
Puis la vapeur se fit plus bleue et plus épaisse,
Puis blanchit; et montant, et grossissant sans cesse,
Elle alla se briser au dur plafond des cieux.

Des plus lointains sommets des Montagnes Rocheuses,
Depuis les lacs du Nord aux ondes tapageuses,
Depuis Tawasentha, le vallon sans pareil,
Jusqu'à Tuscaloosa, la forêt parfumée,
Tous virent le signal et l'immense fumée
Montant paisiblement dans le matin vermeil.

Les Prophètes disaient : " Voyez-vous cette bande
De vapeur, qui, semblable à la main qui commande,
Oscille et se détache en noir sur le soleil ?
C'est Gitche Manito, le Maître de la Vie,
Qui dit aux quatre coins de l'immense prairie :
" Je vous convoque tous, guerriers, à mon conseil ! "

Par le chemin des eaux, par la route des plaines,
Par les quatre côtés d'où soufflent les haleines
Du vent, tous les guerriers de chaque tribu, tous,
Comprenant le signal du nuage qui bouge,
Vinrent docilement à la Carrière Rouge
Où Gitche Manito leur donnait rendez-vous.

Les guerriers se tenaient sur la verte prairie,
Tous équipés en guerre, et la mine aguerrie,
Bariolés ainsi qu'un feuillage automnal;
Et la haine qui fait combattre tous les êtres,
La haine qui brûlait les yeux de leurs ancêtres
Incendiait encor leurs yeux d'un feu fatal.

Et leurs yeux étaient pleins de haine héréditaire.
Or Gitche Manito, le Maître de la Terre,
Les considérait tous avec compassion,
Comme un père très-bon, ennemi du désordre,
Qui voit ses chers petits batailler et se mordre.
Tel Gitche Manito pour toute nation.

Il étendit sur eux sa puissante main droite
Pour subjuguer leur cœur et leur nature étroite,
Pour rafraîchir leur fièvre à l'ombre de sa main;
Puis il leur dit avec sa voix majestueuse,
Comparable à la voix d'une eau tumulteuse
Qui tombe et rend un son monstrueux, surhumain :

II

“ O ma postérité, déplorable et chérie !
O mes fils ! écoutez la divine raison.
C'est Gitche Manito, le Maître de la Vie,
Qui vous parle ! celui qui dans votre patrie
A mis l'ours, le castor, le renne et le bison.

Je vous ai fait la chasse et la pêche faciles;
Pourquoi donc le chasseur devient-il assassin ?
Le marais fut par moi peuplé de volatiles;
Pourquoi n'êtes-vous pas contents, fils indociles ?
Pourquoi l'homme fait-il la chasse à son voisin ?

Je suis vraiment bien las de vos horribles guerres.
Vos prières, vos vœux mêmes sont des forfaits !
Le péril est pour vous dans vos humeurs contraires,
Et c'est dans l'union qu'est votre force. En frères
Vivez donc, et sachez vous maintenir en paix.

Bientôt vous recevrez de ma main un Prophète
Qui viendra vous instruire et souffrir avec vous.
Sa parole fera de la vie une fête;
Mais si vous méprisez sa sagesse parfaite,
Pauvres enfants maudits, vous disparaîtrez tous !

Effacez dans les flots vos couleurs meutrières.
Les roseaux sont nombreux et le roc est épais;
Chacun en peut tirer sa pipe. Plus de guerres,
Plus de sang ! Désormais vivez comme des frères,
Et tous, unis, fumez le Calumet de Paix ! "

III

Et soudain tous, jetant leurs armes sur la terre,
Lavent dans le ruisseau les couleurs de la guerre
Qui luisaient sur leurs fronts cruels et triomphants.
Chacun creuse une pipe et cueille sur la rive
Un long roseau qu'avec adresse il enjolive.
Et l'Esprit souriait à ses pauvres enfants !

Chacun s'en retourna l'âme calme et ravie,
Et Gitche Manito, le Maître de la Vie,
Remonta par la porte entr'ouverte des cieux.
— A travers la vapeur splendide du nuage
Le Tout-Puissant montait, content de son ouvrage,
Immense, parfumé, sublime, radieux !

INDEX TO FRENCH TITLES

NOTES ON THE TRANSLATORS

DOREEN BELL.

English artist and poet; translator from French, Spanish, and Portuguese; contributed to *An Anthology of Spanish Poetry* (ed. Angel Flores, 1961).

KEITH B. BULLEN (d. 1946).

English poet; editor of *Salamander* (Cairo), a poetry review; translator: *Charles Baudelaire, un poète maudit.*

ROY CAMPBELL (1901-1957).

South African poet: *The Flaming Terrapin* (1924), *Adamastor* (1930), *Flowering Rifle* (1939), *Collected Poems* (1949). Translator from Norwegian, Portuguese, French, and Spanish: *Poems of Saint John of the Cross* (1951), *Poems of Baudelaire* (1952). Autobiography: *Light on a Dark Horse* (1951).

ALAN CONDER (1884-1953).

English violinist and translator: *A Treasury of French Poetry* (1951); Baudelaire's *Fleurs du mal* (complete, 1952).

HILARY CORKE.

English poet: *The Early Drowned* (1961); formerly lecturer in Medieval literature in Cairo and Edinburgh.

HENRY CURWEN (1845-1892).

English journalist and novelist, editor of *The Times of India.* Translator of Baudelaire's "Study of the Life and Writings of Poe" (1872); fifty-four poems of Baudelaire in *Echoes from the French Poets* (1870), and *Some Translations from Charles Baudelaire, Poet and Symbolist* (1896).

GEORGE DILLON.

American poet: *Boy in the Wind* (1927); *The Flowering Stone* (1931); translator, with Edna St. Vincent Millay, of Baudelaire's *The Flowers of Evil,* (1936).

MICHAEL FIELD (d. 1914).

Pseudonym of two Victorian ladies, Katherine Bradley and Edith Emma Cooper; their long collaboration ended with the death of Miss Cooper in 1914. Together they wrote many poetic dramas and volumes of verse: *Callirrhoë and the Fair Rosamund* (1884), *Julia Domna* (1903), *Wild Honey from Various Thyme* (1908).

ROBERT FITZGERALD.

American poet: *Poems* (1935), *A Wreath from the Sea* (1943), *In the Rose of Time* (1956). Translator of Greek plays, Paul Valéry's verse plays, and St.-John Perse's *Chronique* (1961); his translation of *The Odyssey* (1961) won the first Bollingen Translation Prize.

JAMES ELROY FLECKER (1884-1915).

English poet, playwright, and novelist: *Collected Poems* (1921); a novel, *The King of Alsander* (1914); and several plays, one of which, *Hassan of Bagdad* (1922) was produced in London in 1923-24 with a Fokine Ballet and music by Delius. Officer in the British Consular Service at Constantinople, Smyrna, Beirut.

BARBARA GIBBS.

American poet: *The Well* (1941), *The Green Chapel* (1958), *Poems Written in Berlin* (1959). Translator: Valéry's *Cimetière marin;* poems of Baudelaire in *An Anthology of French Poetry* (ed. Angel Flores, 1958).

KENNETH O. HANSON.

American poet: *8 Poems* (1958); his poems have been published in *The New Yorker, Sewanee, Botteghe Oscure,* and elsewhere. Professor of English at Reed College, Portland, Oregon.

DESMOND HARMSWORTH.

English poet and painter; his paintings and drawings are in British and American collections, notably at the University of Texas.

ANTHONY HECHT.

American poet: *A Summoning of Stones* (1954), *The Seven Deadly Sins* (1958), and *The Hard Hours* (1962).

PETER HELLINGS.

English poet: *Firework Music* (1950); translator of Baudelaire.

ALDOUS HUXLEY.

Well-known English novelist, essayist, poet; has lived for many years in California. Translator of Mallarmé's "Afternoon of a Faun."

STANLEY KUNITZ.

American poet: *Intellectual Things* (1930), *Passport to War* (1944), *Selected Poems* 1928-1958 (1958).

JAMES LAVER.

English writer; Keeper of Prints and Drawings at the Victoria and Albert Museum. Translator from German and French; editor of *The Poems of Baudelaire* (1940); biographer of J. K. Huysmans (1953).

NAOMI LEWIS.

English writer and critic; her work has appeared in *The New Statesman* and *The Observer,* in London; and in *Harper's* and elsewhere in America. Her translations from Baudelaire were commissioned for broadcasting.

ROBERT LOWELL.

American poet: *Land of Unlikeness* (1944), *Lord Weary's Castle* (1946), *The Mills of the Kavanaughs* (1951), *Life Studies* (1959). Translator: Racine's *Phaedra* (1961); *Imitations* (1961), from Villon, Leopardi, Baudelaire, Rimbaud, Rilke, Montale, Pasternak, and others.

C. F. MAC INTYRE.

American poet: *The Brimming Cup* (1930), *Poems* (1936), *Cafés and Cathedrals* (1939). Translator of Baudelaire, Rilke, Verlaine, Corbière, Goethe.

SIR ERIC MACLAGAN, K.C.V.O., C.B.E. (1879-1951).

Son of the Archbishop of York, Director of the Victoria and Albert Museum, 1924-1945; Charles Eliot Norton Professor at Harvard, 1927-1928. Wrote chiefly on Italian sculpture.

DOROTHY MARTIN.

English poet: *Sextette* (1928) contained translations from French poets; librarian at the Shakespeare Institute, Stratford-on-Avon.

JACKSON MATHEWS.

American translator: René Char's *Hypnos Waking* (1956), Paul Valéry's *Monsieur Teste* (1947), Valéry's *History and Politics* (1962), André Gide's *My Theatre* (1952). Editor of *The Collected Works of Paul Valéry* (Bollingen Series).

EDNA ST. VINCENT MILLAY (1892-1950).

American poet: *Renascence and Other Poems* (1917), *Collected Sonnets* (1941), *Collected Lyrics* (1943). Translator, with George Dillon, of Baudelaire's *The Flowers of Evil* (1936).

THOMAS STURGE MOORE (1870-1944).

English poet, art critic, and wood engraver. Among his books of verse are *The Vinedresser and Other Poems* (1899), *A Sicilian Idyll; and Judith* (1911), *The Unknown Known . . .* (1939). On art he wrote *Studies of Dürer* (1904), *Art and Life* (1910), *Correggio* (1911).

FREDERICK MORGAN.

American poet, translator of Catullus and French Symbolist poets; co-founder and Editorial Director of *The Hudson Review* (New York).

DAVID PAUL.

English poet, playwright, and critic; translator of Paul Valéry's *Degas, Manet, Morisot* (1960) and Valéry's Faust plays (1960).

GRAHAM REYNOLDS.

English art historian, Deputy Keeper of Prints, Victoria and Albert Museum. Author of *Twentieth Century Drawings* (1946), *English Portrait Miniatures* (1951), *Painters of the Victorian Scene* (1953).

LOIS SAUNDERS (1856-1942).

English-born Canadian poet: *Strangers and Foreigners* (London, 1912). Librarian of Queen's University, Kingston, Ontario.

CYRIL SCOTT.

English poet and composer; writer on music and the occult sciences; translator of Stefan George and Baudelaire, *The Flowers of Evil* (London, 1909, 1924 and New York, 1938).

LEWIS PIAGET SHANKS (1878-1935).

American, Professor of French literature at Johns Hopkins University; wrote books on Flaubert, Anatole France, and Baudelaire. First American translator of the complete *Fleurs du mal* (New York, 1926; London, 1931).

KARL SHAPIRO.

American poet and critic: *Poems* (1935), *V-Letter and Other Poems* (1944), *Poems 1942-1953*, *A Bibliography of Modern Prosody* (1948), *Beyond Criticism* (1953), *In Defense of Ignorance* (1960).

RICHARD HERNE SHEPHERD (1842-1895).

English editor and bibliographer; his *Translations from Baudelaire* (1869) were the first to appear in English.

SIR JOHN SQUIRE (1884-1958).

English poet: *Collected Parodies* (1921), *The Birds and Other Poems* (1920), *Collected Poems* (1959). Literary editor of *The New Statesman.*

FRANK PEARCE STURM.

English poet: *An Hour of Reverie* (1905), *Umbrae Silentes* (1918), *The Eternal Helen* (1921). Translator of fifty poems and nineteen prose poems of Baudelaire, *Poems of Charles Baudelaire* (Canterbury Poets Series, 1906).

ALLEN TATE.

American poet and man of letters: *Poems 1922-1947* (1948), *The Fathers* (a novel, 1938), two biographies of Southern leaders in the Civil War, and several volumes of criticism.

RUTHVEN TODD.

English poet and artist: *Until Now* (1941), *The Acreage of the Heart* (1944), *Space Cat Visits Venus* (1955), *Garland for the Winter Solstice* (1962).

RICHARD WILBUR.

American poet: *The Beautiful Changes* (1947), *Ceremony* (1950), *Things of This World* (1956), *Advice to a Prophet* (1961); translator of Molière's *Le Misanthrope.*

YVOR WINTERS.

American poet and critic: *Primitivism and Decadence* (1937), *Maule's Curse* (1938), *The Anatomy of Nonsense* (1943), *In Defense of Reason* (1947), *Collected Poems* (1952).

HUMBERT WOLFE, C.B., C.B.E. (1885-1940).

English writer; translator of Ronsard, selections from *The Greek Anthology,* and Rostand's *Cyrano de Bergerac.* Among his more than forty books are: *Kensington Gardens* (1924), *The Unknown Goddess* (1925), *The Uncelestial City* (1930), and his autobiography, *Now a Stranger* (1933). He was Deputy Secretary of the Ministry of Labour at his death.